Choosing Books
for Young People

• • • • •

Choosing Books for Young People

A Guide to Criticism and Bibliography
1945–1975

• • • • •

John R. T. Ettlinger
and
Diana Spirt

Chicago
American Library Association
1982

Designed by Ellen Pettengell

Text composed by Caron Communications
in Roman P.S. on a Xerox 800 Word
Processor. Display type, VIP Cochin,
composed by Total Typography, Inc.

Printed on 50-pound Antique Glatfelter,
a pH-neutral stock, by
Chicago Press Corporation

Bound in B-grade Holliston cloth
by Zonne Bookbinders

Library of Congress Cataloging in Publication Data

Ettlinger, John R. T.
  Choosing books for young people.

  Includes indexes.
  1. Children—Books and reading—Bibliography.
2. Children's literature—Bibliography. 3. Children's
literature—History and criticism—Bibliography.
I. Spirt, Diana. II. Title.
Z1037.A1E88 1982 [PN1009.A1] 011'.62 82-11659
ISBN 0-8389-0366-5

iv

This work is dedicated to the student assistants, the clerical aides, and the interlibrary loan staff who helped us so much and who rarely get credit for anything in a book (unless they are the author's husband or wife). Although we have already said a personal word of thanks, we would like to add a "literary" thank you for their inestimable help.

Contents

Preface

•••••

The playwrights mouth, the preachers jangle,
   The critics challenge and defend,
And Fiction turns the Muses' mangle--
Of making books there is no end.
                              "A Ballade of Book-Making"

When Justin Huntly McCarthy wrote these words, he not only showed obeisance to the Bible and Bartlett's Familiar Quotations, but he also presaged the lists of materials for young people that have become increasingly commonplace. The history of the book is long and venerable; that of listing books for youngsters came of age in North America and the Continent after World War II. Some lists were available in both Great Britain and the United States much earlier. Mary F. Thwaite has identified those published in England in From Primer to Pleasure in Reading . . . . She also provided an annotated catalog of British books for children (1899-1956) in Children's Books of This Century . . . . The Children's Book Section of the Library of Congress, under the now retired head Virginia Haviland, issued a catalog, Americana in Children's Books, Rarities from the 18th and 19th Centuries. William Sloane's Children's Books in England and America in the Seventeenth Century . . . contains a facsimile of The Young Christian's Library, the first English catalog of children's books. These manuals for choosing books for youngsters can be identified as early entries in what has become an overwhelming public relations promotion to get "the right book to the right child."

H. W. Wilson's Children's Catalog is perhaps the most recognized North American list of books for youngsters to surface during this century. This index was based on the 1909 shelflist of the children's collection of the Pittsburgh Public Library. Other bibliographies of children's books were put out by public libraries and organizations before 1945, coinciding with the establishment of children's departments in publishing houses during the 1920s and 1930s.

Books of quality for young people have always been valued by adults—authors, editors, librarians, teachers, administrators, parents, and other interested people. Richard Darling showed in The Rise of Children's Book Reviewing in America, 1865-1881, that the increase in the reviewing of children's books resulted in an increase in the promotion and selection of children's books. The review is an expression of the gatekeeping interest. The book list is an extension of the tremendous desire of these groups to entice youngsters to read, if not the best books, then at least acceptable ones. Book lists for young people have had a significant influence on the choice of books for youngsters by adults. These lists also show the changes that began in adult society and passed on to the young.

By examining the book lists in this book, one can see this historic trend. The reader will not only be able to tabulate the titles that were recommended in each generation, but also witness the changing attitudes of society on certain issues during the period. Frequently mentioned are realistic fiction, equal rights, and mass media. The books for children that appear in the guides that are described and criticized in this bibliography show drastic changes in society's values on the topics of sex, death, divorce, drugs, opportunities for minorities, and films, recordings, television, computers or any message that is transmitted in a nonprint format. Although society today is now assessing the amount of change that has really occurred, future study of books that are published for youngsters will once again reveal what changes occur and how long they endure.

Currently, adults are caught in the crossfire of conflicting values. The concepts of intellectual freedom and access for minors are undergoing scrutiny, and books for young people are examined for their values. The judgment of adults is sorely tried. "As parents, teachers, and librarians, adults purchase the books that children read. This task offers a real opportunity, but it also carries a load of responsibility." This statement by Iris M. Tiedt in Exploring Books with Children (1979) precedes instruction to select books with the child in mind and to know children's books. Choosing Books for Young People: A Guide to Criticism and Bibliography 1945-1975 indicates that some of the titles in the guides do not follow the former injunction. Additionally, it includes guides that list titles that are controversial to both traditionalists and avant-garde devotees.

Choosing Books for Young People is proof that librarians have been attending to the bibliographic pursuit of aiding book selection for young people over this span of time. A monumental work under the authorship of Virginia Haviland, Children's Literature: A Guide to Reference Books, published in 1966, contains brief annotations of books and articles that have appeared. Although it lists many guides that contain book lists, it also contains many that do not. The serious scholar would have to search diligently to find those guides which contain substantial book lists. Although it is a commonplace that some guides may have been inadvertently overlooked, it is the fervent hope of the authors of this book that the reader will advise them of omissions. Flossie L. Perkins's <u>Book and Non-Book Media</u> . . . (1972), a revision of her husband Ralph Perkins's 1967 book, although far from comprehensive, has been a useful checklist for teachers and librarians and others to well-known guides for materials for young people. The book you are about to read carries on this bibliographic tradition. It is more comprehensive. The authors have made a determined effort to track down all the possible book lists that fit into their delimitations. They have examined each personally, have searched and constructed a bibliographic record, and have described and criticized them. <u>Choosing Books for Young People</u> establishes for interested persons and scholars the guides that have existed between 1945 and 1975. It also includes those guides that are still useful for current book selection and reevaluation, and comments on the purpose for which each guide is best suited.

D.S.

Acknowledgments
•••••

A great deal of time and effort on the part of many goes into producing a work like this, from a gleam of interest in the authors' eyes to the publisher's skills. We all understand or, in the case of some, know by experience the vagaries that enter the scene when one attempts to forge an original work of this nature. The bibliographic work in producing a historical record is prodigious. Resources in many locations from the <u>National Union Catalog</u> to the Bodleian Library have been searched. Those among you who admire the newer tools of technology will be pleased to know that the OCLC data base also contributed. Along the authors' route in the interest of providing bibliographic control in this important area, many groups and individuals helped expedite this work. Our wish is to acknowledge:

The staffs of the following:
> the B. Davis Schwartz Library. C. W. Post Center, Long Island University; particularly Conrad Schoeffling, Ruth Macy, Lisé Rasmussen, Gloria Sharify, Muriel Terry, William Tornow, Frances Volz, Ellen Weinstein, Lorraine Williamson, and Masaka Yukawa
> the Bodleian Library, Oxford University, England
> the Killam Library, Dalhousie University, Canada
> the library of the Library Association, England
> the library of the National Book League, England

The research committees of both C. W. Post Center and Dalhousie University who saw to it that there were typing funds for the authors.

Publishing Services of the American Library Association, particularly Herbert Bloom who first encouraged this work and was understanding throughout its lengthy completion and Mary Huchting who saw this book through to its publication as editor.

There have been innumerable kind people along the way--for example those on the other end of a telephone call. If we have not mentioned you by name, please know that you are recognized by the authors and that some of your good deeds see the light of day on the pages of this book.

We wish finally to acknowledge those who read the following pages with what we hope will be a sense of interest and delight similar to ours.

Introduction

• • • • •

This annotated bibliography is designed to provide a key to the voluminous output of comment and criticism that has appeared since the Second World War about all kinds of books for young people of all ages. The listing of titles here goes beyond the treatment of children's books as literature to include works recommending informational and instructional reading in or out of the school environment. The objectives are to be comprehensive in scope, to record and describe any book published from 1945 to 1975 which selects, criticizes, or lists suitable books for young people, and to comment on their value and usefulness to librarians, teachers, parents, and others who are professionally or personally interested in providing or recommending reading for children and young adults from kindergarten to high-school age.

Emphasis has been placed on identifying tools which provide a subject approach or a selective listing that makes available titles chosen by experienced critics and professionals from the increasing number of publications available for juveniles over the period. Besides those titles which offer currently valid selections, there are many entries that will demonstrate the criteria for book selection of previous generations. Social and literary historians will be able to perceive that the changes of attitude in choosing children's books have been as rapid as the changes in publication pattern and the style of writing in the books themselves.

INCLUSIONS AND EXCLUSIONS

By Date, Language, and Place of Publication   The list includes all relevant books published from 1945 to 1975 in the English language in the United States, Great Britain, and Canada. French-language publications from Canada are included, as are any Australian and New Zealand items that have been located. Titles in other languages and from other countries have been excluded.

By Subject   Subject parameters include all monographs and annuals in which at least one of the principal aims is to recommend or list books for young people. We have included in this category all titles where this criterion forms a major theme or proportion of the text, or where the bibliographical element substantially exceeds a chapter or two or an appendix. On this basis, many titles are listed which ostensibly cover peripheral or related areas, but their inclusion here is due to their bibliographical features or to the degree of relevant comment. Some examples of these related areas are bibliography, black studies, curricular enrichment, disadvantaged readers, folklore, reading guidance, storytelling, and writing and publishing for children.

Books on the following topics are excluded from the list: audiovisual materials, except multimedia guides which include books; free and inexpensive materials; anthologies that do not have a substantial proportion of critical or bibliographical material; individual authors and illustrators; teaching methods; and management of school or children's libraries.

By Format   Monographs, annuals, and works appearing biennially or triennially of sixteen pages or over are included. Excluded are: items under sixteen pages; publications processed from typescript; microform publications and paper prints from these; theses not independently published as monographs; periodical titles (except annuals and works appearing biennially or triennially); periodical articles and offprints from them.

By Agency of Publication   The following types of publication are excluded: sales and advertising material by publishers, jobbers, booksellers, and book clubs; documents produced by state agencies or school systems for their own use or purely local distribution; individual library catalogs and lists, except scholarly publications embodying research or critical comment, which are included.

ENTRY

Arrangement by Author or Main Entry   Entries are arranged alphabetically by author or other main entry. Personal author entries take precedence over institutional or title entries where possible, whether the name appears on the recto or the verso of the title page or is identified in the prefatory matter. The form of name used in the book has been preferred. If authors listed as compilers or editors have functioned in fact as authors, they have been so credited without the use of brackets. All coauthors have been credited in the entry, with the exception of committee members. Committee chairpersons have been given editorial credit. Editors of former editions have been identified in the annotation and in the index, as have institutions whose contributions have exceeded their function as publishers.

Edition   Entries describe the last edition published before the close of 1975. The following qualifications to this rule apply. For books published on both sides of the Atlantic within a year, the edition of the country of origin is given. Entry for a full text is preferred over that for a later abbreviated edition. Unchanged reprints by the original publishers are not cited, but reprints of earlier titles by specialized reprint publishers are treated as later editions. All earlier editions are described in the annotation, including editions under different editors or titles. Editions subsequent to 1975 have been mentioned at the close of the annotation.

ANNOTATION

The primary objectives of the annotation have been to describe the contents of the listed item and to provide bibliographical information. Descriptions have been phrased in terms used by the book's own author, editor, or sponsoring body, whether in direct quotation or in paraphrase. Critical opinions expressed relate particularly to the usefulness of the tool to its potential audience. Readers may presume that standard features such as typographical presentation, illustration, and indexing are of satisfactory quality, unless noted as deficient or as above average in quality or usefulness.

SUBJECT ACCESS

Where appropriate, the subject index uses Sears headings with adaptations for see and see also references from the Library of Congress. However, considerable variations from these lists have been made to suit the nature of the material. See references refer to the whole subject or principal subjects of the books; that is, they will not be analytical in the sense of giving access to individual chapters, etc.

J.R.T.E.

Annotated Bibliography
• • • • •

Adams, Bess Porter. About Books and Children: Historical Survey of Children's Literature. New York: Holt, 1953. 573p.

This historical survey primarily is intended to help parents understand children as well as their books, but it is also directed to teachers and students of children's literature. While competently written in a textbook style, better accounts are available today; however, both choice and comment are interesting in reflecting the selective taste of thirty years ago. The fifteen chapters are supported by an appendix of readings for adults and an extensive bibliography of books for children. These are mainly chosen from titles of the twenties, thirties, and forties and are briefly and well annotated. The author and title index supplements this by referring to titles discussed in the text. Line reproductions of woodcuts and drawings from children's books illustrate each chapter.

Adamson, Catherine E. et al. Inexpensive Books for Boys and Girls. 3rd ed. Chicago: American Library Assn., 1952. 25p.

Low-priced titles that antedate the full impact of the paperback revolution have been selected by the ALA Editorial Committee's Subcommittee on Inexpensive Books for Boys and Girls, and revised up to 1950-51. Sections cover series, picture books and easy reading, and books of general interest for children of grades 4-8. Previous editions in 1936 and 1938 were prepared by the Book Evaluation Committee of ALA's Section for Library Work with Children.

Adcock, June, and Adcock, John. The World in Stories; Books for Young People Selected for Geographical Interest. London: School Library Assn., 1972. 38p.

About 200 stories for young people that have an authentic and readily identifiable geographical setting were selected with the objective of promoting greater awareness of other countries. Authors are either natives or write from excellent first-hand knowledge. The arrangement is geographical, and countries and

1

regions are identified in the index. Brief notes describe the story and the author's background, and indicate likely appeal and age suitability.

Alberta Teachers' Association. English Council and School Library Council. Canadian Books for Schools: A Centennial Listing. Edmonton, Alta.: The Association, 1968. 63p.

Only books published in English and in-print, with the exception of some French-Canadian titles available in translation, were included in this selection. Titles were "chosen on the basis of quality, appeal to students or, in special cases, because of their interesting treatment of particular aspects of Canadian life." Arrangement is alphabetical by author with a title index. The proportion of books written for adults and those written for a juvenile audience is about equal. Brief annotations describe the content. Coded information indicates grade level, broad areas of subject relevance, suggested Dewey numbers, and availability in paperback. When published, this list represented a valuable basic representation of Canadian titles for libraries in Canada and in interested libraries in other countries. Of course, much could be added with the burgeoning of Canadian publication in more recent years.

Alderson, Brian. Looking at Picture Books. London: National Book League, 1973. 64p.

This work was prepared by the author for an exhibition arranged by the National Book League, the aim of which was to show the range of current picture books and to suggest a critical standpoint for their assessment. Selection of the 379 items was not primarily made for a child audience. The principles underlying the creation and criticism of the different types are analyzed, and the annotation forms a running commentary that makes up a thesis of its own. Arrangement stresses key books in a series of broad sections, including alphabet books, counting books, nursery rhymes, simple stories, pictures and play, stories without words, traditional stories, the novel in pictures, and audio-viz.

——. Reading for Enjoyment for 6 to 8 Year Olds. London: Children's Book Centre, 1970. 30p.

The aim of this work is to present books that will bring pleasure to children during their first years of reading--and also to involved adults. Arranged according to reading skill: for children learning to read, readers gaining confidence, and fluent readers. Sections are included on folk and fairy tales, poetry and storytelling.

Alderson, Connie. Magazines Teenagers Read: With Special Reference to Trend, Jackie, and Valentine. Oxford: Pergamon, 1968.

A teacher offers a critical study of the effects of the literary and visual styles of certain mass media on young people in Britain. In spite of a disclaimer to be a sociological analysis, this angry examination of trendy magazines that are popular with young adults is essentially a condemnation.

American Institute of Graphic Arts. Children's Book Show. New York: The Institute, 1942- . Biennial.

Commencing with a catalog covering illustrated books for children of 1937-41, this prestigious design group has sponsored the juried exhibits, usually on a biennial frequency. The titles of the catalog have varied over the years. The degree of annotation provided has been minimal and technical. Retrospectively, the lists form a valuable historical record of American illustrated books for children and their illustrators, judged from an artistic and technical point of view which does not take into account their literary value.

American Library Association. Children's Services Division. Selected Lists of Children's Books and Recordings. Washington, D.C.: Govt. Print. Off., 1966. 48p.

Prepared by a committee for the U.S. Office of Economic Opportunity, this compilation chooses appropriate readings and recordings for professional workers and volunteers who cope with the reading needs of individuals and groups. The title page carries a grammatical motif: "To read, I read, you read, he reads, she reads, we read, you read, and they read." Six briefly annotated and graded lists are designed to "extend boundaries and awaken the imagination of children in Head Start programs, neighborhood centers, and youth activities." Three are useful for preschool through the early grades: "Books for Pre-School Children"; "Stories to Tell"; and "Recordings for Children." Three are for the later elementary grades and older children and emphasize familiar living situations: "Books for Boys and Girls in the City"; "Books for Boys and Girls in Rural America"; and "Books for Those who Need Special Encouragement to Read." Titles include those for Spanish-speaking children of Puerto Rican and Mexican background. Selection of records is restricted and does not cover contemporary or classical music; excerpt types of recordings are avoided. At the time of compilation, this was a sensitive and representative initial selection, and a number of the recommendations retain their validity.

——. Young Adult Services Division. Best Books for Young Adults. Chicago: The Association, 1931- . Annual.

A brief, unannotated, but very influential selection, which has appeared for many years as a small pamphlet and is also published in School Library Journal and more recently in Top of the News, this list is compiled by young adult librarians with thorough knowledge of the books themselves and their audience appeal. Educators and librarians have learned to rely on the annual choices for a broad range of reading levels and reading tastes. The 1981 edition lists fifty titles, and those of previous years remain significant as representative of the best then, and often provide still valid titles for acquisition now.

Anderson, Hugh. The Singing Roads: A Guide to Australian Children's Authors and Illustrators. 3rd ed. Sydney, New South Wales: Wentworth, 1970. 2 vols. 117p., 77p.

First published in 1965, with a second edition in 1966, the third edition incorporates the second part published in 1969. This is a standard bibliographical source for Australian children's literature. Titles are comprehensively listed under their authors and illustrators.

Anderson, William, and Groff, Patrick. A New Look at Children's Literature. Belmont, Calif.: Wadsworth, 1972. 362p.

This work surveys the various doctrines of literary criticism and examines how they apply to children's literature. The authors regard children's literature as a major field of study and a part of the literary mainstream, susceptible to the same critical analysis used when evaluating literature for adults. The first part examines basic concepts, such as structure, plot, character, and style, and illustrates these with extracts from children's books. The second part describes types and uses, analyzing subdivisions of the genre such as mythology, folklore, fantasy, poetry, and picture books, as well as biography and informational works. The third part discusses teaching literature to children, laying stress on the elementary school curriculum. The final part gives an annotated bibliography of 500 good books for children, arranged according to the categories listed in part 2. The titles, many also referred to in the text, carry a full paragraph of descriptive and critical annotation and an indication of age level. This large quarto volume is well printed and generously spaced, with black-and-white illustrations in the text.

Andrew, H. G. et al. Science Books for a School Library. 5th ed. London: Murray, 1968. 70p.

Sponsored by the Association for Science Education, this selection for British secondary modern and comprehensive schools has a long publishing history, the first edition having appeared in 1930, followed by others in 1940, 1949, and 1959. This edition reflects significant changes in science education. Contents are arranged in broad subject groups; general works on the philosophy and history of science and anthologies are followed by biology, chemistry, physics, astronomy, geology, meteorology, and applied science. There is a supplementary list of elementary science books. Brief annotations indicate contents and occasionally criticism of titles listed.

Andrews, Siri. Good Reading for Youth. Concord, N.H.: New Hampshire State Library, 1966. 72p.

Prepared under the direction of the Children's Services Division of the ALA in cooperation with the National Educational Chairman of the U.S. Junior Chamber of Commerce, this is a selected bibliography with brief summary annotations. Nearly 500 titles are arranged in six groups: "Kindergarten to 2nd Grade"; "Books for Beginning Readers"; "Books for Grades 2-4"; "Books for Grades 4-6"; "Books for Grades 6-8"; and "Books for the Family." The last includes Bible stories, poetry anthologies, and storybooks. Starred books are recommended for first purchase. On publication this list was much sought after by school librarians and others for its exceptional quality, and was widely used for selection. A children's librarian could be certain that the titles selected for kindergarten through grade 8 were excellent choices as well as being popular. While some of the authors that youngsters were reading in 1966 have published many more titles, the list is still useful as a checking and reevaluation list.

——, ed. The Hewins Lectures, 1947-1962. Boston: Horn Book, 1963. 375p.

These addresses on literature for the young in nineteenth-century America were initiated at a meeting of the Massachusetts Library Association in 1946. Frederic G. Melcher, who introduces this collection, then suggested "a series of annual papers on the writing and publishing of children's books in New England's fertile years." It was named in honor of Caroline M. Hewins, a longtime librarian in Hartford, Connecticut, and author of Books for the Young. Articles range from Alice M. Jordan's famous "From Rollo to Tom Sawyer" to Margaret Lane's biographical and analytical "Rachel Field." They include an article by the editor on criticism and review of children's books as well as her "The Folklore of New England." Careful references document each article. Eclectic in choice within the period and scholarly in tone, this collection is a valuable aid to the general student and the researcher.

Animal Stories. Topic Booklists. Tunbridge Wells, Eng.: Fenrose, 1974. 63p.

The prime object of this selection of children's novels then available in Britain is to provide a subdivided list under topic, usually a specific kind of animal. Factual nature books and junior picture books are excluded, and there are only a few stories of talking animals. Descriptive annotation is brief, and a letter code designates titles by reading age: under 9, 9-12, and over 12. There is an index of species.

Arbuthnot, May Hill. Children's Reading in the Home. Glenview, Ill.:
    Scott, Foresman, 1969. 374p.

    This introduction to literature for children is written for
parents, teachers, and librarians, and is designed to encourage
children's reading in the home. The text includes a selection of
about 600 titles with descriptive annotations. Grouped into three
parts, "Enjoying Books in the Family," "Growing into Books and
Reading," and "Reading in Special Areas," chapters cover selection of books, the needs of various age groups from very young
children to adolescents, and types of publication and subject
fields. Many parents for whom this volume is intended would no
doubt find it too detailed; others, however, will appreciate its
perceptive book annotations and general information. Arbuthnot
once again proves her excellence in this field. Her sensibilities
toward race and class are remarkable; she even mentions Dr.
Doolittle under fables.

——, and Sutherland, Zena. Children and Books. 4th ed. Glenview, Ill.:
    Scott, Foresman, 1972. 836p.

    First published in 1947 and revised in 1957, the third edition
(1964) was the last to list May Hill Arbuthnot as the sole author.
This fourth edition, as the others, is primarily a textbook for
children's literature courses in teacher-training institutions and
library schools. The needs of teachers in service, parents, and
other concerned adults are also addressed. Every type of reading
interest of children from 2 to 14 is covered and interpreted.
Criteria are presented to help adults evaluate the different types
and their values for children. The work is divided into five parts:
"Knowing Children and Books," "Discovering Books with Children," "Exploring the Types of Literature," "Bringing Children and
Books Together," and "Areas and Issues." Chapters cover book
selection, history, and trends; the work of many individual authors
is analyzed. A strong sampling is given of selections from the
books themselves. Many illustrations are reproduced with critical
comment. This excellent work became a standard, and a pattern
to be followed by others writing in the field. A fifth edition
appeared in 1977 under the principal authorship of Zena Sutherland, and a sixth in 1981.

——, and Taylor, Mark, eds. Time for New Magic. Glenview, Ill.:
    Scott, Foresman, 1971. 300p.

    A revision and expansion of "New Magic: Modern Fanciful
Tales" in Time for Fairytales, this book was published by the same
publisher in 1952 and 1961. It is primarily a "representative
collection of modern fanciful stories for children to be used in the
classroom, home, or camp; especially planned for college classes
in children's literature." The book is arranged in three parts, the
third being a bibliography. Part 1, "Path of New Magic," lists

fifty-six fantasy selections from Hans Christian Andersen to Lloyd Alexander. The selections are grouped under fanciful headings like "Animal Fair" and "The Earth, Sea and Sky." In part 2, "New Magic and Children," adult audiences for fantasy are shown ways to appreciate its importance in the lives of young children. It provides help in evaluating talent, reading aloud, and discussing fantasy with children. A brief history of the genre is also given, as well as biographies of some well-known writers of fantasy. Part 3, the annotated bibliography, which serves well as a fantasy checklist for this age group, is alphabetical by author, and graded by age. The annotations reflect the plot. Also included is a page of adult references. The book includes a few black-and-white reproductions and an author-title index.

———; Clark, Margaret Mary; Long, Harriet F.; and Hadlow, Ruth M. Children's Books Too Good to Miss. Rev. and enl. ed. Cleveland: Press of Case Western Reserve Univ., 1971. 97p.

This is a revised and enlarged edition of a selection that the authors claim is the irreducible minimum of choice books every child should at least look at. A long list of previous editions by Arbuthnot in 1948, 1953, 1959, 1963, and 1966 preceded this posthumous one, which reflects the judgment of a group of collaborating specialists and includes about 300 books, removing out-of-print titles, and including forty new ones. Older classics are combined with recent books, satisfying the test of combining literary distinction with permanent child appeal. A paragraph of annotation for each includes critical comment as well as description. Titles are arranged by topic under four age groups: under 6; 6 to 8; 9 to 11; and 12 to 14. Additional lists cover awards and illustrators of children's books. There are title, author, and artist indexes.

Arnold, Arnold, ed. Pictures and Stories from Forgotten Children's Books. New York: Dover, 1969. 170p.

Illustrations in early children's books make up this anthology, one of the publisher's paperback Pictorial Archives series. Almost 500 illustrations from seventy-five titles in the editor's private collection have been arranged into groups to illustrate contemporary manners and graphic and literary style in juvenilia published in the period from 1750 to 1850. Chapters cover morals and manners, nursery rhymes, street cries, fairytales, anthropomorphism, words of one syllable, robinsonades, humor and riddles, books on sports, games and pastimes, periodicals, and books that teach. The editor is an author-illustrator of children's books and a toy designer. His lengthy introduction acknowledges his indebtedness to Tuer's earlier publication of similar anthologies, but his own choice has stressed "whatever can be read to and with today's children, giving them a sense of kinship with history and sympathy

for their great-great-great grandparents." The quality of reproduction is adequate, considering the poor printing of the originals.
The lack of an index is a limiting factor in the book's usefulness for
bibliographic research. It is perhaps best used as a picture book.

Ashbridge, Jean, and Hubbard, R. A. Classical Studies: Background
Reading for Secondary Schools.   An Annotated Book-List.
London: National Book League, 1968. 25p.
Intended to suggest books that will help children from 11 to 15
acquire a knowledge of life in classical times. This work includes
148 items covering fiction, mythology, ancient life, art and
history and was prepared in consultation with the Joint Association of Classical Teachers to accompany an NBL exhibit.

Ashley, L. F. Children's Reading and the Seventies. Toronto: McClelland, 1972. 102p.
Current influences on children's reading habits are the subject
of this study made by a professor of education. The intended
audience includes professionals as well as those interested in a
more general sense. Conclusions are based on questionnaires
which were answered by 1,500 respondents in grades 4 to 7 in
British Columbia schools. Chapters cover topics such as preferences, dislikes, format, television, books most remembered, and
classics. Each has tables and graphs appended, listing relevant
book titles and their interest level as represented by the questionnaires. Two closing chapters indicate further considerations, and
provide a summarization which includes the comment that children, especially older children, are moving closer to adult literature, and that their choice of reading strongly reflects the society
in which they live. These truisms may be challenged on a national
or personal basis, but the analysis of the children's responses
remains relevant and valuable for teachers and others involved in
reading guidance.

Avery, Gillian. Childhood's Pattern: A Study of the Heroes and
Heroines of Children's Fiction, 1770-1950. London: Hodder &
Stoughton, 1975. 256p.
The author states that the middle years of the period have
received the most attention in this expansion of her 1965 work.
Arrangement follows the various types of heroes and heroines
found in children's fiction and how these changed within the
chronological limits of the study. A valuable source of information on the children's literature of the period, written in an
entertaining and scholarly fashion.

——. Nineteenth-Century Children: Heroes and Heroines in English
Children's Stories, 1780-1900. London: Hodder & Stoughton,
1965. 259p.

The author, who was assisted by Angela Bull, restricts her account to juvenile fiction, examining the attitude of authors to readers, the changing nature of the fictitious child, and the different demands made by adult ideals of behaviour. Period children's literature is looked at from three angles: the child improved, the child amused, and the changing attitude of adults. Half-tone plates reproduce title pages and illustrations from books of the period. The theme was expanded chronologically in Childhood's Pattern (1975), and, like it, is a useful bibliographical source.

Bagshaw, Marguerite, ed.   Books for Boys and Girls.   5th ed. Toronto: Ryerson, 1966. 301p.
This annotated selection was prepared by the Toronto Public Library staff. It first appeared in 1927; succeeding editions were published in 1940, 1954, and 1958 and the last was reprinted with minor corrections in 1966. Emphasis was placed on books of enduring quality, and all titles were reexamined and reevaluated for this edition, with contributions from many staff members. Choice is international in scope within the limitations of the English language, but Canadian titles are not neglected. Arrangement combines conventional types of publication for children with informal subject groupings. Notes are descriptive, occasionally critical, and indicate those children for whom the books will have most interest. Out-of-print books with a few exceptions are omitted, though there are many current editions listed of earlier titles. Its function as a library stock list and a basis for discussion for the librarians of Boys and Girls Services was transcended by its usefulness to other institutions and individuals interested in children's literature. Although a loose-leaf supplement appeared covering books and films from 1965 to 1968, lack of currency has affected the utility of this sound checklist.

Baker, Augusta, ed. Once Upon a Time. 2nd ed. New York: New York Public Library, 1964. 16p.
A committee of the Children's and Young Adults Services Section of the New York Library Association, with Augusta Baker as chairperson, revised this pamphlet first published in 1955. The objective is to inspire and make helpful suggestions for successful storytelling programs, rather than to teach storytellers. Chapters cover the preschool program, the picture book program, the story hour, and suggested programs. Suggestions include some for special groups and for using films and music as techniques. Short bibliographies support the chapters and also list poetry anthologies and collections. This brief but valuable how-to booklet became influential inside and outside its local area.

Baltimore. Public Schools. Bureau of Library Services. Think Black!
A Selected Reading List. Part I, for Young Readers. Part II, for
Young Adults. Rev. ed. Baltimore: The Bureau, 1970. 15p., 16p.
These two annotated lists were written to promote reading on a
major issue among the young people served by this city school
system. Part 1 lists under traditional categories of publication,
part 2 under topical headings appropriate for young adults. Titles
for beginning readers in part 1, and for junior-high use in part 2 are
starred. When published, this was a practical and well-chosen
listing for teachers and librarians.

Banman, Henry A.; Dawson, Mildred A.; and Whitehead, Robert J. Oral
Interpretations of Children's Literature. Brown Education Series.
Dubuque, Ia.: Brown, 1964. 119p.
Children and the oral interpretation of literature are the subjects of this volume by California state college faculty members.
The work is intended as a concise and informative guide for
teachers, students, and parents and explains the principles, techniques, and materials for teaching good oral expression to elementary school children, as a contribution to genuine enjoyment and
literary appreciation. Topics included are choral speaking, creative dramatics, and storytelling. Traditional rhymes are quoted
in the text, and recommended titles, including records, follow
each chapter.

Baronberg, Joan, ed. Black Representation in Children's Books. New
York: Teachers College, Columbia Univ., 1971. 24p.
This bibliographical essay and short annotated bibliography was
prepared as a paper for the ERIC/IRCD Urban Disadvantaged
Series (#21/UD 011 453) with the objective of investigating and
stimulating the portrayal of blacks in children's books. The text
refers to many titles. The bibliography lists only twenty-one
available books, gives grade levels recommended by the publishers, a note indicating any stereotyping of characters, and a star
for those recommended.

Barry, Florence V. A Century of Children's Books. Detroit: Singing
Tree, 1968. 257p.
First appearing in England in 1922, this edition is a photolithographic facsimile of the first American edition published by
Doran in 1923. This survey of English publications written for
children from 1700 to 1825 makes a critical assessment from a
literary standpoint of the types of books available and many
individual authors and titles. Chapters describe chapbooks and
ballads, fairy tales, moral tales and moralists, and "an old fash-
ioned garden of verses." The influence of Rousseau, the tales of
Miss Edgworth, and the little books of Mrs. Sherwood and the
Misses Taylor are singled out. Generous quotations are provided

in the text and a chronological list of all dated works mentioned forms an appendix. This sympathetic and scholarly account of that formative period retains both value and interest.

Barton, Richard. Fiction: 9-13. London: National Book League, 1973. 31p.

Based on an exhibition designed to place an up-to-date selection for enriching the lives of young people before British school librarians, teachers, and others concerned, this booklet offers 243 titles that cater to a wide range of reading and interest levels, which are indicated for each item by a number and letter code.

Bechtel, Louise Seaman. Books in Search of Children: Speeches and Essays. Selected and with an introduction by Virginia Haviland. New York: Macmillan, 1969. 268p.

Compiled as a tribute to the author, an editor of children's books for many years, this collection is sympathetically introduced by Virginia Haviland. The addresses and articles cover a wide variety of topics and stress American children's books from the 1920s on. They are informally grouped under the headings "The Making of Books," "Authors and Artists," "Children and Books," and "Times and Trends." Much background information is supplied. The book gives interesting insights into the history of publication for children in this century.

Becker, May Lamberton. Adventures in Reading. New ed. Philadelphia: Lippincott, 1946. 250p.

First published in 1927, this inspirational title on topical themes was written for young people by a former editor of the famous children's magazine, St. Nicholas. She seeks to inculcate "sound principles on which a beginner might develop a discriminating, individual taste for good literature." The selected lists appended to each chapter include one for a personal collection, and have considerable retrospective interest.

———. First Adventures in Reading: Introducing Children to Books. New rev. ed. Philadelphia: Lippincott, 1947. 286p.

First published in 1936 and reprinted in England the following year with the title Choosing Books for Children, this sharing of personal knowledge and experience by a well-known editor of juvenile books reflects the period in which it was written in attitude and in selection. Sixteen topical chapters cover children's interests in a more-or-less chronological fashion, from "Singing to the Baby" through the "Family in Fiction" to mystery stories. A chapter refers to censorship, in which the author indicates her belief in delaying some types of reading. A selected book list mixing traditional with more recent popular items gives each a brief sentence of descriptive comment. The author is deeply knowledgeable about the classics in the field, as well as the publications of her day, but more modern citations include many now forgotten or out of print. Her opinions are still significant, if read with an understanding of the times that created them.

Benét, Laura. Famous Storytellers for Young People. Famous Biographies for Young People. New York: Dodd, 1968. 159p.

Twenty-two short biographies of English and American authors, mainly of the nineteenth century but a few of the early twentieth, who were judged as outstanding tellers of tales, are included in this work. Written in a simple style, the information is mainly biographical but includes critical comment and itemizes titles in the text. Half-tone portraits are provided of each author. A companion volume in the same series is Famous Author-Illustrators for Young People by Norah Smaridge.

Bennett, Wilma et al. Comprehensive Book Collection for High School Libraries. Santa Ana, Calif.: Professional Library Service, 1963. 386p.

This extensive classified but unannotated listing of over 8000 titles was produced by the staff of a commercial library processing service on the advice of professional librarians, with the objective of providing "the essential core of a well-balanced high-school book collection." Choice was based on existing lists, such as the Wilson catalogs, as well as more personal and less official selection aids. A useful ordering tool when first compiled, it preceded a similar list for elementary school libraries prepared for the service by Margaret H. Miller.

Best, A. M. Story Telling: Notes for the Teachers of History in the Junior School. Teaching of History Leaflet, no. 13. London: The Historical Assn., 1952. 29p.

To aid teachers in choosing authentic titles is the aim of this work. Different topics and types of stories are critically considered. A list of historical stories considered suitable for use in the junior school is given. The emphasis is on British history.

Best Books for Children: A Catalog. New York: Bowker, 1959-72. Annual.

This annually revised selection was culled from the general trade juvenile titles listed in Children's Books in Print, with an emphasis on recent publications. Compilation in the offices of Library Journal was largely based on recommendations in standard selection tools, both periodical and monograph, to reflect qualities of literary excellence, pertinence, and timeliness of subject matter. From 1962, adult books recommended for young people were included, as is noted in the subtitle for 1963. The volume count reached 3,300 in 1960 and 4,000 in 1967, titles being arranged by subject interest topic within five sections based on age: preschool to third grade 3; grades 4-6; grades 7 and up; adult books for younger readers; and special subjects. The brief descriptive annotations have coded references to selection aids such as Booklist and the Children's Catalog, etc. Editors included Mary C. Turner (1st and 2nd eds.), Patricia Hunt Allen (3rd ed. to 8th ed.), Ann M. Currah (9th ed.), Joan Sragow (10th and 11th eds.), Doris Solomon (12th ed.), Eleanor Widdoes (13th and 14th eds.), with coeditors and consultants Aileen O'Brien Murphy (2nd ed.), Kathleen Widdoes (3rd ed.), and Lillian Gerhardt (9th, 10th, and 12th eds.). This inexpensive buying guide, subsidized by book-industry advertising, functioned as a consistent and unexceptionable checking list much utilized by schools and libraries during its span of publication.

Bewick, Elizabeth N. Children's Books. Reader's Guide, new series, no. 81. London: Library Assn., County Libraries Group, 1964. 19p.

This work is intended as a selection guide for parents buying books as presents for children, and as an aid for librarians and teachers with a small amount to spend. Annotations mention other titles by listed authors. All imprints are British. Previous editions were published in 1962 under the same title and in 1958 as Books for Children.

Blanck, Jacob. Peter Parley to Penrod: A Bibliographical Description of the Best-Loved American Juvenile Books. New York: Bowker, 1956. 153p.

A virtually unchanged reprint of what has become a bibliographical classic, this title was first published in 1938; only a few comments have been added and a few errors corrected. Leaning towards historical significance rather than literary quality, Blanck's choice of the outstanding early American juveniles has signposted later collectors. The criterion for inclusion was to list the "books which have withstood the years of change in reading tastes and are favorites still." Over 100 titles receive full title-page transcriptions and collations, with careful and complete physical descriptions and details of publication. There is no other annotation. About 50 selections receive less than full treatment. Publication dates range from 1827 to 1926, and arrangement is chronological.

Blishen, Edward, ed. The Thorny Paradise; Writers on Writing for Children. Kestrel Books. Harmondsworth, Middlesex, Eng.: Penguin, 1975. 176p.

These essays written by well-known British authors for children, such as Richard Adams, Molly Hunter, Rosemary Sutcliff, and John Rowe Townsend, describe in the main their own works and how they came to be written. However, Geoffrey Trease in "The Revolution in Children's Literature" makes incisive general observations on twentieth-century British writing for children.

Blount, Margaret. Animal Land: The Treasures of Children's Fiction. London: Hutchinson, 1974. 336p.

This book examines animal literature for children and its appeal, including fable, fantasy, and factual accounts. Partly a historical overview, the study concentrates on the nineteenth and twentieth centuries and describes extensively the work of better-known authors up to the date of writing.

Bodger, Joan. How the Heather Looks; a Joyous Journey to the British Sources of Children's Books. New York: Viking, 1965. 276p.

A family summer holiday in England that was planned as a literary pilgrimage precipitated this literary journey in print. A book to be read for pleasure that gives en route background and miscellaneous material about authors and illustrators of children's books.

Bomar, Cora Paul, ed. Reference Materials for School Libraries: Grades 1 through 12. 3rd ed. Raleigh, N.C.: State Board of Education, 1968. 216p.

This substantial compilation appeared first in 1959, with a supplement in 1963. A second edition came out in 1965, edited by Margaret P. McCotter. Designed to serve as a guide in selecting and using reference materials in North Carolina schools, this state document "is expected to be of particular value in selecting titles to support the school's curriculum." Three parts cover reference materials in the school library, a classified list of reference materials, and materials on North Carolina. The first part discusses selection, organization, and the teaching of reference skills; the second part comprises the body of the work. The third part is particularly well-developed to satisfy local reference needs. Apart from that, this publication by a state with an early record of fostering school libraries would have been equally valuable for other jurisdictions when it appeared. Now outdated as a general tool, it retains local interest.

Books for Children. London: National Book League, 1955-61. Annual.

Five annual selections, covering the period 1955-61, demonstrate the league's long-standing bibliographical interest in quality literature for children. Each recommended over 100 items of fiction and nonfiction and provided a sentence of descriptive annotation. Arrangement is within broad type-of-publication or subject groups. Works originally published in other countries are included. As an annual review of British publications, it was succeeded by Naomi Lewis's The Best Children's Books . . ., 1963-69, and Elaine Moss's Children's Books of the Year . . . from 1970.

Books for Children: A Select List. 4th ed. Melbourne: Children's Book
   Council of Victoria, 1966. 91p.
   This reading list of books for Australian children is not limited to Australian children's literature. Selected by a committee to be a guide to a personal collection, it is arranged informally into age, interest, and subject groupings. Previous editions appeared in 1955, 1961, and 1963; for this edition, the selection was extensively reexamined and revised.

Books for Children, 1960-1965: As Selected and Reviewed by the
   Booklist and Subscription Books Bulletin, September 1960 through
   August 1965. Chicago: American Library Assn., 1966. 447p.
Books for Children: [1965-66 to 1966-67] Pre-School through Junior
   High School . . . 1967-72. Annual.
   Reviews of young people's titles selected and recommended for purchase in the pages of ALA's prestigious twice-monthly book review were edited by an ALA committee and reissued in this format, to serve as a handy buying guide for librarians and teachers in selecting new children's books for schools and libraries. The substantial five-year cumulation volume incorporates material previously published as Subscription Books Bulletin Reviews in volumes for 1956-60, 1960-62, and 1962-64. The subsequent annuals under the Books for Children title each cover publications from September in one year through August the following year. Over 3,000 reviews in the basic cumulation and from over 700 to over 900 reviews in the annual additions make this a formidable compilation of full critical and descriptive comment by Booklist's contributors and consultants, mostly school and children's librarians chosen for their wide knowledge of the field and including many well-known names. Entries are arranged in a modified Dewey sequence, followed by individual and collective biographies, two sections of fiction--the latter comprising easy-to-read and picture books--and thorough indexing. The excellent selection and a high level of criticism made this a valuable source whose demise must be regretted by librarians. It retains its value for finding critical assessments of publications through these years.

Books for Young People. Adelaide: Libraries Board of South Australia,
   1974. 23p.
   This revised and abbreviated version of a similarly named publication of 1962-63, described as a guide to Christmas buying, appeared originally in 1970, with a further revision in 1973.

Books for Young People: An Annotated List. Adelaide: Libraries
Board of South Australia, 1962, 1963. 2 vols. 87p., 82p.

A revised and expanded edition of the first edition of 1959, this
work is not confined to Australian publications. Part 1 covers
books for children up to 9 years and from 9 to 13. Part 2 caters to
adolescents from 13 to 17 years and includes books written for
teenagers and adult readers. Each age group is divided into fiction
and nonfiction arranged by subject. Brief annotations are descriptive and, where possible, evaluative. A revised and abbreviated
listing was published as a guide to Christmas buying in 1970.

Bos, Gerda. Good Reading: A List of Recommended Books for Grades
K-12. Grand Rapids, Mich.: National Union of Christian Schools,
1963. 100p.

This briefly annotated bibliography was prepared by a committee of teachers to assist in book selection in Christian schools, but
the compilers state "it should be made clear that we have not tried
to compile a list of Christian books." "There is no attempt to
isolate 'evil' that may appear in a child's book, just as 'good
literature' cannot isolate itself from life." Four parts list titles
under primary, intermediate, junior-high and high-school levels,
and there is further subdivision into fiction, poetry, biography,
folklore, and nonfiction. While a few earlier and later titles are
included, the bulk of entries seems to be of earlier vintage than
the publication date would suggest, concentrating around the era
of the 1940s. This perhaps reflects the compilers' own predilec-
tions. Selection appears moderately conservative in tone and has
regard to literary quality, and, as such, the choices can still be
suggestive for current purposes. The union's annual Library Book
Guide was recommended to update the list.

Bowles, Catherine, ed. Good and Inexpensive Books for Children. 5th
ed. Washington, D.C.: Assn. for Childhood Education Internatl.,
1972. 62p.

This briefly annotated list for children in elementary grades
concentrates on inexpensive books. The objective was to help
parents and children shop for inexpensive books of merit for their
personal libraries. Beginning as a bulletin of the association, it
has had a long publishing history under various titles which have
regularly reflected an inflated price ceiling. Children's Books for
75¢ or Less in 1947 and 1950 rose to 85¢ in 1952 and 1953, $1.25 in
1957, 1961, 1963, and 1965, and $1.50 in 1967 and 1969. Former
chairpersons of the compiling committees include Elizabeth H.
Gross (1957), Helen Oeschger (1963), Siddie Joe Johnson (1965),
Sylvia Sunderlin (1967), and Isabel Wilner (1969). Arrangement is
in conventional categories, such as picture books and recreation
and hobbies. All editions were very useful selections at the time
of publication, and many of the titles remain available.

Boylan, Lucile, and Sattler, Robert. <u>A Catalog of Paperbacks for Grades 7 to 12</u>. New York: Scarecrow, 1963. 209p.

Over 1,000 paperbacks to supplement school subjects are listed here. Nonfiction books are arranged according to Dewey; fiction is arranged alphabetically. Brief annotations include indication of grade level. Some provision is made for retarded and advanced students. Selection criteria, although not specified, do suggest that presence on approved reading lists was a basis for inclusion. As a school-oriented selection from the early days of the paperback revolution, the list has some historical interest, but the subsequent flood of paperback publications for young people has superseded its usefulness as a working tool.

Bradshaw, Valerie. <u>Across Time</u>. YLG Storylines, no. 4. Birmingham, Eng.: Library Assn., Youth Libraries Group, 1973. 16p.

This annotated list of fantasy books encourages young readers to try out new ideas. About fifty titles are grouped under objects and devices, atmosphere and emotional disturbance, time travel, and future time stories.

Branston, Elizabeth. <u>Reference Books</u>. London: National Book League, 1974. 26p.

While not stated to be specifically for school use, this selection by a young people's librarian was most valuable for that purpose. Over 200 items published in Britain are arranged by subject and briefly annotated. Canadian and other school libraries outside Britain would find the list useful to supplement American reference works.

Brewton, John E.; Brewton, Sara W.; and Blackburn, G. Meredith. <u>Index to Poetry for Children and Young People, 1964-1969: A Title, Subject, Author, and First Line Index to Poetry in Collections for Children and Young People</u>. New York: Wilson, 1972. 575p.

This publication supplements rather than supersedes its predecessors. The basic volume was published in 1942 with supplements in 1954 and 1965, all with the title <u>Index to Children's Poetry</u> .... The expanded title indicates greater emphasis on covering the needs of grades 7 to 12. Each volume lists and analyzes over a hundred collections and anthologies published since the closing date of the last, with choice of titles directed to those most available in American school and public library collections. It is useful therefore as a selection tool, but the basic objective is to assist librarians and teachers as a literary and topical resource accessible by author, title, subject, or first line. As such, like many of Wilson's standard reference tools, it is unrivaled and indispensable.

British Children's Books. 4th ed. London: National Book League, 1972.
      102p.
      Extensively revised and updated, this exhibition catalog suc-
ceeded those similarly titled in 1963, 1964, and 1967. Over 500
entries provide a historical overview of British publication for
children. An introduction by Eileen Colwell comments on
twentieth-century trends. All books exhibited are by British
authors whose works meet the criteria of a panel of distinguished
selectors, including children's authors and librarians. A sentence
or two of descriptive annotation accompanies each item, arranged
alphabetically within five chronological groupings: pre-1914,
1914-39, 1940-60, 1961-67, and 1968-71, the last three being
subdivided into fiction and nonfiction. The catalog forms a useful
checklist of the best of British books for young people, with stress
on the classics and titles of literary quality.

Broderick, Dorothy M. Image of the Black in Children's Fiction. New
      York: Bowker, 1973. 219p.
      A historical, literary, and critical analysis of the portrait of the
black as portrayed in children's books from 1827 to 1967, this
study originated as a doctoral dissertation at Columbia University. Choice of the books analyzed was confined to those listed in
Jacob Blanck's Peter Parley to Penrod for earlier titles and
editions of the H. W. Wilson's Children's Catalog for later ones.
Arrangement begins chronologically and then examines recurrent
stereotypes in relation to the social milieu of their time. There
are numerous extracts. The author stresses that her book is
written by a white for other whites. This important thesis established through careful research reveals the racist nature of and
social lag in children's literature. As the author admits, using
subject headings other than "Negro" might have produced a less
devastating picture of our society's portrayal of the black. However, everyone should look at the sample bibliographies of children's books that are analyzed and go on to read their explication
in the text. A challenging contribution that comes in an era that
promises some degree of social change in children's literature, and
a warning that the mistakes of the past must not be repeated.

——. An Introduction to Children's Work in Public Libraries. New
      York: Wilson, 1965. 176p.
      Intended as a general textbook for librarians, particularly those
who work by themselves, this slim, subjective volume gives almost
equal attention to the management of children's collections in
public libraries and the discussion of types of literature for children and how to use them with children of all age groups. Space is
devoted to picture books, nonfiction books, easy reading, unusual
books, and books about children's books. It refers often to The
Horn Book and Arbuthnot in its brief treatment of selection, and

to no one save the author for the clever interweaving of book titles to illustrate points. The titles are traditional, and the author's approach to children's literature is better indicated by her chapter on discipline and programming: a philosophy is advocated for public libraries that will compensate for the dominance of middle-class values. A second edition was published in 1977.

Bryant, Sara Cone. How to Tell Stories to Children. Ann Arbor, Mich.: Gryphon, 1971. 260p.

In this practical source book of the old-fashioned type (a reprint of the 1905 original edition), the author shares her knowledge and style in storytelling and enunciates sound, though personal, principles. Chapters cover the art of storytelling, selection, adaptation, and specific schoolroom uses. The latter part of the book lists selected and adapted stories arranged according to grade level from kindergarten to grades 4 and 5. Her choice, though of her generation, is not without interest today.

Burrell, Arthur A. A Guide to Story Telling. Ann Arbor, Mich.: Gryphon, 1971. 336p.

A reprint of the original British edition published by Pitman in 1926, and dedicated "to all who try to educate by the told story," this book was intended for teachers who were not experts in order to remedy the neglect of storytelling in teacher training. The account of the nature and history of storytelling and the different types of stories includes mention of authors and their books, and a list of suitable stories and short stories, with synopses, concludes the work. Difference in time and place from the current American scene makes it an interesting comparative account.

Byler, Mary Gloyne. American Indian Authors for Young Readers: A Select Bibliography. New York: Assn. on American Indian Affairs, 1973. 26p.

This short bibliography is based on the premise that it is essential to be an Indian to write about being one. Therefore, only books written by American Indians are included and, as the compiler points out, there are few of those. The interesting introduction is concerned with negative stereotyping and calls on publishers, schools, and libraries to take another look at books they offer to children. The bibliography lists American Indian authors alphabetically, identifying tribal affiliation, and recommends grade level. Descriptive annotations point out positive American Indian characteristics, and tales based on oral tradition are emphasized. Brief though this list is, it should stimulate practitioners and publishers as well as provide authentic material for a young audience.

Cahoon, Herbert. Children's Literature: Books and Manuscripts: An
   Exhibition. November 19, 1954, through February 28, 1955. New
   York: Pierpont Morgan Library, 1954. 84p.

   A catalog of an important exhibition of early children's books,
especially American ones, this work "attempts to show in an early
form many, but not all of the important works for children." Over
300 books (periodicals and games had to be excluded) chosen from
a wide chronological range are arranged in four thematic groups:
education; fable and fairytales; poetry and nursery rhymes; and
"The Moral Tale to Mickey Mouse." Most were on loan, many from
private collectors, but a highlighted item was the Morgan's own
presentation manuscript of Charles Perrault's Contes de ma Mère
L'Oye. The brief descriptive notes and full citations reflect the
bibliographical expertise of the compiler, making the catalog a
valuable reference source for collectors, librarians, and
historians.

Cameron, B. I.; Barrett, R. E.; and Barton, R. G. Fiction for the Middle
   School. London: National Book League, 1970. 39p.

   This list has been selected for students with an age range from 8
to 13, whose reading abilities and interest levels range from
picture books to adult authors. The aim is to introduce a wide
variety of authors with books that children are known to enjoy,
including some used for creative activity in the classroom. Each
of the 183 items is briefly annotated and carries code notations
for reading ability and interest age. The entries suggest additional titles by many of the authors.

Cameron, Eleanor. The Green and Burning Tree: On the Writing and
   Enjoyment of Children's Books. Boston: Little, 1969. 377p.

   This collection of essays, some based on talks and some "written
out of joy" on the appreciation rather than the criticism of
children's literature, is dedicated to "all those concerned with the
minds and imaginations of children." The author, preoccupied
with the craft of writing since her teens, seeks to identify what
makes books memorable. The essays are grouped under four
headings: "Fantasy"; "Writing Itself"; "The Child and the Book";
and "Vision and Act." The text includes excerpts from distinguished children's books and biographical details about their
authors.

Canada. Department of Indian Affairs and Northern Development.
   About Indians: A Listing of Books. 3rd ed. Ottawa: The
   Department, 1975. 321p.

   First published in 1973, this annotated bilingual list of books
about native American peoples was designed for teachers, librarians, and the general public. A second edition appeared in 1974.
While items cover all of North America, with a few on Central and

South America, Canadian material is emphasized and distinguished by a maple leaf symbol. The long descriptive and critical annotations were composed with the assistance of Indian university students and are often very frank in commenting on books not recommended. Titles are arranged in broad age categories: K to grade 3; grades 3 to 6; grade 6 and beyond; and French-language titles. Some carry more specific age recommendations. The attractive appearance is enhanced by excellent illustrations which concentrate on traditional crafts and artifacts in the second edition, and the social situation in the third edition. This distinguished production is the best comprehensive bibliographical guide to the subject. The fourth edition appeared in 1977.

Canadian Library Association. Canadian Materials [1971-] 1972: An Awareness List for School Resource Centres of Print and Non-Print Materials Issued in the Calendar Year [1971-] 1972. Ottawa: The Association, 1973. 92p. Annual.

Prepared in the belief that the lack of Canadian material for the Canadian student was a "national calamity," two annual editions, for 1971 and 1972, appeared in 1973 of this list. Included are "Canadian produced or oriented materials suitable for inclusion in school resource centres from Kindergarten to Grade 12." Preceded by a subject index which gives grade recommendations, printed and audiovisual items, such as films and games, are arranged alphabetically with a paragraph of descriptive and critical comment. The planned annual companions for succeeding years failed to materialize, but publication resumed on a semiannual pattern in 1975, with a cumulated index. This indispensable aid for the appreciation of Canada in Canadian schools compensates for an inevitable bias in American materials, and is now firmly established. From 1976 there were three, and from 1980 four, issues a year.

Canadian Library Association. Young People's Section. Committee on Canadian Books. Canadian Books. Ottawa: The Association, 1963-72. 36p. Annual.

This annual listing, which first appeared as a brief offprint from typescript in 1955, assumed a standard form in 1963, covering books of 1962. The final 1972 printing combined the sixteenth and seventeenth annual selections, arranging books published in 1970 and 1971 separately under broad subject groupings. A committee of public and school librarians selected Canadian books in English and French--those written by Canadians, and those about Canada and Canadians--for the use of young people in libraries "for reference, study and recreation." Annotations are brief; reference titles are designated with an R, titles judged suitable for senior grades in junior high-schools because of language or complexity with an S, and highly recommended titles are starred.

Dewey classification numbers are provided. The choices represented the response of professional librarians to the growing
movement for Canadian content in young people's reading, together with the growth of Canadian publishing in this area, and so
retain retrospective interest for those interested, in and outside
Canada.

Canadian School Library Association. Basic Book List for Canadian
    Schools. Rev. ed. 3 vols. Ottawa: The Association, 1968-69.
    290p., 145p., 163p.
    First published in 1966, this selection by a committee of the
    association includes books which have proved essential for
    Canadian schools, wherever their place of publication, and is
    intended as a guide for first purchase, not for a complete collec-
    tion. Part 1, the elementary division, comprises 1067 titles for
    use by grades 1 to 6; part 2, the junior division, 871 titles for
    grades 7, 8, and 9; and part 3, the senior division, 947 titles for
    grades 10 to 13. Part 1 is arranged by type of publication, such as
    picture books, fiction and reference, and broad subject divisions;
    part 2 is classified by a simplified form of Dewey. All items have
    a short paragraph of descriptive annotation and grade levels are
    indicated. Having an almost official status, with the imprimatur
    of the sponsoring and the publishing associations, this thorough
    selection reflects a catholicity of taste and interest from the
    classic to the popular. It was influential at a period when
    Canadian school libraries were beginning to expand. Now largely
    outdated, a successor is required which would show the same
    nationality of objective and internationality of scope.

Cane, Suzanne S.; Chatfield, Carol A.; Holmes, Margaret C.; and
    Peterson, Christine C., eds. Selected Media about the American
    Indian for Young Children, K-3. Boston: Mass. Dept. of Educa-
    tion, Div. of Curriculum and Instruction, Bureau of Curriculum
    Innovation, 1970. 21p.
    Originally a project in the Graduate Library School of Simmons
    College, this is an evaluative annotated bibliography of media,
    chiefly books and recordings, with a few films. Prefatory matter
    includes two contributions by American Indians, W. W. Keeler, a
    chief of the Cherokee nation, and Frank James. The list is divided
    into three sections: children's material, including both material
    for children and for the use of adults with children, and a list of
    museums to visit; adult background material; and selected sources
    of additional material. Criteria for inclusion were nonstereo-
    typing, high literary quality, and child appeal. Selection was
    deliberately limited, and at the time of publication the items
    could be purchased for about $200. Consequently, as a core
    collection, the list would now need to be supplemented with other
    choices as well as later publications in this developing area.

Capelle, Elizabeth; Lewis, Susan; and Miles, Betty. Little Miss Muffet
     Fights Back: A Bibliography of Recommended Non-Sexist Books
     about Girls, Compiled by Feminists on Children's Media. 2nd ed.
     New York: Feminists on Children's Media, 1974. 62p.
          The group, disturbed by the stereotyped portrayals of girls and
     women found in children's books, sponsored the first edition of this
     list in 1971, with Pat Ross as compiler. This revision deletes some
     titles and adds many more. The introduction discusses the objec-
     tive: to provide a representative sample of well-written, thought-
     provoking books that show girls and women as vital human beings
     or that indicate an understanding of social conditions that would
     encourage meaningful choices towards self-fulfillment. The bib-
     liography is subdivided into picture books, fiction, biography,
     history, and women's rights.

Caples, Beth. Story Hour for the Three-to-Five-Year Olds. Baltimore:
     Enoch Pratt Free Library, 1958. 26p.
          This pamphlet guide for adults who wish to tell stories to young
     children explains with practical suggestions how one goes about
     giving a story hour. A three-page listing of books that can be used
     successfully with this age group is appended. The advice is still
     sound; the list will serve beginners as a focal point, but requires
     supplementation with more recent titles.

Carlsen, G. Robert. Books and the Teenage Reader: A Guide for
     Teachers, Librarians and Parents. 2nd ed. New York: Harper,
     1971. 247p.
          First published in 1967, this reading guide by an authority on
     teaching English in high schools has become the most consulted
     work on the topic by parents and other concerned lay people, as
     well as youth workers, teachers, librarians, and students of educa-
     tion and library service. This edition is sponsored by the National
     Book Committee, with the professional endorsement of the
     American Library Association, the International Reading Associ-
     ation, and the National Council of Teachers of English. The
     author's key to encouraging reading is the realization that teen-
     agers are individuals with problems and interests of their own.
     The important step of getting them started as readers is depen-
     dent on this central concept, and the book presents basic tech-
     niques for "making a reader out of a human being" by emphasizing
     the joy and fulfillment of reading. The text provides practical and
     specific answers to a wide range of adolescent reading problems,
     supplemented by an annotated descriptive guide to over 1,000
     books selected with the above in mind. Many titles are also
     referred to in the text, which discusses such areas as subliterar-
     ture, the adolescent novel, popular adult books, shockers, signifi-
     cant modern literature, and the place of the classics. The bibliog-
     raphy covers hobbies, personal advice, adventure, reference

books, science fiction, ethnic literature, and books for the college
bound. It makes a very valuable selection tool for schools and
libraries. All editions were published simultaneously in paperback
by Bantam. Another updated edition appeared in 1980.

Carlson, Ruth Kearney. Emerging Humanity: Multi-Ethnic Literature
for Children and Adolescents. Dubuque, Ia.: Brown, 1972. 246p.
    The author is aiming to help teachers from kindergarten to
grade 12 understand ethnic literature, as well as "to humanize
people." Discussion of the general features of ethnic literature
includes definitions, values, basic criteria, and ideas to help interpretation, laying stress on classroom activities. Four ethnic
groups and their literature are singled out: African blacks,
American blacks, American Indians, and Mexican-Americans.
Appended to each chapter are reactions, questions, and projects
stemming from the text, and an annotated bibliography of books
subdivided by level: primary, intermediate, adolescent, and professional and adult. There are illustrations from photographs and
charcoal drawings of representatives of ethnic groups.

——. Enrichment Ideas: Sparkling Fireflies. Literature for Children.
Dubuque, Ia.: Brown, 1970. 109p.
    The author and series editor here seeks to share creative ideas
she has found useful in class and in her work with elementary
grades and students up to grade 12. The approach is refreshingly
imaginative and stimulating for students in education and library
schools as well as for working teachers. Each chapter has a dual
listing of selected books for children and for professionals and
other adults. A feature is the full index of activities.

——, ed. Folklore and Folktales around the World. Perspectives in
Reading, no. 15. Newark, Del.: International Reading Assn.,
1972. 172p.
    This collection of conference papers was prepared by the asso-
ciation's Library and Literature Committee. The eleven contributions are organized on a geographic basis, covering the Western
Hemisphere, Europe, and the Pacific area, but omitting Asia and
Africa. Canadian and American chapters by Sheila Egoff and
Rosemary Weber are thematic rather than descriptive: "Reflections and Distortions of Canadian Folklore in Children's Literature" and "The American Hero in Children's Literature." The book
is designed to bring to the attention of teachers, librarians, and
others interested the rich resources available in folklore. Despite
its geographic restrictions, it deserves the attention of a wider
audience and fills a need about a topic of contemporary interest
and significance. References are appended to each chapter and an
eleven-page bibliography, divided geographically, is given of folklore and tales.

Carpenter, Charles. History of American Schoolbooks. Philadelphia:
    Univ. of Pennsylvania Pr., 1963. 322p.
        A general portrayal of American textbooks up to about 1875 in
    relation to the pioneer day school system, this work is confined to
    books used in common schools--elementary and secondary--and
    ranges from The New England Primer to McGuffey's Readers.
    Spelling, writing, and copybooks are included, and information is
    given on science books and schoolbook publishing. There is an
    annotated bibliography.

Carter, Julia S. Subject and Title Index to Short Stories for Children.
    Chicago: American Library Assn., 1955. 333p.
        The aim of this work is "to assist public and school librarians in
    locating stories on specific or related subjects, and in tracing
    hard-to-find stories." Almost 5,000 stories from 372 titles
    selected for children from grade 3 through 8 have been indexed
    according to subject headings derived from Sears's List of Subject
    Headings and the Children's Catalog. A list of books indexed
    precedes the subject index which takes up over half the volume;
    this is followed by the index of stories under title and author with
    code referencing to the books. Cross references are clear and
    useful. A valuable aid to teachers and school librarians when
    published, new publications and the retiring of old books have
    inevitably rendered it obsolete.

Carter, Yvonne; Jones, Milbrey L.; Moses, Kathlyn J.; Sutherland,
    Louise B.; and Watt, Lois B. Aids to Media Selection for Students
    and Teachers. Washington, D.C.: Govt. Print. Off., 1971. 82p.
    Supplement, 1973. 67p.
        This useful list was sponsored by the Library Resources Division
    of the U.S. Department of Health, Education, and Welfare. A
    forerunner entitled Book Selection Aids for Children and Teachers
    prepared by Milbrey L. Jones and others, was issued in 1966, with a
    supplement, Sources of Audio-Visual Materials, in 1967. Three
    sections cover book selection sources, sources of audiovisual
    materials, and sources of multiethnic tools. In addition to rele-
    vant current bibliographical and reference tools, general and
    subject periodicals that review books and audiovisual materials
    are included. Citations carry descriptive annotation, and items
    and sources are fully indexed. Revisions appeared in 1976 and
    1979.

Cass, Joan E. Books for the Under Fives. London: National Book
    League, 1970. 20p.
        This list of about 180 British imprints modestly claims to be a
    useful list. Each entry has a lively paragraph of critical and
    descriptive annotation. The books are grouped as stories and
    picture books, collections of stories, nursery rhymes and poetry,

and play ideas. An introduction is addressed to parents. The author published a shorter but similar selection in 1973.

——. Books for the Under Fives: A Starter Collection. London: National Book League, 1973. 16p.

Shorter than the author's list of 1970, but arranged similarly, this work aims to share books with children in which they can identify live characters. The frightening, the weird, and the distorted are avoided. Each book is intended to help satisfy a feeling, an idea, wish, or need of a young child. Entries are described critically and annotations often mention other titles by the author.

——. Literature and the Young Child. London: Longmans, 1967. 259p.

This book is written for parents and teachers, and anyone who reads and tells stories for children from 2 to 7 or 8 years of age, or who shares picture books with them. General types of stories are identified, and storytelling techniques are described with examples. Picture books and their illustrators are discussed, and the appeal of poetry to young children is examined. The bibliography includes a representative selection of about 120 mainly British titles, with brief annotations, divided into two sections; books for reading to and looking at with children, and background books on the subject. Although this work is a standard educational book produced for a British audience (with the identifiable Little Black Sambo and sequels), it does present satisfactory bibliographies on the subjects of reading to and looking at books with children.

Cathon, Laura E.; Haushalter, Marion McC.; and Russell, Virginia A. Stories to Tell to Children: A Selected List. 8th ed. Pittsburgh: Univ. of Pittsburgh Pr., 1974. 145p.

All editions of this well-known work since the first in 1916 have been prepared for the Carnegie Library of Pittsburgh Children's Services Division. Four editions were issued before World War II; the sixth and seventh appeared in 1949 and 1960, respectively, under the same principal editorship as this revised eighth edition, compiled with Margaret Hodges as consultant. Titles were chosen for use by libraries, schools, clubs, and radio and television storytellers. The selections are unannotated, but graded, and arranged alphabetically by the title of each story in sections covering preschool children, 6-10-year-olds, older boys and girls, holiday programs (religious and patriotic), and aids for storytellers. Stories from picture books are coded for preschool children. A classified list of topics is provided as well as an author-title list of the books from which the stories were taken. This is a comprehensive collection of tried and true tales that are successful with children. Its high quality, developed over the years, makes it a valuable selection tool.

Catterson, Jane H., ed. Children and Literature. Newark, Del.: International Reading Assn., 1970. 104p.

Intended to help elementary and high-school teachers bring literature into the school curriculum, this selection of papers was originally presented at the association's 1968/69 conference. Grouped in three divisions, "The Point of View," "Choosing the Books," and "Using the Books," the papers reflect the rapidly changing climate for literature and a commitment to the development of worthy reading habits, through providing positive literary experiences which will carry over into the future. Most contributors are educators from a university.

Chambers, Aidan. Introducing Books to Children. London: Heinemann, 1973. 152p.

Written for teachers, particularly student teachers, and others concerned with helping children become willing and enthusiastic readers, this book takes a practical look at the ideas, methods, and various approaches which bring books and young people in contact. The author avoids extensive consideration of the literature of teaching. Chapters describe the importance of reading experience and practical explorations of appropriate methods based on discussions with other teachers. Sources for further reference are indicated at the end of each chapter, and there is a concluding bibliography. The author's lucid statements about how to manage children's reading can be profitably read by all. Although there are other British sources to help the novice teacher confront children and books, the diversity of topics about encouraging children to read recommends this book as introductory reading.

——. Reading for Enjoyment for 11 Year Olds and Up. London: Children's Book News, 1975. 32p.

This is the fourth in a series (see Moss, Reading for Enjoyment with 2 to 5 Year Olds) intended to help parents, teachers, and librarians introduce to young adults books that they can enjoy and which will help lead them into maturity. While controversial issues are not avoided, this is not a list of books about adolescent problems. Selected for a wide variety of tastes, titles are mainly British with some American. Almost all are published specifically for teenagers. Over 100 titles carry perceptive annotations, descriptive and critical. The first edition, entitled Reading for Enjoyment for 12 Year Olds and Up, was published in 1970.

——. The Reluctant Reader. Oxford: Pergamon, 1969. 161p.

Why normal young people can be reluctant readers is the subject of this work. The author, who writes for children, has drawn on teaching experience in English schools by himself and others. His stated emphasis is on people and general requirements rather than on the analysis of individual books. An unannotated selection of five-star books and lists of books for school, public, and personal libraries, adult books for young people, and books for use with classes is included. Always of interest, this book about the slower reader gives practical advice, and lists of titles that may appeal. Because of the general scarcity of such material, the titles are not as dated as they may seem.

Chambers, Dewey W. Children's Literature in the Curriculum. Rand McNally Education Series. Chicago: Rand, 1971. 227p.

The author, an elementary teacher for ten years, pleads the case of children's literature as an integral part of the school curriculum, and stresses its importance as a factor in children's lives. The book is an attempt to bring theory into a practical framework, furnishing models and examples to delight, inform, and instill values. Three sections discuss the role of literature in the elementary curriculum, how books can affect children, and controversial issues in children's literature, including special issues such as book reports, award winners, paperback series, and controlled vocabulary.

Chandler, Martha H. A Bibliography of Books for Young Children Representing Different Categories of Interest. Boston: Eliot-Pearson Alumnae Assn., 1970. 22p.

This unannotated list of selected titles for young children was prepared for the Eliot-Pearson Department of Child Study at Tufts University. Books were chosen for literary and artistic merit and arranged under interest, topic, and type. Age recommendations are given. Supplementary annotated lists are given of adult works of interest to workers with children, parents, and education students.

Charlton, Kenneth. Recent Historical Fiction for Secondary School Children. Teaching of History Leaflet, no. 18. London: The Historical Assn., 1960. 20p.

Over 200 titles published since 1950 and written specifically for children are arranged by historical period with brief descriptive comments. The introduction discusses the value of historical fiction and appropriate selection criteria. Selection has a British emphasis, but not exclusively.

Chase, Judith Wragg, ed. Books to Build World Friendship; An Annotated Bibliography of Children's Books from Pre-School to 8th Grade; Europe. Dobbs Ferry, N.Y.: Oceana, 1966. 76p.

This is a list of briefly annotated titles on how to overcome international tension and misunderstanding, and is designed to assist current social studies through supplemental reading. Coverage of other continents has not been published. Arrangement is alphabetical by country, with a supplementary short list of foreign-language works. Books from an American point of view have been excluded, and limitations have been placed on the inclusion of nonfiction books, works with a historical setting, fantasy, and out-of-print titles. The list is intended as a beginning, not a definitive, selection, and is restricted to those read and evaluated by the author. Titles cover a wide grade level, but reflect the restraints imposed in both quantity and quality. Although the compiler has aimed too high with a very subjective approach, the list, by now dated, is useful in spite of its deficiencies.

Child Study Association of America. Children's Books of the Year. New York: The Association, 1930- . Annual.

With variant titles, this is an annual publication selected by two committees of the association that has covered books of the previous year since 1930. Addressed primarily to parents and those who work with children, the choices have stressed children's enjoyment in reading as well as literary value. Paying special attention to possible emotional and intellectual impact, the credo has been to help children learn to cope, not to shield them. Some 300 to 600 titles a year are grouped in three age groups from preschool to teenage and under general headings such as collections, special interests (e.g., science), reprints, paperbacks, and titles for parents and counselors. Brief annotations include age recommendations. Useful both for current buying and for retrospective checking, this is a quality list by a concerned group.

——. Recommended Reading about Children and Family Life. New York: The Association, 1969. 74p. Supplement, 1970.

Preceded by the association's similar Books of the Year . . . for Children, Selected by the Children's Book Committee; about Children, Parents and Family Life, Selected by the Book Review Committee, with a publishing history under variant titles going back to 1930, this title was first issued in 1966, covering books published from 1960. The selection combines books about children, arranged in special categories such as child development and rearing, sex education, schools and learning, mental health education, and social problems, with books for children, about special situations such as going to the hospital, death, and adoption. Entries carry lengthy critical annotation. It forms a very useful checklist for children's librarians and others because of the quality of the selection, which takes account of changing social values.

——. Book Review Committee. The Children's Bookshelf: A Guide to Books for and about Children. 2nd ed. New York: Bantam, 1965. 194p.

Revised and edited by the same committee that compiles the association's annual list Books of the Year, this is a valuable combination of articles and a bibliography first published in 1962. A publication with the same title, but with the subtitle A Parents' Guide to Good Books for Boys and Girls was issued by the Federal Security Agency in 1946, but the first edition sponsored by this association, published in paperback by Bantam, appeared in 1962. Criteria included literary value and reader appeal in the selection of a wide range of titles for young people from 3 to 14. Nine articles by distinguished writers on books for children are complemented by chapters devoted to age categories: under 3, 3 to 5, 5 to 7, 7 to 9, 9 to 12, 12 to 14, and bridges to adult reading. Titles in the bibliography are briefly annotated and arranged by title under age or topic. Included are books and pamphlets of concern to parents or professionals on family and social issues dealing with children. Changes of cultural attitude, as well as new publications, have tended to outmode a selection made two decades ago. But much remains valid in this widely distributed paperback.

——. Children's Book Committee. Latin America in Books for Boys and Girls. Washington, D.C.: Pan American Union, 1956. 23p.

This list, issued by the union's Department of Cultural Affairs as a supplement to the accessions list of the Columbus Memorial Library, includes earlier titles now hard to locate.

——. Children's Book Committee. Reading with Your Child through Age Five. Rev. ed. New York: The Association, 1972. 40p.

This pamphlet is intended to aid parents and others who want to help preschoolers who enjoy reading find suitable inexpensive books. The first edition appeared in 1970. An introductory article by Josette Frank gives practical advice about reading to young children. The booklist of almost 200 titles then in print is arranged in eight categories by broad topic or type of publication. Entries are briefly annotated and those titles that are easier to read are starred.

Children's Book Council. The Children's Book Showcase. New York: The Council, 1972- . Annual.

These annual exhibit catalogs, timely and functionally produced through the seventies, aim to share and spread the appreciation of quality and beauty in children's books. The selection committees, which have included artists, design directors, and editors, explain their criteria and provide systematic annotation which emphasizes artistic and manufacturing elements. A double-page spread is allotted to each of the twenty to thirty selected titles. Historically, these lists, along with catalogs of the American Institute of Graphic Arts (AIGA) shows, will provide a record of outstanding illustrated work in children's books, and will instill in librarians and others high standards for acquiring them.

——. The World of Children's Books. New York: The Council, 1952. 128p.
Various aspects of the field from literary values and the tastes of parents and children to trade promotion and bookselling are covered in this collection of essays. Authors include such well-known figures as Joseph Wood Krutch, Frederic G. Melcher, and Anne Thaxter Eaton. Some have bibliographies, and examples of children's books are cited in the text.

Children's Books on the Commonwealth. 2nd ed. London: National Book League, 1968. 35p.
This annotated reading list of 200 items was prepared for the 1968 Commonwealth in Books exhibition in London. The books-- fiction and nonfiction--published in Britain and the British Commonwealth cover the overseas Commonwealth and are arranged by continent and country. A similar exhibition was held and a catalog published in 1966 with 248 items.

Chukovskii, Kornei Ivanovich. From Two to Five. Translated and edited by Miriam Morton. Berkeley: Univ. of California Pr., 1971. 170p.
An English translation of this seminal work by one of the deans of Russian children's writers first appeared in Britain in 1963. This is a revised edition, simultaneously issued on both sides of the Atlantic, with a foreword by Frances Clarke Sayers. The original book, entitled Malen'kie Deti, was published in 1925. The author, writing in a conversational style of general appeal, opposes the concept of realism in creating literature for young children. As a poet himself, he uses a poem, "The Roach," as an appendix to illustrate his theories. An extended bibliographical essay in six chapters, it lacks an index and readers will have to read the text for individual references to children's books. The translation is slightly abridged.

Cianciolo, Patricia. Illustrations in Children's Books. Literature for Children. Dubuque, Ia.: Brown, 1970. 130p.
One of the publisher's series directed to elementary classroom teachers, this work provides a thorough and stimulating discussion of the significance of illustration as an art form and as an important factor in the creation of books for children, and the use of such books in the school situation. Chapters cover appraisal, style, media, and techniques. There are bibliographies at the end of each chapter, and many titles are referred to in the text. An

added bibliography of illustrated children's books is a compilation of books with pictures that effectively illustrate the text and exemplify qualities required in appraisal. A second edition appeared in 1976.

——, ed. Picture Books for Children. Chicago: American Library Assn., 1973. 159p.

Compiled with the assistance of the Picture Book Committee, a subcommittee of the Elementary Booklist Committee of the National Council of Teachers of English, this list is intended to serve as a resource and guide for teachers from nursery school through junior high, librarians in school and public libraries, and parents. It also functions as a reference tool for courses in library schools and schools of education. The introduction explores the values, criteria, and uses of the genre today and examines trends in writing and illustration. Stated objectives include identifying and describing picture books that give children enjoyable and informative literary experience, fostering reading, and appreciating graphic art. Each title carries a committee evaluation of the story and the artistic medium, which indicates the age range. The majority are recent publications up to early 1973, but some classics are included. This work constitutes a valuable selection tool and thirty-five full-page illustrations make it an attractive publication.

Cimino, Maria, and Masten, Helen A. Foreign Children's Books Available in the United States. Rev. ed. Chicago: American Library Assn., Children's Library Assn., 1954. 32p.

First published in 1952, this booklet, attractively printed by the New York Public Library, arranges titles under the languages in which they were written. The list is highly selective, the number of items for each country varying from half a dozen to about thirty. Short descriptive annotations stress the illustrative content. High quality and the proportion of children's classics included make this selection still interesting, although the time lag has largely eliminated the availability factor.

Clark, Berna C., ed. Books for Primary Children: An Annotated List. 3rd ed. London: School Library Assn., 1969. 113p.

This basic list for British primary schools, compiled by the association's Primary Schools Subcommittee, aims to help teachers select essential books, both imaginative and factual, for the school library. Nearly a thousand titles are briefly annotated and arranged in four parts: picture books, poems, stories and plays for infants, younger and older juniors; encyclopedias, dictionaries and subject works; series in simple format; and some adult books. First published in 1960 as Primary School Library Books, edited by C. H. C. Osborne, and reprinted with additions in 1961, it appeared in a second edition in 1965, edited by Felicity Sturt. Annual additions selected from reviews in the School Librarian appeared for 1971, 1972, 1973, and 1974 in pamphlet form entitled Recent Primary School Books: A . . . Select List. A standard for British schools, this authoritative selection is valuable for comparison purposes for North American libraries.

——. Children's Stories: Fiction, Verse and Picture Books for the Primary and Middle School. Oxford: School Library Assn., 1974. 87p.

Planned as a replacement for the fiction and poetry element in Books for Primary Children (1969), over 500 current items are briefly annotated and grouped as picture books for infants; poems, nursery rhymes and anthologies of stories for infants; stories, collections and poems for young juniors; and stories and poems for older juniors. A selection of illustrations and an index are provided. This is a helpful British list with many titles unfamiliar to North American libraries.

Clarke, Penelope. Natural Science: A Selection of Books for the Middle and Secondary School. Oxford: School Library Assn., 1973. 43p.

Intended to replace coverage of this area in Eleven to Fifteen (1963), this annotated selection of books currently available in the field of natural science is not a specialist list, but represents books of general interest and value to 11- to 16-year-olds which have proved worthwhile in British schools. Attention has been paid to new developments, and readable text and visual appeal have been criteria of choice.

Cleary, Florence Demon. Blueprints for Better Reading: School Programs for Promoting Skill and Interest in Reading. 2nd ed. New York: Wilson, 1972. 312p.

This "procedure manual and idea book" for improving reading programs is directed to those preparing to teach in classrooms and libraries, as well as to those more experienced. The author, experienced as a librarian in public schools, reaffirms the concept that skill and interest in reading are independent but inseparable, and that neither quality can be reached unless both are pursued simultaneously. By identifying problems and suggesting productive programming and methods, she seeks to enable teachers and librarians to build up reading habits and values in their pupils. First published in 1957, the work is greatly enlarged in this edition, and has benefited by its hypotheses being tested in active research and studies in reading guidance. Appendixes list books for children and young people mentioned in the text, educational films, and records.

Cohen, Munroe D.; Sunderlin, Sylvia; and Jacobs, Leland B., eds. Literature with Children. Washington: Assn. for Childhood Education Internatl., 1972. 64p.

This collection of articles on a broad range of topics relating to literature for children and its relation to the community has been prepared by academics in the field of education, and the audience is likely to be a professional one. Titles range from "Enjoying Poetry with Children" to "Children's Literature in the Content Areas." The articles reflect the experience of experts and contain sage advice. A similar collection was issued by the association in 1946 under the title Literature and Children.

Colby, G. Poindexter. The Children's Book Field. New York: Pellegrini, 1952. 246p.

Many of the personal opinions of the author are found in this explanation of juvenile publishing dedicated to authors of children's books. Editorial methods, reviewing, physical format, design, illustration, and production are examined in the light of publisher's practice in the fifties. As a historical reference in a field that has changed much, it retains some interest.

Colebourn, R. The Greek and Roman World: General and Topic Books, Selected and Annotated for Middle and Lower Secondary Schools. London: School Library Assn., 1971. 26p.

A representative selection of 172 books suitable for pupils aged from 10 and 11 to 14 and 15 years, this book covers every aspect of the classical world and reflects the changing emphasis on the classics in the curriculum. Titles were in print in Britain at the time of compilation.

Colwell, Eileen. To Begin With: A Guide for Reading for the Under-Fives. London: Mason, 1964. 24p.

This list offers guidance to parents and others about some of the best books available for children who have not yet learned to read. Emphasis is placed on picture books and stories for adults to read to children, in addition to nursery rhymes, Bible stories, and informational series. Only one title by each author is included, and there is a brief descriptive annotation for each. The books chosen are of good quality and carefully selected. That Little Black Sambo is the second book listed, however, indicates a British viewpoint and a caveat to some.

——; Green, L. Esmé; and Parrott, F. Phyllis, eds. First Choice: A Basic Book List for Children. London: Library Assn., 1968. 120p.

The aim of the editors of this title was to produce a list of books of high quality as a basic stock for British children's libraries. Only books written for children have been included, and requirements of readers over age 13 are not covered. Fiction is listed in three groups: picture books, for younger readers, and for older readers. Nonfiction is arranged in broad subject areas, subdivided into smaller subject groupings, and call numbers with abridged Dewey classification and Cutter numbers are supplied. Annotations, carefully written in a uniform style by a team of librarians, are evaluative rather than merely descriptive. Entries include original publication date and foreign imprint where appropriate; there are a number of American titles. There is full indexing. An official Library Association publication, this work can be regarded as a sound and slightly conservative British selection, with considerable comparative value for North American libraries.

Commire, Anne. Something about the Author: Facts and Pictures about Contemporary Authors and Illustrators of Books for Young People. Detroit: Gale, 1971- .
    Stylistically directed to young people, and designed to furnish an "almost personal introduction to authors whose books you read," this reference series is continuous and partly derived from the publisher's Contemporary Authors. Each volume runs from A-Z and cumulative indexes link them together. The approach is descriptive rather than critical, and emphasis is placed on providing information about the less-than-famous figures whose careers cannot be researched elsewhere. Author entries are sub-arranged under personal, career, writings, sidelights, and hobbies. Extracts are given from personal interviews, with many half-tone reproductions of portraits and book illustrations. Seven volumes appeared up to 1975, and the series continues.

Conwell, Mary K., and Belpré, Pura. Libros en Espanol: An Annotated List of Children's Books in Spanish. New York: New York Public Library, 1971. 52p.
    Sponsored by the South Bronx Project, an operation of the library aided by federal funds in a depressed urban area with many Puerto Rican immigrants, this selection of over 200 titles is briefly annotated in Spanish and English. Arrangement is in nine broad topical categories, including picture books, young readers, books for children in the middle-age group, books for older boys and girls, folklore, songs and games, anthologies, and bilingual books and books for learning Spanish. This is a carefully chosen starter list for communities with Spanish-speaking younger readers.

Coody, Betty. Using Literature with Young Children. Dubuque, Ia.: Brown, 1973. 174p.
    What is best to use with children from one to eight years of age is the subject of this introduction for prospective teachers to some of the available literature of early childhood. Chapters deal with aspects of the learning process and the incorporation of

literature with them, such as reading aloud, storytelling, and language experience. Each carries a short bibliography relating to the topic and an annotated list of related titles for children. While providing a methodology for teaching literature, the book can also be used as a supplementary textbook for introductory courses in childhood education.

Cook, Elizabeth. The Ordinary and the Fabulous: An Introduction to Myths, Legends and Fairy Tales for Teachers and Storytellers. London: Cambridge Univ. Pr., 1969. 152p.

The author, a lecturer in English, wishes to persuade teachers, librarians, and parents that an understanding of myths, legends, and fairy tales is essential for child development, and that there are many ways of presenting them so they become part of children's lives. The text describes old and new methods of interpretation, gives a survey of European traditions, and describes the practical approach of storytellers to the material. A classified and annotated list of tales suitable for different age groups is provided, but it is stressed that this is a personal selection. Humor and animal fables, and those outside the main European trends, are excluded. While the treatment is strongly literary and historical, anthropological and psychological factors are not ignored. Informative, with a literary approach, this book is suggested for teachers and librarians on both sides of the Atlantic. The British age recommendations, especially for fables for older children, will seem unusual to American readers.

Cooperative Children's Book Center. Materials on Indians of North America: An Annotated List for Children. Madison, Wis.: The Center, 1970. 15p.

A list of eighty-six items for teachers and librarians "to facilitate an appreciation of the North American Indian in the development of our civilization" and "to present a variety of effective literary approaches." Material is arranged by cultural groupings of Indian nations, from California to the Eastern and Northern woodland and from the Southwest and the Southeast to the Eskimo. Descriptive annotations include grade level and coding under basic, curriculum, or exhibit categories. Useful though it is, this small sampling of representational material will require supplementing for building a basic collection. It is also available as an ERIC document (ED 039 991).

Cory, Patricia Blair. School Library Services for Deaf Children. Washington, D.C.: Alexander Graham Bell Assn. for the Deaf, 1960. 142p.

This volume is one in the association's education series, designed to answer inquiries from parents, teachers, librarians, trustees, and supervisory and professional personnel. It aims to provide suggestions for an active library program for the deaf child, comments on the special techniques necessary for introducing the deaf child to the world of books, and inquires into the problems of selecting suitable printed and audiovisual material. The chapters on programs and selection list suitable titles with annotations and age recommendations. There are two concluding lists of professional books and children's books. While the bibliographic material needs supplementary updating, the rest remains valid commentary in a difficult-to-document field.

Coughlin, Margaret N. Creating Independence, 1763-1789, Background Reading for Young People: A Selected Annotated List. Washington, D.C.: Library of Congress, 1972. 62p.

Part of the library's program for the Bicentennial of the American Revolution, this guide was compiled by a specialist in the Children's Book Section, and carries a preface by its then-head, Virginia Haviland. An introduction by Richard B. Morris discusses the American Revolution as a young people's war. Books suitable for young people, including a few adult titles but excluding textbooks, were selected that presented "a point of view that broadens the reader's understanding not only of Revolutionary America, but also of problems still current, such as equal rights and individual freedom." Over a hundred items are arranged in chronological groupings and by subject relating to the period. Annotations are descriptive and interpretative in a style which is scholarly as well as appropriate for young readers.

Countries of the World. Topic Booklists. Tunbridge Wells, Eng.: Fenrose, 1974. 63p.

Each major country represented by children's historical fiction and biography available in Britain is allotted a section in this work. Titles are arranged chronologically within countries and given a brief descriptive annotation.

Crouch, Marcus, ed. Books about Children's Literature: A Booklist Prepared by the Committee of the Youth Libraries Group. Rev. ed. London: Library Assn., 1966. 36p.

This unannotated checklist, first published in 1963, is limited to books of interest to the student of children's books as a form of literature. It is not intended to be a substitute for a full bibliography. The contents cover the history of children's literature, criticism, bibliography, illustration, authorship, and biography.

——, comp. Chosen for Children; An Account of the Books Which Have Been Awarded the Library Association Carnegie Medal, 1936-1965. 2nd ed. London: Library Assn., 1967. 136p.

First published in 1957, this volume marked the twenty-first anniversary of the British award. Entries for the winning titles consist of a page of descriptive and critical assessment, along with a selected passage from the book and personal comment by its author. Illustrations include half-tone portraits of each author and line illustrations from the books. Valuable, as well, for its critical assessments and descriptions, this title is important as an official record of the Carnegie medal books. A third edition was published in 1977.

——. The Nesbit Tradition: The Children's Novel in England, 1945-1970. London: Benn, 1972. 239p.
An experienced British author and critic of books for children gives a personal commentary and appreciation of novels shared with young audiences over twenty-five years. Deploring the unprecedented spilling of so many critical words over children's literature, he enunciates his own view that there are no children's books per se--that is, the novel for children requires the same criteria applied to adult books: narrative, characterization, examination of society, objectives, and style. His criticisms keep in mind the requirements of the "serious English child" for reading fare more English and European than North American. Chapters cover topics such as high adventure, to the stars, foreign scenes, laughter, the open air, school, family, work, self, and society. There are a dozen illustrations and a supplementary list of twenty children's books for adults.

——. Treasure Seekers and Borrowers; Children's Books in Britain, 1900-1960. London: Library Assn., 1962.
Modeled on F. J. H. Darton's work covering the earlier periods, this general historical treatment aims to relate the books to contemporary social and educational ideas. Within the stated limitations, the author does indeed provide, as he hoped, more than a book list, although not a social document in the sense of Darton's title. The short chapter on pre-1900 juveniles serves as a good introduction to the readable narrative that follows about twentieth-century books and their significance. The text opens with Arthur Ransome and closes with Brian Wildsmith, a new author on the scene. Titles are easily retrievable through the index. A short reading list of books about children's literature is supplied.

Cullinan, Bernice E. Literature for Children: Its Discipline and Content. Literature for Children. Dubuque, Ia.: Brown, 1971. 108p.
This volume, intended primarily for elementary teachers and librarians, addresses itself to the task of identifying excellence in children's literature by using the tools of criticism applicable to all literature. It advocates a literature curriculum in elementary schools based on literary values, and suggests that it is entirely

too important a curricular area to be treated in a casual manner.
Examples for comment are selected from narrative fiction only
and citations of appropriate titles are given in the text. An
annotated bibliography on literary criticism and children's literature is included.

Culpan, Norman, and Messer, W. J. Contemporary Adult Fiction,
1945-1965, for School and College Libraries: A List of Books, with
a Short List of Critical Works on the Modern Novel, Chosen and
Annotated for the Use of Sixth-Form and Other Students. 3rd ed.
London: School Library Assn., 1967. 66p.
Primarily for advanced students in British secondary schools,
this annotated selection is also directed to teacher-training
colleges and adult education classes. Arranged alphabetically by
author, nearly 550 titles are distinguished for prior choice, for
mature and advanced readers, and as controversial works.
Allowing for these distinctions, the selection is perceptive and a
useful source for British publications. The descriptive and critical
notes have substance and style. Its very limitations make this a
valuable comparative source for American libraries, and not only
those for young people. First published in 1955 under the title of
Modern Adult Fiction . . . , covering titles since 1918, a second
edition appeared in 1960, and included an appendix of novels from
1955 to 1960. This edition adds nearly 200 titles, but its predecessors are still of value for the 1918-44 period omitted here.

Cundiff, Ruby Ethel. Recommended Reference Books for Elementary
School Libraries. 2nd ed. Chicago: Wilcox, 1951. 35p.
This basic short list proved a useful tool for many elementary
schools, but has now been long outdated.

——. Recommended Reference Books for the High School Library. 5th
ed., rev. and enl. Nashville: Tennessee Book Co., 1955. 28p.
First published in 1936 with revised and enlarged editions in
1940, 1949, and 1950, this list proved useful as a minimal require-
ment for high-school libraries. Features are similar to the author's companion volume for elementary school libraries.

——, and Webb, Barbara. Story-Telling for You: A Handbook of Help
for Story-Tellers Everywhere. Yellow Springs, Ohio: Antioch Pr.,
1957. 103p.
This storytelling handbook of a previous generation admits to
being a personal presentation by the two authors, who are sharing
their experiences with librarians and authors who may or may not
have told stories. Chapters include "The Importance of Storytelling," "Touch-Tell Stories," and "Some Proved Samples," where
the story is written out in full with an introductory comment
which includes the age level recommended. A select bibliography

arranges recommended stories by author under topics such as holidays and picture stories, with brief annotations. The authors' experience in storytelling remains admirable after twenty years, and their book will still be helpful to new storytellers.

Cusenza, Joan. The Eloise Ramsey Collection of Literature for Young People: A Catalog. Detroit: Wayne State Univ. Libraries, 1967. 389p.

This work is a catalog of the Ramsey collection in the university library, selected and organized by Professor Ramsey. Criteria for selection were originality of concept and treatment or unusual or outstanding book production. The volumes, mostly in English, range in date from 1658 to 1967, and are arranged in chronological groups within subheadings: Religion; Subject Matter Books; Literature Adopted by Young People; Sources for the Study of Children's Literature; Children's Periodicals; and Foreign Children's Books. Title-page transcriptions and some descriptive notes are given. While not bibliographically systematic, the catalog is a research guide to a sizable children's collection.

Dale, Joanne, ed. Portraits: Literature of Minorities: An Annotated Bibliography by and about Four Ethnic Groups in the United States for Grades 7-12. Los Angeles: Office of the Supt. of Schools, 1970. 70p. Supplement, 1972. 61p.

One of a series of publications of the office intended to aid teachers in curricular development, this committee project evaluates available literature "that portrays members of minorities in the United States as human beings who share all the experience of their common humanity, and who, at the same time, are in many ways unique." Books representing black Americans, Mexican-Americans, Asian Americans, and North American Indians were considered for language, illustrations, themes, character treatment and literary quality. Lengthy descriptive annotations include suggestions for use. Sections cover fiction, poetry, nonfiction, anthologies and background material. A wide range of reading and maturity level is provided, including titles with adult themes appreciated by young adults. As a resource checklist for teachers and librarians, this selection remains a valuable one.

Dalphin, Marcia. Light the Candles! A List for Christmas Reading. 2nd ed. Boston: Horn Book, 1960. 24p.

This list of books for Christmas reading first appeared in 1944, and is revised in this edition by Anne Thaxter Eaton. Directed to those who wish to use stories at Christmastime, the briefly annotated entries are arranged in informal groups according to various aspects of the Christmas season, such as Christmas carols, animals, Christmas in the family in America, Christmas parties and games, and "Christmas-Home made." A supplement, com-

piled by Sidney Long, entitled And All the Dark Make Bright like
Day: Christmas Books, 1960-1972, was published by Horn Book in
1973.

Darling, Richard L. The Rise of Children's Book Reviewing in America, 1865-1881. New York: Bowker, 1968. 452p.
    This investigation of nineteenth-century reviewing of children's
books in America concentrates on the years following the Civil
War, a period of expanding publishing for children. Thirty-six
literary and critical magazines are given special emphasis, but
religious, pedagogical, and trade journals are also examined.
Reviewing of selected books is analyzed with extensive quotation,
and many other titles are mentioned in the text. A bibliography of
over 2,000 reviews, arranged on an annual basis, forms an appendix. A detailed study in an unexploited area of research, originally
a dissertation.

Darton, F. J. Harvey. Children's Books in England: Five Centuries of
Social Life. 2nd ed. Cambridge: Cambridge Univ. Pr., 1958.
367p.
    First published in 1932, when the author believed it would
furnish a minor chapter on English social life, Darton's account of
English children's literature has become a landmark. In the
preface to this edition, Kathleen Lines points out that this work
was the first to tell the story of children's books in England
written as a continuous whole and as part of the history of English
social life. While viewing children's literature as a lively part of
contemporary literature in each generation, attention is directed
to those books which were printed ostensibly "to give children
spontaneous pleasure and not to teach them, nor solely to make
them good, nor to keep them profitably quiet." He exemplifies his
belief that "children's books were always the scene of a battle
between instruction and amusement, between restraint and freedom, between hesitant morality and spontaneous happiness."
Many titles are cited in the text, and stress is laid on carefully
researched bibliographical detail, with frequent comment on
publishing practices, which as a member of an old family business
in the field Darton was in a position to know well. While an
introductory survey gives an account of the earlier period, the
bulk of the narrative deals with the eighteenth and nineteenth
centuries, and not much is traced after 1901. Chapter arrangement is by chronology and genre. This edition does not add to the
story, confining textual changes to a few of the author's own
corrections and appending a select book list of books of general
and specific interest published since 1932. Supplements are also
made to the bibliographies at the end of each chapter. A few
illustrations are taken from early editions. Scholarly and humane,
Darton's work has classic standing in the field, and, in the words of

Percy Muir, "will never be supplanted." Because of his accuracy and taste, it remains a major authority in matters of fact and criticism and is essential for collectors and collections, students, and the general public.

Davies, Alan. Literature for Children. Open University Educational Studies. Bletchley, Buckinghamshire, Eng.: Open Univ. Pr., 1973. 49p.

The author of this instructional booklet intends to raise three questions for student discussion: what is the educational value of reading literature; what is literature for children; and what is the role of the teacher. He is also interested in the application of linguistics to the teaching of reading.

Davies, John. Christmas Stocking: A Select List. YLG Pamphlet, no. 14. Birmingham, Eng.: Library Assn., Youth Libraries Group, 1973. 17p.

Selected for librarians, teachers, and others, this is a list of books to expand the Christmas experience that does not include the "well tried or well rejected." Coverage includes picture books, fiction, anthologies, drama and music, and topics such as customs, handicrafts, and the Nativity. Entries have brief critical annotations.

Davis, Dorothy R., ed. The Carolyn Sherwin Bailey Historical Collection of Children's Books: A Catalogue. New Haven, Conn.: Southern Connecticut State College, 1966. 232p.

This is a description of 1,880 English and American children's books, dating from 1657 to 1930, presented to the college library by and in honor of Carolyn Sherwin (Bailey) Hill, children's author and Newbery Award winner. Coverage includes the conventional types of literature for the young, but only unusual books of instruction are listed. Arrangement is alphabetical, with some supplementary lists of anonymous material such as toy books and games. Many brief bio-bibliographical notes are supplied, with a generous sampling of half-tone reproductions.

Davis, Joan A. M., and Wood, Helena E. S. Books for School Libraries. London: National Froebel Foundation, 1950. 26p.

This unannotated listing arranged under subject topics is intended for British junior and secondary school teachers. Choice was limited to British publications of the previous twenty years that were judged interesting to older and abler primary school students, middle and lower secondary and grammar school students, and particularly to boys and girls in secondary modern schools.

Dawson, Mildred et al. Children, Books, and Reading. Perspectives in Reading. Newark, Del.: International Reading Assn., 1964. 150p.

This collection of conference papers aims to cultivate in elementary school teachers a strong desire to get children to read and appreciate worthwhile reading materials. Well-known American specialists represent different roles affecting children's reading. Robert Karlin, May Hill Arbuthnot, Margaret Edwards, Charlotte Huck, and Helen Huus are among the ten contributors. The latter's Interpreting Research in Children's Literature includes a useful bibliography. The concluding bibliography of 150 children's books, although unannotated, comprises an excellent small basic selection of value to teachers and students.

——, and Pfeiffer, Louise. A Treasury of Books for the Primary Grades. Teacher's Guide Series. San Francisco: Chandler, 1959. 32p.

Designed for professionals ordering books in schools and libraries, and also for parents and other purchasers, this list includes 300 books recommended for use as a basic library for children in the kindergarten and primary grades. The list is a secondary one, derived from a list of 1,200 titles cited in other selective and reviewing tools. Emphasis is on "high-grade literature most likely to have general appeal to young readers." Titles, with brief annotations and recommended grade levels, are arranged in eight topical categories. A chapter of suggestions on book selection is apposite and readable. Because of the careful selection of quality books, the choices given are an excellent guide to the titles current in the late fifties.

Deason, Hilary J. The A.A.A.S. Science Book List: A Selected and Annotated List of Science and Mathematical Books for Secondary School Students, College Undergraduates and Non-Specialists. 3rd ed. Washington, D.C.: American Assn. for the Advancement of Science, 1970. 439p.

Because of its authority, this guide has gained wide currency throughout the English-speaking world as a reference and acquisition tool in the sciences. First published in 1959 and reedited in 1964, it had its origin in a book list for a traveling high-school science library project set up by the association's Science Library Program and supported by the National Science Foundation. It is designed to provide a guide to recreational and collateral reading and to basic reference works in the sciences and mathematics for students and nonspecialist adults. This edition, revised with the aid of recommended book lists in Science Books: A Quarterly Review, increases the number of titles to 2,441 from the 1,376 of the second edition and 900 of the first edition. The system of starred ratings has been abandoned, and broader scope reflects interdisciplinary development and popular interests. Paperbound editions are indicated and some British and out-of-print titles are included. Subjects are listed according to the seventeenth edition of the Dewey Decimal Classification; however, only the section headings, not individual works, carry the Dewey number. The one-paragraph annotations are thorough, systematic, and critical. Excellent for school and college libraries, its value for public library selection should not be underestimated. A supplement was published in 1978.

——. The A.A.A.S. Science Book List for Children: A Selected and Annotated List of Science and Mathematics Books for Children in Elementary Schools, and for Children's Collections in Public Libraries. 3rd ed. Washington, D.C.: American Assn. for the Advancement of Science, 1972. 253p.

First published in 1960, with a second edition in 1963, this is a companion volume to the compiler's similar title for secondary school students. It is a selected and annotated list designed to aid elementary school teachers in planning the curriculum and assigning collateral reading for enrichment. It also serves as an acquisition guide for school library or public library collections for children. The objective is to maintain adequate, balanced, and up-to-date holdings in the sciences, including mathematics, in order to help young readers develop "intensely inquiring minds." Over 1,500 titles bear letter notations indicating the level of difficulty for kindergarten, primary, intermediate, and advanced elementary students. Individual subgroups, not the books, carry modified Dewey classification numbers. Carefully written descriptive and critical annotations often derive from reviews in Science Books: A Quarterly Review. Indexes are provided for authors and for subjects and titles.

The scope of this third edition reflects the increasingly inter-disciplinary nature of science education and popular interest in the sciences. The asterisks used in previous editions to indicate priorities for purchase have been abandoned. Long considered the basic source for young people to keep abreast in the field of science, this list exhibits magnificent strengths in traditional scientific subjects, for example, meteorology and reproduction—and a few weaknesses. Areas such as addiction and health reflect the problems that recent upheavals and social values in flux can exert on even the best list.

——. A Guide to Science Reading. 2nd rev. ed. New York: New American Library, 1966. 288p.

This annotated bibliography of over 1,000 paperbacks on science for students from kindergarten to grade 12 is its third appearance under this title. The first edition appeared in 1963; the second in 1964. Its predecessor, An Inexpensive Science Library, initiated by the American Association for the Advancement of Science under its Science Library Program, appeared in

five editions annually from 1957 to 1961 and was compiled by
R. W. Lynn and William Blackton. In addition to forewords and
instruction for use, four essays are contributed by well-known
scientists, including Margaret Mead. Titles are arranged by
Dewey. Descriptive annotations are written for the student
reader and level of reading difficulty is identified. Author and
title indexes are provided. While many scientific books for young
people have dated, many of the paperbacks on this list have not,
and in-print status should act as an indicator of this if the guide is
used for selection in a school library today.

De Boer, John J.; Hale, Paul B.; and Landin, Esther. Reading for
Living: An Index to Reading Materials for Use in Human Relations
Programs in Secondary Schools. Springfield, Ill.: State Supt. of
Public Instruction, 1953. 170p.
A curriculum program bulletin intended to aid teachers in
locating, selecting, and using suitable materials, this annotated
bibliography lists over 1,000 books for young people under the
categories of a problem index, such as family and home relationships, financial problems, personality development, etc. Many
titles are idealistically motivated and conventionally positive;
some are classics. Today's publications available for children will
offer a changed perspective.

Detroit Public Library. Books to Own: Recent Books and Old Favorites for Any Child's Bookshelf. Detroit: The Library, 1938- .
Annual.
This annotated and graded list of books for a child's personal
ownership has been selected by staff members for many years.
Arrangement has varied, but generally new titles and traditional
favorites are contrasted under broad age groups. A sentence or
two of annotation is accompanied by a grade annotation. This
attractively produced list has been a useful checking aid for those
beyond the library's local area because it has drawn on the expertise and experience of the practitioners in this large library
system.

———. Children's Service. Human Rights: Books for Boys and Girls
Highlighting the Principles Set Forth in the Universal Declaration
of Human Rights. 3rd ed. Detroit: The Library, 1975. 19p.
First published in 1963, this classified and annotated bibliography was prepared by the children's department of the library,
and appeared in a revised edition in 1966. Compiled at the request
of the Children's Services Division of the American Library Association, it received national distribution. A limited selection of
about 100 titles aims to publicize the United Nations principles on
human rights adopted in 1948. Books chosen because of their
popularity with young people, combined with accuracy of portray-

al, are arranged in four general topical categories: "Heritage of Hope"; "Freedom Bearers"; "In My Brother's Shoes"; and "Tomorrow's World." Brief descriptive annotations include grade levels, mostly from grade 5 and up. The quality of the selection makes it a valuable tool for larger collections which have many of the titles, and a foundation checklist for smaller school and children's libraries.

De Vries, Leonard, comp. Flowers of Delight: Culled from the Osborne Collection of Early Children's Books. Toronto: McClelland, 1965. 232p.

This anthology of extracts--words and pictures--has been compiled from children's books in the collection dating from 1765 to 1830. Regrettably, there is no introduction or commentary, only an appendix of notes on writers, publishers, and illustrators. But the 750 reproductions, 125 of them in color, give this compilation reference, as well as enjoyment, value.

——, ed. Little Wide-Awake: An Anthology from Victorian Children's Books and Periodicals in the Collection of Anne and Fernand G. Renier. Cleveland: World, 1967. 240p.

This anthology, selected from a distinguished English collection, can be regarded as the chronological successor of the editor's similar work derived from the Osborne collection (above). An introduction by M. F. Thwaite gives a general picture of Victorian children's literature. The profusion of illustrative material reproduced, together with the biographical and bibliographical notes, constitutes a useful source for research.

Dobler, Lavinia G. The Dobler World Directory of Youth Periodicals. New York: Schulte, 1966. 37p.

A successor to the Dobler International List of Periodicals for Boys and Girls, 1960, this directory is designed to bring together in one place the magazines read by the youth of the world. The editor's descriptive foreword and a short essay, "Youth Magazines in the United States" by Muriel Fuller, precede the text. Over 400 titles are arranged alphabetically within five divisions: general, religious, school and classroom, foreign periodicals in English, and foreign-language periodicals. Annotation provides publishing details, circulation figures, audience and grade ratings, and important features. When issued, much of this information was hard to locate, but is now largely superseded.

Dodds, Barbara. Negro Literature for High School Students. Champaign, Ill.: National Council of Teachers of English, 1968. 157p.

This study, undertaken when the author faced the problem of finding literature by and about blacks suitable for high school students, represents a reaction against stereotyping and discriminatory patterns. The introduction decries the lack of such material in the schools. Five chapters cover a historical survey, listing writers and their dates; works about blacks; the junior novel, which lists titles for boys and girls with an evaluation and indication of reading difficulty; biography; and classroom uses of black literature. This final chapter lists other sources as well as a suggested library collection. Written at the time that genuine interest in black literature was beginning to surge, its bibliographical element is interesting historically, and its advice to teachers still valid.

Doyle, Brian. The Who's Who of Children's Literature. London: Evelyn, 1968. 380p.

Described as a labor of love, this reference guide seeks to give basic information about the most widely read and approved authors and illustrators of children's books. Some 300 entries represent mainly British and Americans, although Europeans are included if translations of their works have become English classics. Biographies, averaging a page in length, are critical and make references to books and characters. The hundred illustrations are for the most part portrait photographs. The compilation is based partly on the author's Boys' Writers and Illustrators, privately published in typescript form in 1964, though coverage is not identical.

Duff, Annis. "Bequest of Wings": A Family's Pleasures with Books. Rev. ed. New York: Viking, 1954. 207p.

Not really a book about children's literature, this simple tale of a family's pleasures with books was first published in 1944, and frequently reprinted. Chapters include poetry, funny books, and fairy tales. Individual books, mainly for young people, receive comment in the text. An appendix lists titles appropriate to each chapter and is revised to late 1954.

——. "Longer Flight": A Family Grows Up with Books. New York: Viking, 1955. 269p.

This work is a continuation of the author's "Bequest of Wings." Very readable and interestingly personal, it weaves book titles into the text with comments. The criteria for inclusion are family interest and successful use by the author, and, while they include some unashamedly conservative classics, her choice will be stimulating for the book selector.

Dunn, Anita, and Jackman, Mabel E. Fare for the Reluctant Reader. 3rd ed. Albany, N.Y.: State Univ. of New York, 1964. 277p.

A project of the Capital Area Development Association, this bibliography is designed to be read by young people themselves. It appeared as a mimeographed booklet in 1950 and expanded into a

second edition in 1952, both with the coauthorship of Bernice C.
Bush.   An article on secondary school reading programs was
written for this third edition by J. Roy Newton. Young people in
grades 7 through 12 are the anticipated audience.   Titles are
arranged in informal subject categories that represent teenage
interests, each subdivided by grade groups, 7 and 8, 9 and 10, and
11 and 12. Titles range in date from 1945 to 1963 and carry brief
annotations written to tempt the reluctant reader. Supplementary lists are provided of series, abridgments, and periodicals.
There are still useful titles in this extensive list.

Eakin, Mary K., ed. Good Books for Children: A Selection of Outstand-
    ing Children's Books Published 1950-1965. 3rd ed. Chicago: Univ.
    of Chicago Pr., 1967. 407p.
    This outstanding aid, valuable both for the selections and the
quality of the annotations, is based on the pooled judgment of the
staff of the Center for Children's Books and the Book Evaluation
Committee of its Bulletin, from which most of the reviews are
drawn. Restricted to books written for children from preschool
age through high school, a majority are appropriate for grades 4 to
9, preschool and primary interest ranking next, and only a small
number for senior high.   All inclusions are judged noteworthy,
though many have qualified recommendations. Approximately
half are fiction and half nonfiction, the latter not being intended
as a balanced subject selection. Choice was based on the annual
lists of a hundred children's books recommended to the University
of Chicago reading conferences.   The alphabetical author
arrangement is supplemented by full indexing where subject
entries group titles by grades. The preface stresses the importance of good selection principles, gives general criteria for
evaluation, and outlines a method of analyzing books for children.
This edition drops pre-1950 and out-of-print titles; consequently,
the previous editions (1959, covering 1948-58, and 1962, covering
1948-61) retain retrospective value. This anthology of reviews
drawn from one of the most prestigious American children's book
reviewing journals enables parents, teachers, and librarians to
discover the best titles published over these years. Especially
noteworthy is the attention paid throughout to the developmental
needs of children from their earliest days.

——. Library Materials for Beginning Independent Reading. Instruc-
    tional Material Bulletin. 2nd ed. Cedar Falls, Ia.: Iowa State
    Teachers College, 1966. 19p.
    First published in 1959, this is an aid for teachers and
librarians who select material for independent reading that will
encourage children to progress toward full-length books.
Almost 200 titles for grades 1 to 3 are given brief annotations
and assigned a reading level according to the Spache formula.

Not a comprehensive list, the selection is based on literary quality. The compiler's introduction explains the criteria and gives her thoughts about the value of independent reading. Both editions have been popular with teachers and librarians looking for this type of material.

——. Subject Index to Books for Intermediate Grades. 3rd ed. Chicago: American Library Assn., 1963. 308p.

Intended for use by teachers and librarians in identifying books that can supplement and enrich both teaching and individual reading programs for pupils in grades 4 to 6, this index lists some 1,800 books in print in 1961. All are recommended titles. Only books with a specific subject value or special type of appeal are included for the fiction category. The list of books indexed gives grade level and a simplified Dewey classification. Previous editions published in 1940 and 1950 were compiled by Eloise Rue. This is a useful tool that parallels the author's similar index for primary grades (see below).

——. Subject Index to Books for Primary Grades. 3rd ed. Chicago: American Library Assn., 1967.

Parallel to the compiler's similar work for intermediate grades, this work is intended to give librarians and teachers access to sources of instructional and supplementary material for use with children up to grade 3. Titles covered are mostly trade editions, rather than textbooks, selected from the period from 1950 through 1965, but some go back as far as 1905. Most fantasy, folklore, and poetry are eschewed as these areas were judged to be of little instructional help. The author list of books cited indicates reading aloud grade levels, as well as interest levels. The subject list uses subject headings which, in this edition, have been revised to correspond with those used in the Wilson Children's Catalog. First compiled in 1938 by Eloise Rue as Subject Index to Readers, the first edition under this title was prepared by her in 1943. A much expanded second edition appeared in 1961 by the present editor and Elinor Merritt. This edition has been a standard reference tool.

Eaton, Anne Thaxter. Reading with Children. New York: Viking, 1963. 354p.

This inspirational title by a well-known children's librarian retained its popularity through many reprintings since its original appearance in 1940. It can still be recommended for its social commentary and for checking children's books of historical interest. Titles discussed in the text are supplemented by unannotated lists at the end of each chapter. The author's conviction in relation to children's reading that the world may change but children do not may be open to question today.

——. Treasure for the Taking: A Booklist for Boys and Girls. Rev. ed.
New York: Viking, 1957. 322p.

This annotated bibliography was prepared for any adult concerned with children's reading by an author well-known in librarianship. This edition, unlike the first published in 1946, is
restricted to books in print at the time of publication. Sixty-four
sections under broad informal subject headings are briefly introduced and list titles by author. Each has a descriptive annotation
and an indication of the age most likely to enjoy it. The selection
constitutes a very good representation of books available at the
time, and as such retains current interest for the researcher.

Education Book Guide. London: Councils and Education Pr., 1956.
110p.

This work was compiled by the National Book League as a
record of new books for the benefit of teachers and others who
want to make their own selection. The objective was not to draw
up a list of recommended books, but to introduce more children to
the world of books. Intended to appear annually, succeeding
volumes, covering new British educational publications suitable
for all ages up to 18, were published in 1957, 1958, 1959, and 1960.
Arrangement is by subject in alphabetical order with indication of
age and grade suitability and some brief explanatory annotations.

Educational Research Council of America and the American Associa-
tion for Jewish Education. World Jewish History, Religion and
Culture . . . pt. 1.; The American Jewish Experience . . . pt. 2.;
Jews in Israel and Other Lands . . . pt. 3.: A Graded Annotated
Bibliography for Grades 7-12. Cleveland, Ohio: The Council,
1972. 24p., 23p., 17p.

This collaborative bibliographical project in three parts was
designed to provide informative guides for students and teachers,
primarily in public schools, and to advance the knowledge of Jews
and Judaism today. Arrangement is within broad conventional
subject and literary categories. Annotations include recommendations for reading level. Selection was dictated "by space
restrictions and by the objectives and judgment of those who
prepared them." While some groups, notably fiction, could be
expanded, those titles included reflect well the aims of the collaborators.

Edwards, Margaret A. The Fair Garden and the Swarm of Beasts. Rev.
ed. New York: Hawthorn, 1974. 195p.

First published in 1969, this examination of goals and problems
in using books with young adults reflects the personal philosophy
of its author, for many years a coordinator of work with young
adults at the Enoch Pratt Free Library of Baltimore. The author
concedes in a new introduction to this edition that her attitude to

encouraging young adults to become readers in the public library may not suit everyone. "Growing Season," "Branching Out," "Fighting Weeds and Insects," and other horticulturally oriented chapter headings reflect the metaphor of the title and are supplemented by the "Tool Shed," which covers such library-related functions as criteria for book selection, annotation writing, and useful activities drawn from the author's experience. Some brief lists of titles that reflect the nature of young adults occasionally seem dated. However, readable style and sage advice based on experience combine to make this an enjoyable and rewarding book for young adult librarians and others professionally and personally interested in this age group.

Egoff, Sheila A. Children's Periodicals of the Nineteenth Century: A Survey and a Bibliography. Pamphlet no. 8. London: Library Assn., 1951. 55p.
    Covering the period from 1752 to 1900 chiefly in Britain, this account was based on work submitted for the Fellowship of the Library Association. The survey stresses two parallel streams, Sunday school magazines and boys' adventure stories. The bibliography is a chronological listing. An alphabetical index is added.

——. The Republic of Childhood: A Critical Guide to Canadian Children's Literature in English. Toronto: Oxford Univ. Pr., 1967. 287p.
    One of the most constructive and accessible accounts of Canadian children's literature, this volume started off as a centennial project. The author, a library school faculty member, drew on her own decade of experience in Toronto's Boys and Girls House, and also credits Canadian school and children's librarians and her own students for their contributions. Chapters cover the genres in Canadian books for children--Indian legends, history and biography, fairy tales, and "all the rest" stories--and also illustrations, design, and early Canadian books. Each is followed by a list of titles with short descriptive and critical annotations, in addition to comment on individual titles in the text. A few book illustrations are reproduced.

——; Stubbs, G. T.; and Ashley, L. F., eds. Only Connect: Readings on Children's Literature. Toronto: Oxford Univ. Pr., 1969. 471p.
    This is an influential anthology of essays, articles, and critical reviews that regard children's literature as an essential part of the whole realm of literary activity, to be judged by the same standards. The editors, eschewing any special scale of literary values, have chosen a broad representation by English and American writers, mostly the products of the 1960s, although a few seminal pieces from an earlier period have been included (such as essays by T. S. Eliot and C. S. Lewis). Byways, as well as more familiar

ground, are explored. Forty contributions are ranged under six headings: "Books and Children," "Fairy Tales, Fantasies and Animals," "Historical Fiction," "Some Writers and Their Books," "Illustration," and "The Modern Scene," which includes two articles by the senior editor, "Science Fiction" and "Precepts and Pleasures: Changing Emphases in the Writing and Criticism of Children's Literature." Notes on the contributors, a few illustrations, a select bibliography, and a full index complete the volume. A second edition appeared in 1980.

——, and Belisle, Alvine. Notable Canadian Children's Books. Un Choix de Livres Canadien pour la Jeunesse. Ottawa: National Library, 1973. 91p.

Originally prepared for a National Library exhibition, this bilingual annotated catalog, with the help of later supplements, has come to represent an official selection of the best of Canadian children's literature. With the objective of showing the historical development of Canadian children's literature, the chosen books have been arranged chronologically by date from 1825 to 1972 in the English-language section, and from 1931 to 1972 in the French-language section, so as to "most aptly illustrate trends and changes." Each language section has its own topical subdivisions, introduction, and supplementary lists of prizewinning books. The paragraphs of annotation, in English for English books and French for French books, are bibliographical and critical as well as descriptive. The original volume is handsomely produced and illustrated in black and white. The revised edition of 1976, prepared by Irene E. Aubrey, and annual supplements for succeeding years are reproduced from typescript.

Elkin, Judith. Books for the Multi-Racial Classroom: A Select List of Children's Books, Showing the Backgrounds of India, Pakistan and the West Indies. YLG Pamphlet, no. 10. Birmingham, Eng.: Library Assn., Youth Libraries Group, 1971. 66p.

This annotated book list, produced in collaboration with the Birmingham Public Libraries, is intended to be used by educators, librarians, and social workers for children growing up in a multiracial community. The objective is to develop awareness and understanding by making available worthwhile children's books on the geographical, cultural, and religious backgrounds of three large immigrant groups in Britain. Entries are arranged on a biographical and national basis and short, descriptive, critical notes indicate possible use and suggested reading level. A second edition appeared in 1976.

Ellis, Alec. The Family Story in the 1960's. London: Clive Bingley, 1970. 105p.

In an era that stresses realism in literature for young people, this examination of a select list of British stories about families represents a solid, though brief, treatment that relates a large area of popular fiction to everyday life in Britain in the 1960s. The evolution of the family story is explained. Titles are described in the text and also listed alphabetically, and the index gives a subject approach.

——. A History of Children's Reading and Literature. Oxford: Pergamon, 1968. 233p.

The author relates his topic thematically to the development of working-class education in England and Wales from the nineteenth century to the 1960s, and shows the interaction of educational legislation, literacy, and publishing for children. Four chapters give a chronological review from 1860-90, 1890-1920, 1920-45, and 1946-65. Illustrations reproduce pages from representative books. Some authors and significant titles are mentioned in the text. However, using the golden-age theory of children's literature to trace the education of the working class is similar to losing the baby in a very large bath.

——. How to Find Out about Children's Literature. 3rd ed. Oxford: Pergamon, 1973. 252p.

A general introduction from a British point of view, not specifically for, but most useful to, students in library schools and colleges of education. First published in 1966 with a second edition in 1968, this edition has been further expanded. The introduction comments on the growing importance of children's books; chapters cover history, subject approaches, and general tendencies. Chapters on guidance form a valuable source of information on selection aids, organizations, etc., many of which are British, but will be of interest for comparative and reference reasons in North America. First issued when interest in children's literature was increasing, this volume proved useful in Great Britain and to some extent in the United States. Revisions include many additions on current books, translations, and organizations, mainly British.

English Historical Fiction. Topic Booklists. Tunbridge Wells, Eng.: Fenrose, 1973. 61p.

This volume of the publisher's series includes historical novels and biographies written for young people that were then in print, nearly all of the former having brief descriptive annotations. Arrangement is in fifteen chronological groups from ancient Britain to the second world war, with a supplementary general reference section. The index includes persons, places, and themes. Almost all authors are British, and, since some are masters of their craft, the list will remain useful, particularly the fiction titles.

Enoch Pratt Free Library. <u>Unassigned Reading: Teen-Age Testimony</u>
<u>2, 1970</u>. Baltimore: The Library, 1970. 36p.

The successor to a small pamphlet, <u>Teen-Age Testimony</u>, published by the library in 1960, this booklet analyzes the responses of
30,000 students in Baltimore's public and private high schools
about the books they had read and enjoyed. Both the 1960 and
1970 surveys were carried out by the staff as part of National
Library Week. The ten favorites of 1970 are listed along with the
ten favorites of 1960 and favorites of teenagers of the past. Their
choices reflect primarily the current interests and concerns of
each generation and the adolescent search for values in contemporary society (such as love and marriage and the human situation
of black Americans). Included are the choices of individual high
schools and interesting testimony from several Baltimore teenagers of the past, now educators, politicians, novelists, and
editors. Naturally influential within the local area, the report was
used in other areas as a selection checklist, if only to confirm
what many already knew, as the titles were part of many collections in school libraries.

Eyre, Frank. <u>British Children's Books in the Twentieth Century</u>.
London: Longmans, 1971. 208p.

First published in much briefer form for the British Council in
1952 as <u>20th Century Children's Books</u>, this expanded edition was
completely rewritten and affords a more inclusive study of British
juveniles during the first seventy years of this century. But the
objective remains the same--to examine developments in
publishing and their influence on the trends in writing for children,
and then to analyze the more significant original work by British
writers and artists. Starting with a historical survey, contents
include books with pictures, in-between books (fantastic and
impossible adventures), and fiction, thematically subdivided.
Appendixes cover regional writing and awards in Commonwealth
countries. A select bibliography of books about children's books
includes only a few American titles. The list of titles in the index
is impressive, but the narrative bio-bibliography is even more so.
The temperate but concrete criticism provided for many titles, in
addition to the up-to-date perspective, recommends this volume.

Fader, Daniel N., and McNeil, Elton B. <u>Hooked on Books: Program and</u>
<u>Proof</u>. New York: Putnam, 1968. 244p.

This "sweeping program for getting even the most bored and
apathetic students to enjoy reading and writing" has as an
essential feature the identification of the kinds of literature and
individual books that underprivileged young adults themselves will
choose to read and enjoy. First appearing as <u>Hooked on Books</u> in
1966, then coauthored by Morton H. Shaevitz, it was based on
Daniel Fader's cooperative research project for the U.S. Office of

Education published in 1966 as <u>English for Reluctant Learners,</u> <u>Grades 7-9: English in Every Classroom</u>. The 1968 edition was extensively rewritten and reorganized and summarizes two years of research by the new coauthor. While the findings concern children in poorer public schools and penal institutions, the authors stress that it is the "poverty of experience" found in all groups in this television-dominated age that affects children's feelings about reading. The reading list of 1,000 paperbacks has been doubled from the previous edition and there are many textual references to authors and titles that have personal appeal to young adults. This revision was also published as a paperback by Berkley, as the original edition was, and reprinted in England by Pergamon in 1969, when a reading list of paperbound books available in Britain, compiled by Aidan Chambers, was substituted. From the moment of first publication this seminal enquiry tapped a dynamic field--paperbacks and delinquents. Aimed at classroom teachers of nonreaders, its proven thesis appealed to the book industry as well as to librarians and educators. Frequent reprintings in paperback testified to its influence. A new edition appeared in 1976 under the title <u>The New Hooked on Books</u>.

Faissler, Margaretta. <u>Key to the Past: Some History Books for Pre-</u> <u>College Readers</u>. 2nd ed. Washington, D.C.: American Historical Assn., 1959. 77p.

This annotated bibliography was compiled at the Service Center for Teachers of History and first appeared in 1957. Intended to help high school students enjoy and benefit from history and social studies courses, it aims to make these more interesting and to encourage boys and girls to find pleasure in reading biography, social history, and even political history. It is planned for use by the students themselves with or without teachers' supervision. Criteria for choice were accuracy, readability, and conform-ity with high school curricula. A chronological framework by countries is adopted within three main divisions, "Europe and the Near East," "The United States," and "Other Parts of the World." Topics are each divided into general and special categories, books in the latter being chosen to "compell the attention of the pupil from beginning to end." This selection of standard titles will now require supplementary updating but, because previous contributions to the subject remain substantially valid and also because of the authoritative sponsorship of the American Historical Association, this is still a useful source for school libraries.

Fenner, Phyllis Reid. <u>The Proof of the Pudding: What Children Read</u>. New York: Day, 1957. 246p.

Intended for parents who want to buy and borrow books for their children, the author has selected "some of the best-liked books of all times, telling you a little about them, why a child likes them,

and approximately how old a child is when he reads them."
Eighteen unconventionally titled chapters basically represent the
traditional types of publication for children, such as picture
books, humor, and adventure. Two essays that the author explains
have been a source of inspiration are reprinted: Padraic Colum's
"Imagination and Children's Literature" and Henry Barnes's "The
Winged Horse." For those who wish to research what was popular
with children or what was recommended for them in the late
1950s, this is a very useful volume; it also deserves a good read by
today's practitioners.

———, ed. Something Shared: Children and Books: A Personal Treasury
of Stories, Articles, and Cartoons, Selected and with Comments.
New York: Day, 1959. 234p.
    An anthology of things that the editor has found useful in
working with children, teachers, parents, and librarians, this work
blends tales by well-known authors with articles on the joys and
problems of reading and the importance of books in a child's
background. Topical cartoons illustrate these themes.

Fenwick, Sara Innes, ed. A Critical Approach to Children's Literature:
The Thirty-First Annual Conference of the Graduate Library
School, August 1-3, 1966. University of Chicago Studies in
Library Science. Chicago: Univ. of Chicago Pr., 1967. 129p.
    This series of addresses by writers, library educators, and other
concerned professionals first appeared in print in Library
Quarterly. The theme of the conference was "continued search
for the ingredients of knowledge, understanding and sensitivity
fundamental to serious criticism and interpretation of children's
literature." Children's literature was regarded as a segment of all
literature, and emphasis was placed on what "can provide satisfying and worthwhile experiences of joy, inspiration, self-realiza-
tion, and increased wisdom." Studies included investigation of
children's reading and adult values, the psychological significance
of children's literature, social values, poetry, science for children,
evaluation of children's responses to literature, current reviewing
and criticism. While there is a scarcity of references to individual
books, the scholarly nature and the qualifications of the contributors make this a significant volume for those interested in different aspects of literature for children.

Ferris, Helen, ed. Writing Books for Boys and Girls: A "Young Wings"
Anthology of Essays by Two Hundred Sixteen Authors Who Tell
How They Came to Write Their Special Kinds of Books for Young
Readers. Garden City, N.Y.: Doubleday, 1952. 320p.
    The editor-in-chief of the Junior Literary Guild's organ Young
Wings wrote the introduction to this collection of essays by
twentieth-century children's authors, almost all American, dis-

tinguished and not so distinguished. The selection is grouped in three sections, those writing for 6-8-year-olds, for 9-11-year-olds, and 12-16-year-olds. Many titles and their backgrounds are commented on by their authors.

Fiction-Faction: Books for the Family. A List Compiled by Children's Librarians in Buckinghamshire. YLG Pamphlet, no. 9. Birmingham, Eng.: Library Assn., Youth Libraries Group, 1971. 16p.

This random selection, varying from reference books to stories, is arranged in informal interest groups with very brief notes and a subject index. It lists currently available British books for the family to use and enjoy together, suitable for borrowing, buying, or giving.

Fidell, Estelle A., ed. The Children's Catalog. 12th ed. New York: Wilson, 1971. Annual supplements, 1972-75.

First published in 1909, this catalog was based on the book catalog in the children's department of the Carnegie Library of Pittsburgh and the catalog of books for public school libraries in New York City. It was edited by Marion E. Potter. The second edition of 1917, edited by Corinne Bacon, was based on fifty-four selective library lists. It has three supplements. The third edition, edited by Minnie Earl Sears, was published in 1925. It has five supplements. The following chart lists the editions, year of publication, and the editor(s).

4th	1930	Minnie E. Sears
5th	1936	Siri Andrews
6th	1941	Siri Andrews, Dorothy E. Cook, Agnes Cowing
7th	1946	Ruth Giles, Dorothy E. Cook, Dorothy H. West
8th	1951	Ruth Giles, Dorothy E. Cook
9th	1956	Marion L. McConnell, Dorothy H. West
10th	1961	Dorothy H. West, Rachel Shor
11th	1966	Rachel Shor, Estelle Fidell

Subtitles have varied over the years, especially in the early editions.

The fourth edition of 1930 was arranged in two parts: alphabetical and classified lists. The format remained this way until the ninth edition (1956) when it was divided into three sections: the classified catalog, the alphabetical index, and a new list by grades. This list does not appear in the twelfth edition.

Throughout its history, the purposes of the catalog have remained the same, ". . . as an aid in purchasing, as a cataloging aid, as a reference aid, as an aid in rebinding and discarding and replacing, and as an aid in library schools." Both the practicing librarian and teacher, as well as students in library schools, are the audience for this standard book selection tool.

In the twelfth edition, the work is divided into three parts. Part 1 is the classified catalog and contains the descriptive annotations; citations, including the price; grade levels; the Dewey classification numbers; and subject headings. Part 2 contains the author, title, subject, and analytical index. Part 3 is a directory of distributors and publishers. An attempt is made to keep the selections current. This is partially accomplished by issuing annual supplements which are included in the initial price.

The twelfth edition of this book selection catalog has made significant strides in some areas. For example, there has been a sharp curtailment of the duplication of titles with Junior High School Library Catalog. Starring some highly recommended titles has been abolished. Over 2,400 new titles have been added; titles from the past have been examined carefully and for the most part eliminated.

This classified list was an original book selection aid for public and school libraries, and as such highly regarded. As with many things, it became less highly thought of with time because of its lack of comprehensiveness and apparent unwillingness to treat the issues of the times in its selections. Since these problems have been addressed and corrected in the twelfth edition, the aid is once again worthy of resuming its position as a standard selection source in the children's book field. The thirteenth and fourteenth editions were published in 1976 and 1981, annual supplements being continued.

——, and Berger, Toby M., eds. Senior High School Library Catalog. 10th ed. New York: Wilson, 1972. Annual supplements, 1973-76.

This recognized classified and annotated bibliography attempts to place a representative core collection of books before librarians and others for their use in acquisitions. The first edition was published in 1926 under the title Standard Catalog for High School Libraries. This title was retained through the eighth edition. From the beginning, this work has been published every five years (quinquennially) and kept current by the issuance of annual supplements. The following chart lists the edition, the year of publication and the editor(s) prior to the tenth edition.

1st	1926-28	Zaidee Brown
2nd	1932	Minnie E. Sears, Isabel S. Monro, Dorothy Cook
3rd	1937	Dorothy Cook, Agnes Cowing, Isabel Monro
4th	1942	Isabel Monro, Ruth Jervis
5th	1947	Dorothy Cook, Anne T. Eaton, Dorothy H. West
6th	1952	Dorothy H. West
7th	1957	Dorothy H. West, Marion L. McConnell
8th	1962	Dorothy H. West, Estelle Fidell, Rachel Shor
9th	1967	Rachel Shor, Estelle Fidell

This catalog also had a separate Roman Catholic supplement beginning in 1942 that coincided with the publication of the fourth edition. This separate catalog was discontinued in 1977.

In the tenth edition, the format is the same as it has always been. The first section is based on the abridged Dewey decimal system and contains the titles listed by author with a full citation including the price and the subject headings. The subject headings are taken from Sears List of Subject Headings. A descriptive evaluation from a book evaluation source follows. The second section consists of the analytics key to the volume. It is an index of authors, titles, subjects, and analytics with a referral to the appropriate citation in section 1. Section 3 contains a directory of publishers and distributors of the materials that appear in the pages of this volume.

This work has been and remains valuable as a core collection guide. It is also useful as a reference tool because of the analytic index. Since the work is kept up-to-date with annual supplements, it is beneficial as a checklist for senior-high librarians, teachers or others interested in reading for these ages. The eleventh edition (1977) was edited by Gary L. Bogart and Karen R. Carlson. Annual supplements continue.

Field, C., and Hamley, D. C. Fiction in the Middle School. London: Batsford, 1975. 143p.

Concerned with the teaching of literature and its relationship to the emotional and cognitive development of children, the authors seek to help teachers appreciate fiction within a framework of educational theory, minimizing anecdotal evidence derived from classroom practice. The latter part of the book is taken up by annotated book lists which suggest appropriate titles in developmental sequence for the age groups 7-8, 8-9, 10-11, and 11-12. Their recommendations, while personal, are based on twenty years of experience in British schools.

Field, Carolyn W., ed. Subject Collections in Children's Literature. New York: Bowker, 1969. 142p.

Prepared for the National Planning Committee for Special Collections of the Children's Services Division of the American Library Association, with Virginia Haviland and Elizabeth Nesbitt as consultants, this directory is designed to assist the researcher into children's books as literature. Two sections list collections by subject, arranged alphabetically and including personal names as well as types of literature, and by institution, in an alphabetical sequence of states, followed by Canadian entries. Descriptive annotations include statistical information as well as availability, cataloging status, photocopying, and interlibrary loan. There is a supplementary bibliography of books and articles relating to the collections listed. This is an indispensable tool for researchers, particularly those concerned with the historical aspect of children's books.

Field, Elinor Whitney, ed. Horn Book Reflections on Children's Books and Reading: Selected from Eighteen Years of the Horn Book Magazine, 1949-1966. Boston: Horn Book, 1969. 367p.

For this successor to Norma Fryatt's Horn Book Sampler (1959) articles have been culled from later volumes of The Horn Book to stimulate discussion, encourage new concepts, and remind readers of the literary heritage of children. Contributors include writers, illustrators, librarians, teachers, parents, and others concerned about children and their books; to understand these people, over twenty pages of notes and comments about them have been added. The articles and reviews are grouped under general topics: inspiration, goals and guidelines for writers and illustrators, history, poetry, fantasy, people and places, family reading, and storytelling.

Field, Louise Frances. The Child and His Book: Some Account of the History and Progress of Children's Literature in England. 2nd ed. Detroit: Singing Tree, 1968.

In spite of the claim on the title page, this is an unaltered photolithographic facsimile of the first edition published in London by Wells, Gardner, Darton and Co. in 1892. The later and greater historian of the field, Harvey Darton, pointed out that Mrs. E. M. Field's work was the first account of English children's books with any claim to completeness. Arranged on a chronological basis, the story stops almost entirely at the accession of Queen Victoria. Her opinions about, and the many bibliographical references to, early works remain sound after seventy-five years.

Fisher, Janet. Five to Eight. YLG Pamphlet, no. 12. Birmingham, Eng.: Library Assn., Youth Libraries Group, 1972. 43p.

This is an annotated list of 138 best titles available in Britain for 5-8-year-olds to read and understand. Criteria for inclusion include good writing, clear and accurate illustrations, and scope that is not beyond the age group.

Fisher, Margery. Intent upon Reading: A Critical Appraisal of Modern Fiction for Children. 2nd ed. Leicester, Eng.: Brockhampton, 1965. 416p.

In this critical overview, first published in 1961, an experienced reviewer of children's books seeks to illustrate general points of significance rather than write a definitive survey. Many individual titles are analyzed and extracted in the text, and there are extensive book lists to support each of the chapters which treat informal themes found in the literature, such as witches, magic carpets, good chaps, and bad chaps. Two chapters, "Realism and

Reality" and "Standards and Achievements, 1961-1964," are added to this second edition. An excellent source for titles, brief annotations, and textual information within her categories, this is the British literary equivalent--or superior--to Arbuthnot's work.

——. Matters of Fact: Aspects of Non-Fiction for Children. Leicester, Eng.: Brockhampton, 1972. 476p.

This is an analysis of nonfiction books written for children, in particular those that set out to teach. The author holds that such books are still irreplaceable for learning as well as for teaching. Chapters cover types of publication as well as subject groups, including biographies and career books. Brief reading lists are given with each chapter. Although not as outstanding as some of her other works, this work does attempt to give the same type of treatment to nonfiction that the author gives to fiction elsewhere. Fisher develops sound guidelines with her usual critical sense. However, information books come off second best. Useful, nevertheless, for all the types and categories that are included. Also published in the United States in the same year by Crowell.

——. Who's Who in Children's Books: A Treasury of the Familiar Characters of Childhood. London: Weidenfeld & Nicholson, 1975. 400p.

As many as possible of the characters in children's books that have become household names have been included in this Who's Who. Excluded are nursery rhyme characters and those found in myths, fairy tales, and history. Articles are often lengthy and largely descriptive, but also analytical and critical of characters and their authors. Well-chosen illustrations, some in color, support the text, and are attractive in their own right. Illustrations and indexes ensure its use for reading and for reference.

Fitz-Gerald, Carolyn, and Gunter, Dolores. Creative Storytelling for Library and Teacher Aides. Dallas, Tex.: Leslie, 1971. 133p.

This how-to-do-it text is designed to teach effective story selection and storytelling skills to teacher and library aides who work in elementary schools, especially with ethnic groups. The authors are themselves teachers and two contributors come from a journalism and an education background. An introduction for potential storytellers and a model course syllabus precede the text. Chapters, ranging from one on storytelling techniques to another on the child and his image, deal with specific situations and give concrete examples. Aside from the simple approach, the guide is of interest as a regional expression of teachers.

Flandorf, Vera. Books to Help Children Adjust to a Hospital Situation. Chicago: American Library Assn., 1967. 55p.

Prepared for the Association of Hospital and Institution

Libraries, this bibliography of over 750 books for hospitalized children stems from a project started in 1956 to help volunteer workers. An objective was to help sick children find ideas in books to assist in meeting the emotional problems they encounter in a hospital situation. Titles, briefly annotated, are arranged under seven subject headings: "Adjustment and Understanding," "Cooperation with Others, Fear and Reassurance," "Hospitals," "Doctors and Nurses," "Loneliness and Homesickness," "Making New Friends," and "Just for Fun," and subdivided by the age groups 3-6, 6-9, 10-13, and 13-16.

Flynn, Alice H. et al. Read Your Way to World Understanding: A Selected Annotated Reading Guide of Books about the United Nations and the World in Which It Works for Peace and Human Welfare. New York: Scarecrow, 1963. 320p.

The chairperson of the Editorial Committee of the American Association for the United Nations responsible for this graded bibliography explains how the concept will be helpful to teachers and pupils in schools. Three parts, "The United Nations--The Family of Nations Dedicated to World Peace," "The United Nations Works in a Changing World--People and Places," and "Resources for Individual and Group Participation Programs," are subdivided topically and geographically. All titles have descriptive annotation and are appropriately recommended and graded in broad age groups. These age recommendations tend to be rated higher than suitable for many average readers in the school system. Fairly comprehensive when published, developments in the world and in publishing have now outdated this list.

Flynn, Barbara; Bernath, Kathleen; Ewing, Robert; Wyatt, Margaret; and Albright, Cora. Chicano: A Selected Bibliography. Riverside, Calif.: Inland Library System, 1971. 93p.

This bilingual list of materials by and about Mexican-Americans includes a substantial number of titles for children and young adults as well as adults. Selection centers on contemporary interests and problems of the Chicano community. Books, pamphlets, periodicals, and media are included. Some items are annotated. Arrangement is by Dewey and subject access is provided in English and Spanish. Although a partial union list of library holdings in San Bernardino and Riverside counties, in practice this work will serve as a useful resource checklist for other collections.

Ford, Robert. Children's Rhymes, Children's Games, Children's Songs, Children's Stories: A Book for Bairns and Big Folk. Detroit: Singing Tree, 1968. 287p.

A photolithographic facsimile of the first edition published by Alexander Gardner in 1904, this is a collection of what the author termed the national literature of the children of Scotland. It includes nursery rhymes, counting-out rhymes, children's songs, stories, games, and humor, mostly reprinted verbatim from old chapbooks. The author contributes a general introduction and a commentary on each group of selections.

Francis, Shelagh. Romans to Vikings, 55 BC-1066 AD. YLG Storylines, no. 3. Birmingham, Eng.: Library Assn., Youth Libraries Group, 1973. 16p.

Designed to meet the needs of teachers and others looking for a well-written story to illustrate this age of British history and give background information for the period, this selection aid is oriented to mature children of about 10-15 with good reading ability. Arrangement is in two sections: fiction arranged chronologically by subject, and background books arranged alphabetically. Each of over forty items has a paragraph of descriptive annotation which tells the story.

Frank, Josette. Your Child's Reading Today. New and rev. ed. New York: Doubleday, 1969. 368p.

First published in 1954 and reedited in 1960, this aid is the successor to the author's What Books for Children: A Guide Post for Parents, first published in 1937 and revised in 1941. Both works stemmed from the author's forty years of experience with the Child Study Association of America, and draw on the book evaluations of its Children's Book Committee. She seeks to bring about an alliance between children and books by suggesting ways "to open up to boys and girls the varied roads they may travel in reading, from their earliest childhood to the world of adult books." The point of view is realistic. The first part stresses the relationship of parents, children and books, and is followed by analyses of what children like to read, giving attention to age differences between the under 5s, 5-8-year-olds, 8-11-year-olds, and young adults. Examination of special kinds of reading includes the classics, realism, books that affect emotion and character, religion and poetry, a child's private library, and the comics. The effects of radio and television are also analyzed. Over a hundred pages are occupied with selected and briefly annotated lists for various ages and topical interests. Her work is based on many assumptions, a primary one being that books today are an instrument for much more than just literary experience. With this in mind, the work serves adequately to give parents a set of general principles about reading and how to encourage it, as well as many titles. Choices in many cases now need reconsideration.

Freeman, Graydon La Verne, and Freeman, Ruth Sunderlin. The Child and His Picture Book. 2nd ed. Watkins Glen, N.Y.: Century, 1967. 111p.

Updated from the original edition of 1933, this study concentrates on the child's own choice of illustration and subject matter
in picture books, rather than the fitting of these to educational
practice. Originally a seminal study in the field, the revision was
sparked by renewed interest in day-care programs for nursery age
children. Its demonstration that the very young favored color in
illustration has been amply borne out by today's lavish picture
books. Appendixes list some 125 tested titles, describing their
illustration techniques and starring the most notable, and also
give notes on illustrators and their style.

Freeman, Ruth Sunderlin. Children's Picture Books, Yesterday and
Today; An Analysis. Watkins Glen, N.Y.: Century, 1967. 200p.
This overview of the history, genre, and collecting of picture
books, with attention given to children's illustrators and publishers, draws on the author's own collection, as well as public
ones.

Frend, Patricia. Junior Fiction Index. 2nd ed. London: Assn. of
Assistant Librarians, 1971. 55p.
Designed to meet the needs of librarians and teachers for a
subject index to good quality children's fiction, this selective list
includes younger children's books only when portraying a country,
historical period, or way of life. References, mainly to current
British titles, are minimal, and the informal subject headings,
which are arranged alphabetically, are not cross-indexed, but
serve quite usefully for ready access. The first edition appeared
in 1964.

From Morality and Instruction to Beatrix Potter: An Exhibition of
Books for Children from the Collection of Edgar Osborne Held in
Connection with the Annual Conference of the Library Associa-
tion 23 May-12 June, 1949. Eastbourne, Sussex, Eng.: Towner Art
Gallery, 1949. 34p.
This is a checklist of a distinguished collection subsequently
given to the Toronto Public Libraries Board. The list is arranged
by type of publication.

Fryatt, Norma R., ed. A Horn Book Sampler on Children's Books and
Reading: Selected from Twenty-Five Years of the Horn Book
Magazine 1924-1948. Boston: Horn Book, 1959. 261p.
Representative articles from early issues of the famous Ameri-
can magazine of children's literature are included in this sampler.
Selected for appeal to present-day parents, librarians, authors,
and illustrators, each article has been chosen for the vivid quality
of the writing and has stood the test of frequent rereading.
Contributors include Beatrix Potter, Lois Lenski, Edward Ardiz-
zone, and Anne Carroll Moore. The introduction by B. Mahony

Miller terms the collection a "sampler of the creative spirit." The selections recapture some of the milieu and culture of the now almost remote first half of this century. Déjà vu at its best.

Galisdorfer, Lorraine. Educational Reading Guide for the Partially Seeing. 2nd ed. Buffalo: Foster & Stewart, 1951. 83p.
——. Educational Reading Guide for the Partially Seeing, 1965-1969. Buffalo: Stewart, 1959. 20p.

First published in 1950, and brought up to date by its supplement (1959), this list, compiled to help young people with visual impairment in the regular classroom situation, is directed to teachers and workers with the visually handicapped and parents. It was developed from the author's mimeographed Reading Guide for Boys and Girls with Partial Vision which was revised for the fifth time in 1949. Titles are arranged in general content areas which are compatible with curricular requirements, and within these by author. Annotation includes a descriptive sentence, indication of grade level, and a note on type face (frequently Caslon Bold) and size, either very large (18 pt.) or oversize (24 pt.). A second part includes publisher information and an author index, with a list of reference works and books on reading measurement. With the supplement, the selection remains a useful checklist which can be updated from other sources.

Gallagher, James Joseph. An Annotated Bibliography of Anthropologic Materials for High School Use. New York: Macmillan, 1967. 135p.

Designed to document courses in social studies, this list is subdivided by conventional academic divisions of anthropology and by geographic and cultural areas. A paragraph of descriptive annotation accompanies each item.

Gates, Brian E. World Religion in Education. London: National Book League, 1974. 24p.

Limited to books judged reliable by religious groups and by academics, this selection seeks to tempt young readers, fast or slow, to study and inquire about the range of man's religious traditions. The emphasis is principally, though not exclusively, on living rather than historic faiths. Nearly 250 items, which are not annotated, comprise books written at a popular level and some specialist studies.

Georgiou, Constantine. Children and Their Literature. Englewood Cliffs, N.J.: Prentice-Hall, 1969. 501p.

A substantial volume with numerous illustrations, this title is intended to survey all fields of children's literature for a wide variety of groups, ranging from school administrators to prospective teachers and librarians. Its textbook style of presentation makes it more appropriate for students than advanced readers. Twelve chapters give an overview of the historical approach, literary criticism, forms of publication, and types of children's literature. Concluding sections cover realism and subject information. Each chapter includes references to further reading and an annotated list of typical titles.

Following an approach in educational texts initiated by May Hill Arbuthnot, one of the individuals to whom this book is dedicated, has its pitfalls. The book's good qualities, the design, readability, and illustrations do not necessarily offset its deficiencies, e.g., the homogeneity of the titles at the end of each chapter and the unrealistic assignment of reading patterns. The treatment of realism in the book suffers most, however, because of nonrecognition of the fact that social change recognizes the child's ability to read about and deal with life's recurrent problems. The author's inspirational streak and use of standard titles both add and detract from this volume's appeal.

Gerhardt, Lillian N., ed. Issues in Children's Book Selection: A School Library Journal/Library Journal Anthology. New York: Bowker, 1973. 216p.

Twenty-nine articles on current questions in library book selection for minors are included in this selection by the editor of School Library Journal. The revised reprints from the two Bowker periodicals are by a wide range of librarians, authors, and faculty members, many of them prominent in the profession. Social problems rather than literary concerns are the fare, including court cases, propaganda images, racism, sexism, and ethnicity. There is something for everyone here. The emphasis really is on timely and longstanding issues. For example, in the article on sexuality, two recognized writers scarcely mention a title; however, in one the author says that what is being talked about is political--an apt description for this work. Most contributions append a list of references, some have substantial bibliographies, others mention a few titles in the text.

Gersoni-Stavn, Diane, ed. Sexism and Youth. New York: Bowker, 1974. 468p.

A representative anthology that includes many ground-breaking articles in the field, a number with substantial application to books for young people, the objective of this title is "to make absolutist inflexible sex-role stereotyping a thing of the past." The selection is directed to parents, educators, and other concerned groups, and includes analytical essays, personal reminiscences, studies, reports, and resource lists. Both male and female stereotyping is considered. Four divisions comprise "Socialization/Indoctrination," "Dear Old Sexist School Days," "Books: Propaganda and the Sins of Omission," and "Media Mix and the

Games Children Play." Most articles mention titles in the text, and some append extensive book lists. The whole work serves as a landmark in the field for both reevaluation and checking.

Gillespie, John T., and Lembo, Diana. Introducing Books: A Guide for the Middle Grades. New York: Bowker, 1970. 318p.
This companion volume to Juniorplots (1967) is designed "to help teachers and librarians who are giving reading guidance and booktalks to children and young adults between the ages of 9 and 14." The work adds titles published since 1967 and some previously overlooked as well as lowering the age range covered in order to provide more material for readers in grades 4 and 5. Titles are arranged according to developmental stages of childhood: "Getting Along in the Family"; "Making Friends"; "Developing Values"; "Understanding Physical Problems"; "Forming a World View"; "Respecting Living Creatures"; "Evaluating Contemporary Problems"; "Identifying Adult Roles"; "Learning to Think Abstractly"; and two categories that deal with interest; appreciating books and reading for fun. Eight titles within each chapter were selected by children, teachers, and librarians who determined the reading preferences. The material on each book is divided into four sections: plot analysis; thematic material; book talk material; and additional suggestions. The latter contain many media, more so than in Juniorplots. An author and title index lists all of the over 350 books mentioned in the text. The subject index lists the main titles and those summarized. The foreword by Lloyd Alexander is an excellent introduction to an author's experience in giving reading guidance. Practitioners can use the titles that are summarized for reading guidance.

——, and Lembo, Diana. Juniorplots: A Booktalk Manual for Teachers and Librarians. New York: Bowker, 1967. 222p.
To aid teachers and librarians in giving reading guidance and book talks, particularly to children and young people between the ages of 9 and 16, is the aim of this book. Eighty books are summarized and suggested as models of book talks, and are presented under eight chapters which correspond to adolescent reading interests: "Building a World View"; "Overcoming Emotional Growing Pains"; "Earning a Living"; "Understanding Physical Problems"; "Making Friends"; "Developing Self Reliance"; "Evaluating Life"; and "Appreciating Books." The basic selection criteria were quality, pertinence to chapter theme, and provisions for various reading levels and areas of interest. Ten titles listed alphabetically by author are arranged under each chapter and receive similar treatment. There is an extensive author and title index of over 300 titles mentioned in the text. A special feature is Doris M. Cole's "Introduction to the Booktalks," a practical guide. The subject index of the eighty main titles, combined with the

suggestions on use, make a comprehensive checklist for practitioners. Little of the advice has dated since publication.

——, and Spirt, Diana Lembo. Paperback Books for Young People: An Annotated Guide to Publishers and Distributors. Chicago: American Library Assn., 1972. 177p.

A spin-off of the authors' The Young Phenomenon: Paperbacks in our Schools (below), this work lists information about publishers and distributors of paperbacks useful to librarians, teacher-training institutions, library schools, parent-teacher groups, and others interested in the format. There are three parts, each introduced by a page or two of background, covering publishers and distributors in the United States and an annotated list of current selection aids. The directory of paperback publishers lists them alphabetically and gives information about the types and series of paperbacks each publishes that are suitable for public and school libraries and young people, special services provided, and ordering information. Comparative see and see also references are made. The directory of distributors is preceded by general information about channels of distribution, including bookstores and book clubs. For each distributor, listed alphabetically by state, information about services, specialties, promotional aids, number of suitable titles, and minimum order accepted was compiled in reply to a survey questionnaire. This work provided a comprehensive checklist of appropriate paperbacks when published, but the rapidly changing character of paperback publishing will now require careful rechecking.

——. The Young Phenomenon: Paperbacks in Our Schools. ALA Studies in Librarianship. Chicago: American Library Assn., 1972. 140p.

This study is based on a comparison of the 1967 school paperback survey by the School Improvement Committee of the American Association of School Librarians and a 1970 survey made by the authors. In addition to comparing the two surveys, it gives an "overview of the place of the paperback and of the changing usage patterns that had evolved in America's schools during the past few years." Another purpose is to provide "a practical guide to help librarians in their use of paperbacks, especially with those problems that the survey uncovered." Directed to school librarians, teachers, administrators, and community groups, the authors hope that it will give insight into the problem to publishers and distributors of paperbacks. Eight chapters cover the history of the paperback phenomenon; survey analyses in schools; case studies of paperback programs; selection; administration of collection; sale of paperbacks in the schools; and recommendations. Bibliographies, current, retrospective, and specialized are included. Appendix A contains the questionnaires for the two surveys, while appendix B contains directory information on the binders and manufacturers of paperback books and racks. Anyone wishing to use paperbacks, especially in school libraries, should read this basic volume. The practical advice on this very changeable field holds true today. From the school library viewpoint, it complements Marie T. Curley's The Buckram Syndrome: A Critical Essay on Paperbacks in Public Libraries in the United States.

Gillespie, Margaret C. History and Trends. Literature for Children. Dubuque, Ia.: Brown, 1970. 128p.
   One of a useful series edited by Pose Lamb and designed for elementary teachers, this volume gives a historical sketch that treats fantasy, poetry, and realism, as well as identifying landmarks in literature for children. The text includes extracts from early books, biographical notes, and some reproductions of illustrations. Each chapter carries a list of questions and suggestions and selected references for further reading. As a pragmatic pedagogical tool, the guide is true to its purpose.

——, and Conner, John W. Creative Growth through Literature for Children and Adolescents. Columbus, Ohio: Merrill, 1975. 405p.
   This text is "designed to provide a full semester's work for students of children's and adolescent literature." The theme is the relevancy of literature to each of the developmental stages of children. The first part includes chapters exploring the relation of literature to the nature of the child and the development of responses through library encounter. These are essentially bibliographical essays analyzing books, and each is accompanied by title listings and related readings. The second part is preceded by a chapter on book selection, followed by five chapters on each period of childhood development from preschool through late adolescence with supplementary title listings, and a final selected annotated bibliography which emphasizes developmental characteristics and literary themes. While books cited range from the 1930s through the 1970s, the majority are from the sixties. Appendixes give suggestions for group and individual activities, an annotated list of current selection aids, awards, and a list of publishers of children's material. Indexes include subject, authors, illustrators, and titles. Many reproductions are given of well-known illustrations. A useful work for beginning students, it will be less helpful to practicing librarians, except to help plan programs based on a developmental stage approach.

Gilmore, Dolores D. People: Annotated Multi-Ethnic Bibliography, K-12. Rockville, Md.: Montgomery Co. Public Schools, 1973. 344p.
   Prepared in the Evaluation and Selection Division of the school system's Department of Educational Media and Technology, this is a supplementary volume to its Negroes in American Life. In separate sections, it covers immigrants from most European

countries, including Jewish Americans, along with those from Asia, Mexico, and Puerto Rico. Titles are descriptively annotated and graded from elementary to senior high-school levels. A substantial proportion of nonprint media is included, providing exceptionally thorough coverage of hard-to-locate material.

Glancy, Barbara Jean. Children's Interracial Fiction: An Unselective Bibliography. Washington, D.C.: American Federation of Teachers, AFL-CIO, 1969. 124p.

Supplementary to Dharathula Millender's Real Negroes, Honest Settings . . . and, like it, sponsored by the labor association, this bibliography incorporates the compiler's research findings. Her objective is to annotate all current interest children's books that have black characters. Indication of interest level, reading level, and status of recommendation is given for each title, as well as a short descriptive paragraph. Almost 400 titles were selected, excluding literary merit as criterion, and chronologically numbered. A categorized index under headings such as black authors, ghetto settings, and school integration refer to these numbers. There are valuable comments and comparisons, and a noteworthy essay, "Black Barbecue," accompanies the bibliography. The whole serves its purpose well in treating the black and society, and should be widely used by teachers in a classroom situation and as a checklist by librarians.

Good, David. A Catalogue of the Spencer Collection of Early Children's Books and Chapbooks, Presented to the Harris Public Library, Preston, by Mr. J. H. Spencer. Preston, Eng.: Harris Public Library, 1967. 307p.

The children's librarian of Preston compiled this catalog of an extensive collection formed by a local book collector. Entries, with brief bibliographical notes, are arranged in categories representing twenty-two traditional types of children's books. Appendixes include a chronological listing to 1800. The introduction by Percy H. Muir, distinguished antiquarian, bookseller, and historian of children's literature, gives a biographical and bibliographical background.

Good Housekeeping. Children's Books of Yesterday, The Good Housekeeping Collection: An Exhibition of Children's Books Mainly of the 18th and 19th Centuries. New York: Good Housekeeping, 1949. 27p.

Part of a collection earlier exhibited at the National Book League in London (when the catalog was compiled by Percy Muir-- see below) is presented in this annotated catalog and carries an introduction by Karl Kup, rare-bookman extraordinary of the New York Public Library. The American exhibit was circulated under the auspices of the American Federation of Arts.

Good Reading for Youth: Children's Book List. Akron, Ohio: Pilgrim
    Book Society, 1968? 24p.
    This short selection was prepared under the direction of the
    American Library Association's Children's Services Division at
    the request of the national "Good Reading for Youth" program co-
    ordinator for the Jaycees.

Gottlieb, Gerald. Early Children's Books and Their Illustration. New
    York: Pierpont Morgan Library, 1975. 263p.
    An exhibit staged by the Morgan Library resulted in the produc-
    tion of this catalog, at once a bibliographical work of reference,
    an album of illustrations, sumptuously reproduced in color and
    black and white, for students and collectors, and a scholarly
    history of early children's literature. The preface by the Morgan's
    director, Charles Ryskamp, outlines its objectives: "This book
    attempts to show us, by work and picture, how and where chil-
    dren's literature originated and which kinds of stories were chosen
    for children--and by children--over the centuries. We show you
    what the text of the most celebrated children's stories looked like
    in its earliest form, how it was first printed and illustrated, and
    then the development of the illustrated text." The 225 items, all
    illustrated, tell this story with the aid of Gerald Gottlieb's notes,
    which combine erudition and style and include detailed biblio-
    graphical collation.   Arrangement is in thirty-four separately
    introduced sections, basically chronological, from Aesop's fables
    to Beatrix Potter. Many sections represent early types of publish-
    ing, such as primers and readers, and individual authors and works.
    The emphasis is Anglo-American, but there are many exceptions,
    some outstanding ones. An accompanying essay by historian J. H.
    Plumb, "The First Flourishing of Children's Books," describes the
    social history of children, their schools, their books and their
    publishers during the eighteenth century. This catalog does not
    completely supersede its predecessor, edited by Herbert Cahoon
    twenty years previously, since the former largely represented
    loans and the latter principally the Morgan's own collection, much
    of it the donation of Miss Elizabeth Ball.   Text, notes, and
    illustrations combine to make this an indispensable sourcebook, as
    well as a beautiful volume.

Grade, Arnold E. The Merrill Guide to Early Juvenile Literature.
    Columbus, Ohio: Merrill, 1970. 43p.
    One of the publisher's series of bibliographical guides, mostly of
    individual authors, this work was designed for teachers and library
    students. This volume is a very readable, albeit slight, sketch of
    American writing for juvenile audiences from its beginning to the
    nineteenth century. Treatment is anecdotal in tone and largely
    biographical, with many titles and their dates of publication
    incorporated in the text. The selective chronology and author-

and-title index will make a useful checklist for historical collections of children's literature and for collectors.

Green, Elizabeth Alden. What to Read before College. Cleveland, Ohio: Press of Case Western Reserve Univ., 1970. 47p.

To encourage reading by high-school students who are planning to go on to college is the aim of this bibliographical essay. The fiction part of the list is an expansion of one prepared by the director of admissions at Mount Holyoke College. Written out of personal experience with students, it is a traditional and literary selection that does however include titles currently read and enjoyed by this age group. Sections cover fiction, poetry, epics and plays, nonfiction, mysteries, and young people's classics. Each is garnished with photographs of famous art works in the Cleveland Museum of Art. Titles mentioned in the text are not indexed; consequently, its use as a checklist is limited.

Greene, Ellin. Stories: A List of Stories to Tell and to Read. 6th ed. New York: New York Public Library, 1965. 78p.

A famous storytelling list, first published in 1927 and issued by the library's Children's Services branch, this work commemorates the storytellers of the New York Public Library. Postwar editions appeared in 1949, compiled by Eulalie Steinmetz Ross, and 1958, compiled by Augusta Baker. Because later editions drop out-of-print titles and editions, and because some items were replaced by later works judged of greater value for the story hour, the previous editions, all quality selections, retain practical interest and considerable historical value. The avowed objective is "to introduce the beginning storyteller to folk and fairy literature in which children have a claim, and to lead him to source materials which help him develop his arts." Picture books are included "only when the story can stand without pictures." The principal section is one on stories, arranged by title. In this edition, the "For the Story Teller" section includes recordings, the "For Reading Aloud" section includes poems as well as stories, and a striking cover illustration has been drawn by Fritz Eichenberg. All sections carry brief annotation, and detailed indexing is provided; subject indexes list by country of origin, hero, and appropriate festivals, and the expanded name index includes authors, editors, translators, illustrators, storytellers, composers, and collections. This has been an invaluable tool since its inception for storytellers, teachers, and librarians.

Green, Roger Lancelyn. Tellers of Tales: Children's Books and Their Authors, 1800-1968, with a Chronological Table of Famous Children's Books to the Present Day, and Lists of Titles by Each Author. Rev. ed. London: Kaye & Ward, 1969. 320p.

This account of the British authors of children's stories of the

nineteenth and twentieth centuries by a well-known author of
books for children has been constantly revised and expanded since
its first appearance in 1946. Continuous extension of chronological coverage is expressed in the changed subtitles for the
editions of 1953, 1956, 1965 (with separate British and American
editions), and 1969. These changes reflected substantial rewriting
and revision of the original, intended for young readers in their
early teens, not as a scholarly history of children's literature. The
1969 edition was entirely rewritten for the adult reader, retaining
less than ten percent of the original. The text still "tells about
each of the authors, and how they came to write their books, as
well as describing and criticizing the books themselves." Chapters originally about single authors now treat related authors
together in roughly historical order. Choice is confined "almost
entirely to authors whose books are still read and enjoyed by
children"; and, although only British authors are represented, the
appeal of the books is universal throughout the English-speaking
world. This informed and sensitively written study now forms a
very valuable critical and bibliographical account of its genre and
period. Appendixes include bibliographical notes, a list of authors
with their works, and a chronological list of famous or representative children's books from 1800 to 1968.

———, and Schoenfeld, Madalynne. A Multimedia Approach to Children's
Literature: A Selective List of Films, Filmstrips, and Recordings
Based on Children's Books. Chicago: American Library Assn.,
1972. 262p.
   Intended as a buying guide to book-related, nonprint material
for use with children from preschool to grade 8, this work was
compiled for librarians, teachers, media specialists, recreational
leaders, and teachers of children's literature. Selection was based
on first-hand evaluation of use with children. Some 425 books, 175
16mm films, 175 filmstrips (sound and silent), and 300 recordings
on disc and cassette are briefly annotated. All were available in
mid-1971, and buying information is included. Types and topics
include picture books, folk literature, fairy tales, fiction, drama,
poetry, song, and background material about children's books,
authors, and illustrators. Arrangement is alphabetical by title
without distinction of format. Author and subject indexes are
provided, and often indicate how book titles can be enhanced by
corresponding films and records. A highly selective listing, which
stresses the author's own perception of the criteria of inclusion. A
second edition appeared in 1977.

Griffin, Louise. Multi-Ethnic Books for Young Children: Annotated
Bibliography for Parents and Teachers. Washington, D.C.: Assn.
for the Education of Young Children, 1970. 74p.
   Addressed to those responsible for children from nursery

through elementary grades with an emphasis on the younger child, this work treats various groups: American Indians, Eskimos, and Afro-Americans; those from Appalachia, Hawaii, the Philippines, Latin America, and Asia; and those of Jewish and continental European origin. Material was field-tested in four day-care centers. Selections--the list does not attempt to be comprehensive--are given brief descriptive annotations and a grading symbol. A competent compilation of titles largely from standard sources, it constitutes a useful buying guide as most titles can be used currently. Many are familiar to children's librarians, though others are not and may require individual evaluation. Some sources for nonsexist materials are given. Also available as an ERIC document (ED 046 519).

Growing Up with Books. New York: Bowker, 1952- . Annual.
    About 300 in-print children's books, both classic and contemporary, are listed and revised annually in this publication by professional librarians and reviewers in the offices of School Library Journal. Titles, briefly annotated, are arranged by subject and by age groups. Intended for parents, teachers, and librarians, its nominal price has made it useful in bookstores. The brevity which makes it less valuable as an acquisition tool for libraries does provide an interesting sidelight on popular titles and best sellers over the years.

Growing Up with Paperbacks. New York: Bowker, 1967- . Biennial.
    Titles for this pocket-size list are selected from Paperbound Books in Print by staff members and professional librarians reviewing for School Library Journal. Arrangement combines subject and age groupings. Though choice is creditable, the small scale of the selection, some 200 titles, makes it more useful to booksellers and teachers than to librarians. One of a series, it is available at a nominal price through the cooperation of participating publishers.

Growing Up with Science Books. New York: Bowker, 1955- . Biennial.
    The titles included in this graded list of about 200 of the best science books for children are selected by the staff of School Library Journal with the assistance of science educators, and made available at a nominal charge. Briefly annotated and arranged by subject and age, they form a useful core checklist for small library collections, particularly at the elementary level, and also for booksellers, teachers and parents.

Guilfoile, Elizabeth. Books for Beginning Readers. Champaign, Ill.: National Council of Teachers of English, 1962. 73p.
    Concerned adults are the intended audience for this introduc-

tory text with two appended bibliographies, "undertaken primarily to explore a new movement in the children's book field, that of providing interesting material for children with relatively immature skills to read on their own initiative." The study answers four questions about appropriate books: "What are they like," "How to identify them," "What they are about," and "What they offer for first grade." Authors and titles are cited in the text and discussed. A short bibliography for adults is followed by a list of over 300 titles accompanied by an indication of reading difficulty, graded from the first semester of first grade to superior readers. Nearly all books were published after 1950 and three quarters since 1957. A supplement entitled "One Hundred More Books for Beginning Readers" is reprinted from Elementary English (April 1963). Because of the high quality of the selection, the work is still useful as a checklist when supplemented by later publications suitable for this group.

Hadlow, Ruth, ed. Building Together: A Selected Reading List. 2nd ed. Chicago: American Library Assn., 1968. 30p.

First published in 1960, this graded and briefly annotated bibliography of over 200 titles was prepared "for school and youth groups and to use in the education of boys and girls for social responsibility." Directed to librarians and educators, it was compiled for the United Community Funds and Councils of America by a committee from the Cleveland Public Library and chaired by the supervisor of the children's department. The first edition was prepared by Adeline Corrigan. Entries under title are arranged alphabetically within four grade categories: kindergarten and primary, upper elementary, junior high, and senior high. Both editions were helpful for reading guidance when published.

Haebich, Kathryn A. Vocations in Biography and Fiction: A Selective, Annotated List of Books for Young People. 2nd ed. Chicago: American Library Assn., 1962. 77p.

To help librarians, teachers, and other advisers "encourage young people to read for a better understanding and appreciation, not only of a vocation, but also of an individual in a given situation" is the aim of this work. The first edition of 1953 was entitled Vocations in Fact and Fiction, and the change in the title reflects the second edition's policy of listing fiction only if available biographies do not supply adequate coverage. Over 1,000 titles are included with a paragraph of descriptive annotation, under a wide variety of vocations chosen from the U.S. Department of Labor's Dictionary of Occupational Titles. Readers envisaged are students from grades 9 to 12, but some titles below a grade 8 reading level, but with a higher interest level, have been indicated. Vocations for the handicapped receive special attention. Since the date of publication vocations have changed drastically, as has their nomenclature, as well as the aspirations of young people and appropriate publications for them.

Hall, Elvajean, ed. Books to Build On: First Books to Buy for School Libraries: Elementary, Junior High, High School. How to Spend $750, $1000, $1500, etc. New York: Bowker, 1957. 79p.

This is a reprint of contributions made in 1955 to the publisher's periodical Junior Libraries, later School Library Journal. Designed to encourage school administrators, educators, and librarians in starting school libraries, it includes over a dozen articles by superintendents of schools, state librarians, and school library consultants. Three basic articles on how to start school libraries are contributed by the editor. An unannotated topical list of titles occupies half the work. While this standard selection has now become completely outdated, the articles retain validity for their practical advice.

Haller, Elizabeth S. American Diversity: A Bibliography of Resources on Radical and Ethnic Minorities for Pennsylvania Schools. Harrisburg, Pa.: State Dept. of Education, 1970. 231p.

Compiled "to assist school personnel in locating resources to implement the curriculum regulations" for inclusion of "the major contributions made by Negroes and other racial and ethnic groups" in elementary and secondary school courses is the objective of this annotated bibliography. It updates the department's publication, From Slavery to Protest (1968), which was confined to Afro-American materials, and provides for other minorities. Background content and suggested methodology are given. Entries, with brief annotations and coding for suggested grade level, are arranged within major ethnic groups, by categories, including social interpretation, history, biography, art, fiction, guides, teaching units, bibliographies and audiovisual materials. Afro-American inclusions not formerly listed are asterisked. Attempting to be definitive for Pennsylvania, the selection is generally applicable for use in other regions. An example of its quality can be seen in the fiction category relating to the Amish.

Hallworth, Grace, and Marriage, Julia. Stories to Read and to Tell. YLG Pamphlet, no. 13. Birmingham, Eng.: Library Assn., Youth Libraries Group, 1973. 20p.

To introduce librarians and teachers to books available in Britain for storytelling to children from 3 to 8 or 9 years of age is the aim of this annotated list. Part 1 caters to preschoolers up to 7-year-olds and includes picture books and anthologies; part 2 indicates age suitability. A revised expansion of Stories to Tell (compiled by Mary Junor, 1968), this publication includes material for story-reading as well. All of the over 100 items have been used successfully in schools.

Halsey, Rosalie V. Forgotten Books of the American Nursery: A History of the Development of the American Story-Book. Detroit: Singing Tree, 1969. 245p.

A photographic reprint of the Goodspeed edition of 1911, this account of the books published for children in colonial times and the early nineteenth century in America and their publishers was a seminal work and greatly influenced scholars, librarians, and collectors. Unfortunately, this reissue has poor reproductions of the original illustrations drawn from contemporary sources.

Haman, Albert C., and Eakin, Mary K. Library Materials for Elementary Science. An Educational Service Publication. Cedar Falls, Ia.: Iowa State Teachers College, 1964. 68p.

Intended to help teachers "obtain interesting reliable books in science to supplement a specific unit or topic of study in their classroom teaching," this bulletin covers elementary physical science, biological science, and biographies of scientists. Over 700 titles--some with brief annotations--chosen for grades 1 through 8 were selected according to criteria of reliability, interest, suggested activities, scientific explanation, and accuracy. A good checklist when published, subsequent publication in these developing areas has reduced its usefulness, but some standard choices remain available.

Hardendorff, Jeanne B. Stories to Tell: A List of Stories with Annotations. 5th ed. Baltimore, Md.: Enoch Pratt Free Library, 1965. 83p.

This selection "based on the actual stories which have been successfully used with children" in the story hours at the Enoch Pratt Free Library has proved to be valuable to professionals and parents alike over a long period. Two editions were reproduced from typescript in 1940 and 1942. The third, edited by M. Salome Betts, appeared in 1948, and the fourth, edited by Isabella Jinnette, in 1956. An alphabetical list of the stories identifies the source collections in which they can be found and provides descriptive annotations with hints for use. Supplementary material includes a subject list of the stories, recommended picture books for television storytelling, suggestions for story hour programs, a list of poetry collections, and a list of source collections for stories. Great care has been paid to the quality of the tales and their success with young audiences.

Hardgrove, Clarence Ethel, and Miller, Herbert F. Mathematics Library: Elementary and Junior High School. 3rd ed. Reston, Va.: National Council of Teachers of Mathematics, 1973. 70p.

First published in 1960, with a second edition in 1968, this annotated bibliography suggests a selection of books to teachers and librarians that "may serve to enrich the instructional program

by providing sources of information and recreational reading."
Most of the books for primary children are general literature
which gives special attention to mathematical ideas; those for
intermediate and junior-high students are devoted largely to
science and mathematics. Brief descriptive annotations vary
from a phrase to a paragraph, and grade recommendations are
provided. The necessary updating in this area of growing educational interest was effected by a new edition in 1978.

Harrington, Mildred Priscilla. The Southwest in Children's Books: A
Bibliography. Baton Rouge, La.: Louisiana State Univ. Pr., 1952.
124p.
Designed "to review the customs, culture, geography, history
and flavor of this unique and picturesque region," this is a local
bibliography for boys, girls, and parents, as well as librarians and
teachers, selected for quality and a sense of identity. An introduction by Siddie Jo Johnson forms a bibliographic essay on the
children's literature of the region. The chapter arrangements
correspond to the states of Arizona, Arkansas, Louisiana, New
Mexico, Oklahoma, and Texas, local librarians and bibliographers
having local responsibility for the choice. Short annotations
summarize the plot, grading recommendations are added, and
books of superior interest are distinguished with a star. The local
interest of this list still remains strong, though doubtless many
appropriate titles could now be added.

Harrison, Nancy. The Story Hour: Reading Aloud for All Ages.
London: National Book League, 1972. 46p.
First published in 1970 as Reading Aloud to the Family, this
provides a list of books for family or group reading that was
chosen with the objectives of stimulating imagination and building
up vocabulary. Criteria sought were the capture of attention,
style, and wit. Items with brief annotations are grouped by
literary genre, such as realism, fantasy, humor, animal stories,
folk and fairy tales, and collections. Interest age is indicated by a
simple code: A, up to 8; B, from 8 to 11; C, 11 and older.

Harrod, L. M., ed. Books for Young People. Group III: Fourteen to
Seventeen. London: Library Assn., 1957. 85p.
This annotated and classified list, compiled by librarians in the
London and Home Countries Branch of the association, was revised by a subcommittee of the Youth Libraries Section under the
editorship of Joan Butler. Titles in Group II, edited by Edgar
Osborne (see below), were omitted here, as were most out-of-
print books. Fiction, arranged alphabetically by author, is followed by a classified sequence of about 120 subject groups, under
headings likely to appeal to young people. Each title carries brief
descriptive and critical annotation. Because of the careful anno-

tation and arrangement, this was regarded as an official selection by many British school and public libraries. Some titles remain significant.

Harshaw, Ruth H., and Evans, Hope Harshaw. In What Book? New York: Macmillan, 1970. 130p.

The genesis of this literary quiz with the questions designed to stimulate interest in children's literature was a Chicago radio program, "The Battle of the Books." A predecessor, What Book Is That?, was published in 1948. The senior author drew on long experience as an educational consultant working with children's librarians, radio programs, and book clubs. A foreword in her memory is contributed by Mildred Batchelder, and the volume was completed by her daughter, Evans. Questions are in graded groups for ages 3-6, 4-8, 8-12, and over 12. Answers, in number form, are provided at the conclusion of each group. An author-title index relates the book to the questions. In general, the selection today retains its liveliness and popularity, and literary quality. Librarians and teachers find the game approach constructive in generating enthusiasm for books among children.

——, and MacBean, Dilla W. What Book Is That? Fun with Books at Home--at School. New York: Macmillan, 1948. 96p.

The originator of a Chicago radio program "The Hobby Horse Presents" and the Director of School Libraries for the Chicago public schools based this how-to book on improving children's reading interests through literary quizzes on a successful local radio contest, "The Battle of the Books." Four parts cover: how to run a quiz, "Fun with Books"; questions taken from well-known books, "Book Information Please"; sketches taken from famous books, "Name the Book"; and a suggested script for a radio program, "You're on the Air." Frequent reprintings without change testify to its success with teachers and community workers.

Hart, Joan Alvis, and Richardson, J. A. Books for the Retarded Reader. 2nd U.K. ed. London: Benn, 1975. 120p.

Intended not only for remedial teachers and those in special schools, but also for regular teachers, parents, and those who deal with people who speak English as a second language, this work tackles the complex problem of reading disability and describes the essential qualities necessary in books for retarded readers. The conviction that good teaching and good books remain essential in the fight against illiteracy, in spite of the increase in technical aids, is urgently expressed. Book lists provided are arranged on a functional rather than on a subject basis and call attention to specially written series publications. Pre-reading material for infants and reading schemes for older backward pupils are included. First published by the Australian Council for

Educational Research in 1959, an English edition was published in
1971. This edition follows the fifth Australian edition.

Have You Read This? A Wide Range of Books for Parents, Teachers
    and Librarians to Read and Consider Suggesting to Teenagers.
    London: National Book League, 1967. 57p.
    The presumption that the title would indicate this briefly anno-
tated list to be conservative and insular would not be fair to the
league's knowledgeable and careful selection, still of interest to
those seeking young adult titles beyond the current American
output.

Haviland, Virginia, ed. Children and Literature: Views and Reviews.
    Glenview, Ill.: Scott, Foresman, 1973. 461p.
    Haviland has compiled an anthology of articles, including
several of her own, "for those concerned with the creation, distribution and reading of children's books." The selection makes
available contributions on the historical background and a broad
range of subjects and issues in the field of children's literature.
Twelve chapters group articles pertinent to the topics: "Before
the Twentieth Century"; "Of Classics and Golden Ages"; "Children, Their Reading Interests and Needs"; "Writers and Writing";
"Illustrators and Illustrations"; "Folk Literature and Fantasy";
"Poetry"; "Fiction and Realism"; "History"; "The International
Theme"; "Criticism and Review"; and "Awards." Many titles are
referred to in the text, and these are indexed by author and title.
Some appropriate black-and-white illustrations are added. For
knowledgeable librarians and teachers, many of the articles will
be familiar but worthy of perusal again, while for students the
whole forms a valuable text for course readings. An English
reprint appeared the following year.

——. Children's Books. Washington, D.C.: Library of Congress,
    1964- . Annual.
    This sixteen-page annotated selection of 200 books for children
from preschool through junior high-school age was first issued
under the same editor, with the aid of a committee of children's
librarians, by the Children's Book Section of the library in 1964.
Each selection lists the books of the previous year that are
considered best by the editor and consultants. The books are
listed alphabetically by author under various categories: "Picture
and Picture-Story Books"; "Stories for the Middle Groups"; "Fiction for Older Readers"; "Folklore"; "Poetry"; "Arts and Hobbies";
"Biographies"; "History"; and "Nature and Science." Each entry
contains the author, title, illustrator, publisher, pagination, price,
and Library of Congress card number. A short descriptive annotation with a grade recommendation follows. The annual continues
with its original plan and purpose for children's librarians and

others interested in children's reading. It is valuable as a current acquisition list, and the previous issues are useful for study.

——. Children's Books of International Interest: A Selection from Four Decades of American Publishing. Chicago: American Library Assn., 1972. 69p.

This annotated summary list of about 350 exemplary titles was intended to promote international understanding and cooperation in the spirit of UNESCO's International Book Year and draws on an initial list compiled in 1955 (with added annual listings) of books of international interest put out by the International Relations Committee of the Children's Services Division of the American Library Association. The editor was assisted by members of this committee in making a reevaluated selection of about half the total number of fiction and nonfiction titles which were written or translated in America, and identified as intrinsically excellent, enriching, and enduring. The list suggests a basis of selection to teachers of children's literature, librarians abroad, and Americans sending gifts abroad, among others, and also to potential translators in other countries.

——. Children's Literature: A Guide to Reference Sources. Washington, D.C.: Library of Congress, 1966. 341p.
——, and Coughlin, Margaret N., eds. First Supplement, 1972. 316p.

Compiled from the rich resources of the Library of Congress's Children's Book Section with the unrivaled experience of its head, Virginia Haviland, this annotated bibliography, prepared by section staff under her direction, immediately took its place as one of the most authoritative works in the field, a reputation which succeeding supplements, planned on a five-year cycle, have enhanced. Coverage includes books, pamphlets, and articles selected, as the preface states, "on the basis of their estimated usefulness to adults concerned with the creation, reading, or study of children's books." Children's literature is regarded as comprising "books for boys and girls up to the age of 14, or in grades through the 8th." Books about textbooks and other non-literary and scholastic areas which are concerned with children's publications, such as reading techniques, are excluded. Entries are arranged under eight broad topics, with closer sectioning within each: history and criticism; authorship; illustration; bibliography; books and children; the library and children's books; international studies; and national studies. The full descriptive annotations, accompanied by Library of Congress call numbers, indicate the "relative importance and value as well as the usefulness and interest of the various items" and are supplemented by cross references and analytical entries for important parts of general works. The index includes author, title, and subject entries, and a directory of associations and agencies is provided. Black-and-white illustrations from children's books embellish the text. The original volume covers publications up to and including 1965.

The First Supplement, adding 746 entries to the initial 1,073, extends coverage through 1969 and provides two new sections on the publishing and promotion of children's books and the teaching of children's literature. The Second Supplement appeared in 1977, covering the period from 1970 to 1974 and adding 929 more entries. For librarians, teachers, students of literature, education and librarianship, and others with such diverse interests as publishing, writing, and illustrating, this work with its supplements is an essential and indispensable source. The only reservation as to its use arises from the very proliferation of coverage through successive supplementation. Occasional lack of uniformity in treatment, particularly when different contributors analyze periodical articles whose inclusion sometimes seems to exceed the original parameters, scarcely prejudices the consistently high quality of annotation. Users will regard this major bibliographical tool not as a selective guide, but as a virtually complete coverage of the field.

——. The Wide World of Children's Books: An Exhibition for International Book Year. Washington, D.C.: Library of Congress, 1972. 84p.

An exhibition in honor of UNESCO's International Book Year is the subject of this catalog. Over 100 books in their original languages represent thirty-eight countries. Items are arranged by country. In the preface, the compiler, head of the Children's Book Section, indicated that, in selecting only a few of the many children's books received by the Library of Congress's Worldwide Acquisitions Program, the emphasis was put on contemporary writing and illustration, although classics were included that were "notable for continuing importance and their new illustrations by contemporary artists." Lively annotations include background notes and bibliographical references to other editions. As a sampling, the selection will serve as a checklist for libraries seeking a beginning representation of children's literature in languages other than English.

——, and Coughlin, Margaret N., eds. Yankee Doodle's Literary Sampler of Prose, Poetry, & Pictures: Being an Anthology of Diverse Works Published for the Edification and/or Entertainment of Young Readers in America before 1900. Selected from the Rare Book Collections of the Library of Congress. New York: Crowell, 1974. 466p.

A sumptuously produced volume, this is an anthology of the books produced for young readers in America in the eighteenth and nineteenth centuries. Most of the work consists of excellent full-size reproductions in color and black and white of early books in the collections of the Library of Congress. A number of pages are reproduced from each book. Selections include both literary classics and popular mass-market publications. Three parts, covering "Works Intended to Instruct and Improve," "Works Intended to Entertain," and "The Magazines," are subdivided into chapters covering types and forms of publication. The compilers have supplied historical and critical introductions to each section and individual selections. Regrettably, the annotation on Yankee Doodle impugns its indubitably American origin.

———; Gagliardo, Ruth; and Nesbitt, Elizabeth. McCall's List of 100 Best Books for Children, Selected for McCall's. New York: McCall's, 1956. 18p.

The informed taste of the mid-fifties is reflected in this selection for the benefit of the readership of this popular magazine, compiled by three prominent figures in the world of children's literature.

———, and Smith, William Jay, comps. Children and Poetry: A Selective, Annotated Bibliography. Washington, D.C.: Library of Congress, 1969. 67p.

The combined talents of the head of the Library of Congress's Children's Book Section (who writes the preface) and its Consultant in Poetry (who writes the introduction) create an unusual government publication, whose attractive oblong format is greatly enhanced by a generous quantity of illustrations discriminately culled from the selected books. The compilers explored the holdings of the library to recommend "the best that is available today." Traditional poetry has largely been omitted. Five sections cover rhymes, poetry of the past, twentieth-century poetry, anthologies, and world poetry. A discerning paragraph of annotations for each book usually includes excerpts from the poetry and occasionally paraphrases of reviews. This lavishly produced booklet accompanied the Library of Congress's Festival of Poetry for its fiftieth anniversary during Book Week, 1979. It is a delight to read and also acts as a valuable checklist for children's collections.

Haynes, John. Books and Publications Recommended for Use with Dull and Backward Children. 2nd ed. Maidstone, Kent, Eng.: Kent Education Committee, 1960. 24p.

Based on British teachers' recommendations, class books, supplementary readers, library books, and books for teachers are included with a few brief annotations. This booklet was previously published in 1954 with two later supplements. Publications included are British, and are now difficult to obtain in most cases.

Hazard, Paul. Books, Children and Men. Boston: Horn Book, 1960. 176p.

This seminal contribution by a distinguished historian of comparative literature and member of the Académie first appeared in France in 1932 as <u>Les Livres, les Enfants et les Hommes</u>. The translation by Marguerite Mitchell was published in 1944, the year of Hazard's death, with subsequent editions in the same year, 1947, and 1960, all with an introduction by Horatio Smith and a preface by Bertha Mahoney Miller. The last edition adds Miller's memorial tribute to the author's greatness as a scholar-teacher and to his love of childhood, and completes the story of his life in World War II in France. Addressed to all concerned with the world republic of childhood--a phrase coined by Hazard--the book was a labor of love. Within the framework of a brief and selective world survey of books written for children, concentrating on France, Germany, Italy, Scandinavia, Britain, and America, the author's hortatory approach and vigorous style enshrine literary and human values. Five chapters focus on the following themes: "Men Have Always Oppressed Children"; "Children Have Defended Themselves"; "The Superiority of the North over the South"; "National Traits"; and "The Soul of Man." A short bibliography lists critical works relating to each. While the milieu is one of a former generation and children's needs and attitudes have changed, this book will remain a source of inspiration to the practitioner, as well as cogent criticism for the literary scholar.

Heeks, Peggy. <u>Books of Reference for School Libraries: An Annotated List</u>. 2nd ed. London: School Library Assn., 1968. 54p.
    In this guide for British school librarians, reference books that have contents arranged for quick reference, rather than for continuous reading, are listed. Entries, carefully and fully annotated, are arranged in a general category and eight broad subject groups, each subdivided. An article is included on the treatment and selection of reference materials. While some publications of other countries are included, items are mainly British and form a useful comparative list for North American libraries. This new enlarged edition testifies to the work's continued value as an aid in British schools. The first edition appeared in 1961.

——. <u>Eleven to Fifteen: A Basic Book-List for Secondary School Libraries</u>. 3rd ed., rev. and enl. London: School Library Assn., 1963. 115p.
    This selection, aimed at British school librarians, is designed to be a basic nonfiction list for children of this age group, but tools for quick reference are omitted as these are listed in the author's <u>Books of Reference for School Libraries</u>. Over 1,000 entries are arranged in Dewey sequence with brief descriptive annotation provided. This edition doubles the size of the third edition of 1961. The list was first published in 1950, with a second edition in 1953. A careful and useful compilation, mainly of British publications, which was a dependable guide when published, will now require substantial updating.

Heller, Frieda M. I Can Read It Myself! Rev. ed. Columbus, Ohio: Ohio State Univ. College of Education, 1965. 46p.

Three lists, covering grades 1-3 and beginning readers and graded according to reading ability, include fiction and nonfiction selected to provide appropriate material for individualized reading programs. Items carry short descriptive annotations. The objective is to foster the child's feeling of accomplishment in order to lead to more independent reading. This edition enlarges the first of 1960, which bore the subtitle Some Books for Independent Reading in the Primary Grades.

Hewins, Caroline M. A Mid-Century Child and Her Books. Detroit: Singing Tree, 1969. 136p.

This delightful recollection by a venerated children's librarian at the turn of the century of her own Massachusetts childhood and the reading available in the 1850s is informative. The introduction by Anne Carroll Moore, for years head of Children's Services in New York Public Library, the charming depiction of the author's growing years, and the invaluable aid her story provides for checking children's reading of that period commend this book. The retelling of Peter Piper's Alphabet--Hewins's one great storytelling "parlour trick"--is a distinct plus. Unfortunately, this photographic reprint of the original Macmillan edition of 1926 poorly reproduces the numerous illustrations from the nineteenth-century books.

Higgins, James E. Beyond Words: Mystical Fancy in Children's Literature. New York: Teachers College, Columbia Univ., 1970. 112 p.

The literary quality of children's literature, seen as a combination of beauty of form and emotional impact, and not divorced from literature as a whole, is treated in this critical work. The author, preferring the term fancy to fantasy, examines "books that lead forth," their writers and the ways in which they are written, and how they relate to the child and the world within, around and beyond him. The work of two nineteenth-century authors, W. H. Hudson and George MacDonald, and two twentieth-century authors, J. R. R. Tolkien and C. S. Lewis, are specially analyzed.

Hildick, Edmund Wallace. Children and Fiction: A Critical Study in Depth of the Artistic and Psychological Factors Involved in Writing Fiction for and about Children. Rev. ed. London: Evans, 1974. 212p.

The author, a prolific British author of juvenile and adult books, presents a refreshingly honest and sometimes contentious expression of opinion about writing fiction for young people and its place in education. His views are arguable, but founded on experience and study. Points are illustrated with literary extracts, not all of which are drawn from children's books. Full appreciation requires textual reference to titles appearing in the index which represent a core British and American collection. The first edition was published in London in 1970 and New York in 1971.

Hill, Janet, ed. Books for Children: The Homelands of Immigrants in Britain. London: Institute of Race Relations, 1971. 85p.

This critically annotated survey of all children's books, except textbooks, in print in Britain in 1970, about countries from which many people emigrated to Britain: Africa, Cyprus, India, Pakistan, the West Indies, Ireland, Italy, Poland, and Turkey, is not a list of recommended titles. The conclusions supplied by fourteen contributors are intended for people concerned with community relations and connected with children. Titles, with annotations, are arranged by country and a grading system is applied (A means wholeheartedly recommended; B not inspired but useful; C not recommended; biased, prejudiced, or dull). Readers are warned that outstanding books are few, and mediocrity abounds.

Hill, Janet. Reading for Enjoyment for 8 to 11 Year Olds. London: Children's Book News, 1975. 32p.

The third in the series (see Moss, . . . 2 to 5 Year Olds, 1975), this work is designed to be useful to parents, community workers, teachers, etc., so they can help children positively in discovering and enjoying books for themselves. A level of maturity and understanding, rather than precise age limits, is presumed. About 100 items are arranged alphabetically by author, with a paragraph of descriptive and critical comment, and bibliographical mention of other titles by the same author. This list was first compiled by Jessica Jenkins in 1970 for 9- to 11-year-olds.

Hinman, Dorothy, and Zimmerman, Ruth. Reading for Boys and Girls--Illinois: A Subject Index and Annotated Bibliography. Chicago: American Library Assn., 1970. 128p.

To provide a reference tool for librarians, teachers, and boys and girls in Illinois to locate material readily for "a thorough and enjoyable study of their state" is the aim of this work. A wider purpose is to enable young readers everywhere to "learn much about America." Titles included in the annotated bibliography were selected to contribute an appreciation of heritage, and carry a full paragraph of lucid descriptive and critical annotation. Biography and fiction predominate, with an emphasis on the hard-to-find material for the lower four grades. The subject index to Illinois materials provides a key to use. Appendixes furnish additional help, including a list of suggested reference books, another of free and inexpensive materials, and a sports and athletics bibliography.

History of the World. Topic Booklists. Tunbridge Wells, Eng.: Fen-
     rose, 1974. 63p.
     One of a publisher's series, this selection for teachers of history
aims to present "brief details of all the principal children's books
set in historic times outside the British Isles." The emphasis is on
novels. Arrangement is by geographical areas, subdivided chronologically. Titles carry brief annotations and a letter code indicating the appropriate reading age: under 9, from 9 to 12, and
over 12. This is a companion to English Historical Fiction in the
same series.

Hodges, Elizabeth H. Books for Elementary School Libraries: An
     Initial Collection. Chicago: American Library Assn., 1969. 321p.
     A basic selection tool, with a long list of forerunners under
various titles going back to 1922. Its immediate predecessor, A
Basic Book Collection for Elementary Grades (the 5th and 6th
editions being in 1951 and 1956 and the 7th edition in 1960, edited
by Miriam Snow Mathes), was "designed as a buying guide to a
quality collection of books for initial library service to elementary pupils in kindergarten through 8th grade." The selection is
closely related to the curriculum as well as the interests of the
children in elementary school. Advice was given by two committees, one of consultant school librarians and library educators, the
other the Subcommittee for School Libraries of the ALA Editorial
Committee. Over 3,000 titles with brief descriptive annotations
are listed in a classified topical arrangement based on the Dewey
Decimal Classification. Fiction is broken down into "Stories for
Intermediate and Upper Grades" and "Picture Books and Stories
for Primary Grades." These cover the valid titles from previous
lists and more recent publications up to 1968, chosen for excellence of literary quality and content, suitability of subject matter, appropriateness of format, and inclusion in other standard
selection aids. Primarily hard-bounds were chosen, with paperbound editions only if those were unavailable. Excluded are out-
of-print titles, professional books, periodicals, pamphlets, and
audiovisual materials. The editor appends her choice of professional tools for building book collections. The full index includes
subject headings. Now a standard tool for elementary schools,
this official selection remains valid with necessary additions and
reevaluations.

Hoffman, Miriam, and Samuels, Eva, eds. Authors and Illustrators of
     Children's Books: Writings on Their Lives and Work. New York:
     Bowker, 1972. 471p.
     A bio-bibliographical anthology of modern children's writers,
this work aims to make periodical articles that will provide
background material for librarians, teachers, students, and
children permanently accessible. The authors attempt "to make

children's books more meaningful not only for the students but most especially for the children with whom they will be working." Fifty articles represent each author or author-illustrator from varied national origins. Excluded are children's poets and illustrators who are not also authors. Editors' notes supplement the biographical information. The choice of individuals selected reflects those most commonly called for by school assignments. The bibliographical information given in the text and the appendix about in-print titles and the first editions of out-of-print titles is invaluable for both reference and selection purposes.

Hollindale, Peter. Choosing Books for Children. London: Elek, 1974. 187p.

Addressing teachers and librarians, the author poses the questions, "What should we provide?" and "How should we provide it?" and proposes some specific answers. After examining some problems of choosing and consumer reaction, the role of the teacher and the librarian are assessed vis-à-vis different age groups, topics, and types of books. Book lists for children from preschool age to adolescence are provided with explanatory introductions. Some individual titles are sharply criticized. Persuasive in his arguments, literate in his narrative writing, and discerning in his recommendations for different ages, the author will convince many. This is an excellent study, especially for his analysis of well-known stories on both sides of the Atlantic.

Hollowell, Lillian, comp. A Book of Children's Literature. 3rd ed. New York: Holt, 1966. 580p.

An anthology which incorporates a substantial element of criticism and bibliographical material about children's books, first published in 1939 and again in 1950, this work retains its original purpose as a textbook for teachers and librarians in training, as well as a source book for parents and others interested in reading for children from kindergarten to grade 9. Treatment is based on the compiler's long teaching experience in the field. Introductory material stresses social background and provides criteria to selection and evaluation. Ten chapters of short and long anthologized passages divided into traditional types and themes of children's books each carry lengthy introductory remarks, a selected annotated bibliography and black-and-white reproductions of illustrations. Supplements include a historical summary, appraisal of illustration and illustrators, biographical sketches of authors, and references for further reading. As a comprehensive source book of samples and comment, this edition maintains its value as a single-volume teaching text, as well as being of general interest to others.

Hopkins, Lee Bennett. <u>Books Are by People: Interviews with 104 Authors and Illustrators of Books for Young Children</u>. New York: Citation, 1969. 349p.

A curriculum and editorial specialist for Scholastic Magazines, Inc., Hopkins brings a lively personal touch to the interviewing of current American writers and illustrators. Many quotations from the interviewees are incorporated in the text. Each author is provided with an identifying photograph. Bibliographic references are plentiful. As the not-so-famous are not excluded, much of the information here may be inaccessible elsewhere.

——. <u>More Books by More People</u>. New York: Citation, 1974. 410p.

A follow-up to the author's 1969 volume, this work has sixty-five additional interviews of authors of books for children. Choice of subject remains predominantly current and American; interviews are on the average longer and scope for inclusion has been modified: illustrators are excluded, authors are no longer restricted to those for the younger child, and both favorites and lesser-knowns are represented. The treatment remains as vivid and the bibliographical lists for each author as convenient for librarians, students, and lay people as in its predecessor.

Horn, Thomas D., and Elbert, Dorothy J. <u>Books for the Partially Sighted Child</u>. Champaign, Ill.: National Council of Teachers of English, 1965. 80p.

Reprinted from a series of periodical articles in <u>Elementary English</u> (Dec. 1975-March 1975), this annotated bibliography is intended for visually impaired children from kindergarten to grade 8. Criteria for choice included typography (size of type, typeface, and leading), illustrative method, and literary qualities. Annotation is descriptive, with attention given to special appeal for the reader group and to technical print considerations, such as size of type. Nonfiction, fiction, and easy books are divided into topics arranged alphabetically within these. A system of asterisks is the key to recommendation. All choices were personally examined at two Texas libraries, and mainly consist of titles from the late fifties and early sixties. Because of the scarcity of suitable material, this list is still a useful tool, though later sources must be used to supplement it.

Hotchkiss, Jeannette. <u>European Historical Fiction and Biography for Children and Young People</u>. 2nd ed. Metuchen, N.J.: Scarecrow, 1972. 272p.

This annotated book list was designed to foster enthusiasm for history in young people, from elementary readers to young adults. Over 1,000 titles are arranged in eight geographical groups, the first and largest of which is the British Isles; each is subdivided by century. Titles carry a short descriptive note and an indication of reading level. This second edition includes biographies, omitted from the first edition of 1967, making it a useful access tool to a wider literature.

Huber, Miriam Blanton, ed. Story and Verse for Children. Rev. ed. New York: Macmillan, 1955. 812p.

First published in 1940, this anthology was intended for prospective teachers, teachers in service, librarians, and parents. A beginning section covers the enjoyment of literature, selection, children's reading interests, the history of books for children, and the illustrated books. The selections are arranged under traditional categories, each with an introduction, and a selected bibliography is arranged by grades. The guide is now only of interest retrospectively.

Huck, Charlotte S., and Kuhn, Doris Young. Children's Literature in the Elementary School. 2nd ed. New York: Holt, 1968. 792p.

This substantial and attractively produced volume, first published in 1961, is intended to help teachers and school librarians to become familiar with the available literature for children of elementary school age, and to develop criteria in selection and skills in guiding a literature program. The numerous titles discussed in the text have bibliographic references to lists at the close of each chapter, where suggested activities and related readings are also recommended. Appendixes list children's book awards and book selection aids. There are many illustrations in half-tone and line.

Hunt, Gladys. Honey for a Child's Heart: The Imaginative Use of Books in Family Life. Grand Rapids, Mich.: Zondervan, 1969. 127p.

A guide on Christian principles for parents and others who wish to encourage children to read is the purpose of this work. The introduction endorses the author's wide reading tastes and her persuasive arguments that books are beneficial. She gives personal reminiscences of a family Bible-reading tradition that led to the love of reading and cultivation of sound adult values. Six chapters comment on her experiences with books that are familiar choices with children's librarians and parents. A supplementary bibliography classifies recommended titles under five broad topics: general, poetry, Christian (fiction, biography, and missions), books for teens, and family reading. Within each, books are categorized for the young, the middlers (grades 4-6), teens, and mature readers. While highly selective to accord with Christian ethic, the list represents a sound but personal selection of traditional titles, although a few, such as The Voyages of Dr. Doolittle, do not find favor in some current educational thinking.

With this caution, librarians can use it as a source of recommendations to the group for whom it is intended.

Hürlimann, Bettina. Picture Book World: Modern Picture Books for
   Children from Twenty-Four Countries. Translated by Brian W.
   Alderson. With a Bio-Bibliographical Supplement by Elizabeth
   Waldmann. London: Oxford Univ. Pr., 1968. 216p.
      First published in Zurich by Atlantis in 1965 as Die Welt im
   Bilderbuch, this international survey of present-day picture books
   stresses works of high artistic quality. The author has not forgotten the viewpoint of the users, the children. An initial discussion
   of the age of picture books includes photographs of children
   reading from many parts of the world, and is followed by a
   country-by-country resumé. The volume is virtually an anthology
   of color and black-and-white reproductions. Valuable originally
   for its international coverage by a recognized authority, this
   edition has expanded coverage of English and American works in
   the bio-bibliographical supplement.

———. Three Centuries of Children's Books in Europe. Translated and
   edited by Brian W. Alderson. London: Oxford Univ. Pr., 1967.
   297p.
      Translated from the second German edition of 1963, this histor-
   ical survey modifies the strictly chronological approach by examining the literary and sociological backgrounds of children's
   literature in different countries. Insistence on personal examination of the books described and a subjective approach character-
   ize the author's methodology, which is supplemented by many
   carefully selected reproductions. Bibliographies list children's
   books mentioned, biographies, and selected books about children's
   literature in a national arrangement. This edition supplies information on how European titles were received in England and
   provides references to translations. The volume is, for continental literature, a necessary complement to the more easily
   available information on English-language works. An important
   general introduction and the sympathetic personal interpretation
   of individual works make this a classic in the field. This title was
   published in the United States by World in 1968.

Huus, Helen. Children's Books to Enrich the Social Studies for the
   Elementary Grades. 2nd ed. Washington, D.C.: National Council
   for the Social Studies, National Education Assn., 1966. 201p.
      A revision and enlargement of the first edition (1961) of this
   NCSS Bulletin, this work is directed primarily to teachers. The
   compiler advocates the use of trade books for children, rather
   than school texts, as supplementary tools to teach social studies in
   the classroom. The bibliography is organized by concepts and
   ideas, and five chapters are "Our World," "Times Past," "People

Today" (including twentieth-century America and other parts of the world), "The World's Work," and "Living Together." Folk tales are excluded. Titles out of print since the previous edition have been deleted. A fairly detailed annotation includes grade level, based on reading level and appropriateness of subject matter. The compiler warns against future dating of information in the books on account of changing world conditions. While this must be allowed for, the list remains a high quality selection, useful to librarians and students, as well as teachers.

——. Evaluating Books for Children and Young People. Perspectives in Reading. Newark, Del.: International Reading Assn., 1968. 137p.
    Number 10 of the association's helpful series brings together a first-rate assortment of specialists in the teaching and library fields. Ten essays cover a broad range of topics in children's literature and book selection. A primary objective is to help teachers assist the learners in their classrooms to make some evaluations. A caution: the unannotated bibliography at the end is a mixed bag of books referred to in the text, and not a selection of best books.

Information Center on Children's Cultures, United States Committee for UNICEF. Africa: An Annotated List of Printed Materials Suitable for Children. New York: The Center, 1968. 76p.
    This annotated booklist--compiled by a joint committee of the American Library Association's Children's Services Division and the African-American Institute, chaired by Anne Pellowski and coordinated by Elizabeth Gardiner, is a "unique effort to evaluate all in-print English-language materials for children on the subject of Africa." It includes African publications as well as those from English-speaking countries. Arrangement is under each African country, usually subdivided as fiction, nonfiction, and folklore. Brief annotations give grade level and evaluate stereotyping or bias. Supplementary unannotated lists for each section indicate non-recommended books on the one hand, and, on the other, titles specially selected for use in Africa itself. A very helpful list when published, it still retains its value for reference, although many relevant titles have appeared since.

——. Latin America: An Annotated List of Materials for Children. New York: The Center, 1969. 96p.
    Compiled by a committee of librarians, teachers, and area specialists, this annotated booklist represents an effort to evaluate all English-language materials for children on the subject of Latin America. It also includes relevant Spanish-language materials obtainable in the United States, but excludes language teaching aids. Arrangement is under geographical areas and individual countries, and subheadings such as "History Today," "Folklore,"

"Songs," "Inter-American Programs," "Spanish Speaking Americans," and "In Spanish." Some late arrivals are noted as not reviewed at the end of each section. Brief annotations give grade levels and apply criteria of accuracy of factual content, up-to-dateness, and lack of condescension or bias. While supplementation with subsequent publications will be required, the selection will be useful for background reference in areas such as sociological study.

——. Near East and North Africa: An Annotated List of Material for Children. New York: The Center, 1970. 98p.

All the then in-print English-language materials for children on the Near East, including North Africa, Greece, and Turkey are included in this annotated booklist of about 500 titles. There are also some appropriate selections in the languages of the various countries. Compilation was done by knowledgeable individuals rather than by reviewers sponsored by organizations because of the current tensions in the area. Numbered entries are arranged by geographical area and country. The brief annotations pay attention to accuracy and attitude, non-recommended titles being indicated. Grade levels are given from kindergarten to grade 9. Some late arrivals are listed without review at the end of each section. More recent area developments, particularly in the oil-rich countries, will inevitably require supplementation to the list by more recent publications.

Ingram, Anne Bower. It's Reading Time: Books for the Under Fives. Happy Family Series. Hornsby, New South Wales: Hodder & Stoughton, 1972. 94p.

Some, but not a majority of, Australian titles are found in this informally arranged and briefly annotated selection of picture books.

Ireland, Norma Olin. Index to Fairytales, 1949-1972, Including Folklore, Legends and Myths, in Collections. Westwood, Mass.: Faxon, 1973. 741p.

A successor to Mary Huse Eastman's long-established Index to Fairytales (1st ed., 1900, 2d ed., 1926) and its two supplements (1937 and 1952), this substantial volume indexes the stories in over 400 collections published since 1949, and expands the scope to cover folklore, legends, and myths. The first part lists alphabetically the collections indexed--separately published tales are outside the scope--and the second part, the stories themselves, arranged under subject and author. Long an invaluable tool for public and school librarians and teachers, all parts together give access to a vast body of popular tales and retellings, although they are not intended to serve the scholarly researcher of folklore. A supplementary volume, covering 1973 to 1977, appeared in 1979.

Irwin, Leonard B. Black Studies: A Bibliography for the Use of School
Libraries and the General Reader. Brooklawn, N.J.: McKinley,
1973. 122p.

This select bibliography for general use identifies items for
young people by symbols placed before the brief descriptive annotations, and indicates usefulness for high school or grades 6 to 10.
Paperback editions are noted. Sections cover the history of the
black experience in America; biography and memoirs; essays,
anthologies and books on current problems; Negro culture; and
African background and history. More informative guides are
available specifically for school and young people's purposes.

Izard, Anne. Children's Books: Awards and Prizes. 4th ed. New York:
Children's Book Council, 1975. 156p.

First published in 1969, compiled by Ingebord Boudreau, with
succeeding editions in 1971 by Margaret Colbert, and 1973 by
Christine Stawicki, this compilation of honors awarded in the
children's book field can be regarded as the official list of major
international and foreign awards and all those located in English-
speaking countries, given by organizations, schools and universities, publishers, and newspapers. Arrangement is by award. Each
entry carries a brief history and a list of all winners from the first
to the most recent. Runner-ups are noted, as are honor books for
the Newbery and Caldecott medals and finalists for the National
Book Award. Illustrators are listed only when the prize is for
illustration. Awards discontinued since the last edition are re-
moved, so earlier editions retain some value. An informative
introduction, and title and author/illustrator indexes add to the
value of this guide, indispensable as a checklist and for selection.

Jackson, Miles M., Jr. et al. A Bibliography of Negro History and
Culture for Young Readers. Pittsburgh: Univ. of Pittsburgh Pr.,
1968. 134p.

Directed to teachers and librarians, this listing of books with
some audiovisual materials derives from a report (ERIC Document ED 015 091) prepared in connection with the Institute on
Materials by and about Negro Americans, sponsored by Atlanta
University in 1965. Items are grouped by type of publication, and
carry brief descriptive annotations with a recommended elementary or secondary reading level. Supplementary material includes
a foreword, an introductory essay, and a list of biographies of
famous Negroes. The selection was less than comprehensive at
the time of publication, and requires updating with later publications that are relevant.

Jacob, Gale Sypher. Independent Reading Grades One Through Three:
An Annotated Bibliography with Reading Levels. Williamsport,
Pa.: Brodart, 1975. 86p.

Nearly 850 hardcover trade books, half of them published after 1970, were included in this guide for "both teachers and librarians to identify titles appropriate for independent reading and covering twenty-nine subject areas for grades one through three." The advisory committee to the compiler largely relied on the ninth edition of the publisher's more substantial The Elementary School Library Collection, but many titles appear that are not in that work's reading level appendixes. Annotations include a reading level for each grade according to the Spache reading formula, and there is careful cross-referencing from subject headings. The explanatory preface, which describes the compilation procedure and the criteria of choice, and two indexes, one under reading level within the grades and the other by author and title, facilitate the use of this conveniently planned tool.

Jacobs, Leland B., ed. Using Literature with Young Children. New York: Teachers College Pr., 1965. 63p.

Topics that vary from enjoying and providing literature for young children to storytelling, poetry, and drama, are addressed in these twelve essays by well-known educators. While useful titles receive mention in the text, there is no further bibliographical component.

Jan, Isabelle. On Children's Literature. Translated from the French, edited and with a preface by Catherine Storr. London: Lane, 1973. 189p.

First published in Paris by Éditions Ouvrières in 1969 as Essai sur la littérature enfantine, this French study seeks to establish if children's literature actually exists, what are its hallmarks, and how do we recognize it. Chapters are essays on the different genres of children's literature and have considerable comparative value àpropos English-language treatments.

Jeffery, J. Betty. Growing Up with Books. 3rd ed. London: National Book League, 1972. 42p.

This frankly personal list was compiled to help parents choose books for their children to own and to borrow. It was first published in 1966, with a second edition in 1969. Priority is given to less expensive books and those that appeal to young children. In some cases a rough guide to age range is given, and all entries have a sentence of descriptive annotation. Entries are grouped according to the usual types of children's publication, and include nonfiction and books and journals about children's literature.

Johnson, Edna; Sickels, Evelyn R.; and Sayers, Frances Clarke, eds. Anthology of Children's Literature. 4th ed. Boston: Houghton, 1970. 1,289p.

This substantial anthology, first published in 1940 with succeeding editions in 1948 and 1959, is selected primarily for students of children's literature, and includes substantial critical material in the form of introductions and appendixes. The foreword to this edition comments on changes in children's publishing and in society. Among the topical subdivisions, poetry, fiction, and science have revised introductory material, and there is a new essay on picture books. Appendixes discuss storytelling, the history of children's books, illustrators, book awards, and graded reading lists of books and of the selected extracts. Illustrations by Fritz Eichenberg and N. C. Wyeth add to the continued attractiveness of this volume for students informal and formal, teachers, and parents.

Johnson, Harry Alleyn, ed. Multimedia Materials for Afro-American Studies: A Curriculum Orientation and Annotated Bibliography of Resources. New York: Bowker, 1971. 353p.
    Planned as a standard source book to "assist educators in planning and executing necessary curriculum changes," these two bibliographical lists on the Afro-American in the United States and on the peoples of Africa are preceded by four position papers by black educators. The 1,400 entries, with full descriptive annotations, are subdivided by format within the lists, including 16mm and 8mm films, filmstrips, kits, recordings, slides, videotapes, and paperbacks. While not exhaustive, it represented the most comprehensive multimedia selection available on the topic, and with the necessary allowance for later publications, constitutes a very valuable resource tool.

Johnson, James P. Africana for Children and Young People: A Current Guide for Teachers and Librarians. African Bibliographic Center, Special Bibliographic Series. Westport, Conn.: Greenwood, 1971. 172p.
    This finding list for current Africana includes nearly 900 unannotated items. The compiler, a librarian, attempts to be comprehensive, mainly for American publications, by selecting from library and trade tools, such as Books in Print, and appropriate reviewing periodicals, such as the Africana Library Journal. Sections on current bibliography, background reading, update sources, and the regions of Africa--Central, East, North, South, and West--are subdivided under nonfiction and fiction, and printed and audiovisual material. As a current tool, it is now superseded, but can be referred to for titles now unavailable.

Jordan, Alice M. Children's Classics: With a List of Recommended Editions by Helen Masten. 4th ed. Boston: Horn Book, 1967. 16p.
    Famous and limited, this selection first appeared in the February 1947 issue of The Horn Book, and was issued as a separate in the same year. Succeeding editions were revised and added to by

Helen Adams Masten in 1952 and 1960. This fourth appearance increased the list to 136 recommended editions of children's classics issued up to September 1967. This alphabetical list, which the authors state has "no claim to be final or definitive" includes "some of the best books ever written for (or adopted by) children, [that] will enrich the reading tastes of any child." All the editions are invaluable guides to the best in children's books, selected from a literary point of view. A fifth edition appeared in 1976.

——. From Rollo to Tom Sawyer and Other Papers. Boston: Horn Book, 1948. 160p.
     Twelve essays treat aspects of children's literature in America during the nineteenth century. Half of them, including the well-known title paper, originally appeared in The Horn Book. The author's work there as an assistant editor, and as Supervisor of Children's Work at the Boston Public Library, gives her interpretation of famous and typical authors of the last century a personal note, sharing her knowledge and inspiration with all devotees of children's literature. Fascinating reading throughout, the text includes mention of many titles deserving the attention of researchers and collectors in the field. This unchanged work was reprinted in 1974 with the same attractive decorations and end papers by Nora S. Unwin.

Junior Arts and Crafts. London: National Book League, 1970. 18p.
     This book list is useful in the teaching of arts and crafts by modern methods in primary schools, and was selected by Scottish teachers. Eighty-five items, some of them American imprints, carry brief annotations and are arranged alphabetically. Many are suitable for student use at several levels.

Karl, Jean. From Childhood to Childhood: Children's Books and Their Creators. New York: Day, 1970. 175p.
     In a pleasant conversational style, the editor of many prize books details the many facets in the process of writing and publishing children's books. Chapters examine the why and wherefore of children's books, the author's task, criteria of quality, and the contribution of editors and publishers. The chapter on "Children's Books from Yesterday to Tomorrow" is literate and rich in titles. The work is valuable also for the perceptiveness of the author's concluding words about the reading of children's books by all ages.

Keating, Charlotte Matthews. Building Bridges of Understanding. Tucson, Ariz.: Palo Verde, 1967. 140p.
     This is an annotated list of over two hundred books which present opportunities for children from different ethnic back-

grounds in the United States to become acquainted. Choice has been directed to those appealing books which provide insights into the feelings and cultural values of individual children from a variety of ethnic groups, but those describing life in countries outside the United States have been excluded. Sections include titles about Negroes, American Indians, Spanish-speaking ethnic groups, Chinese-Americans and Japanese-Americans. A final section covers Hawaiians, Jews, other minority groups and multi-ethnic situations. The descriptive and critical annotations vary in length from a paragraph to a page and reflect the author's personal impressions of each title.

Kelly, R. Gordon. Mother Was a Lady: Self and Society in Selected American Children's Periodicals, 1865-1890. Contributions in American Studies, no. 12. Westport, Conn.: Greenwood, 1974. 233p.

A study of cultural transmission, directed to historians of culture, this work examines the literature intended to edify the young and inculcate adult values. It concentrates on the narrative fiction produced by what the author calls the American gentry class in the Gilded Age, a period of rapid social change. Stories, some by famous authors in periodicals such as St. Nicholas, Our Young Folks and The Youth's Companion, are analyzed. The author's distinction between the books read by children and those offered to them, and his sympathy with the thesis that reality is socially constructed, enable him to use children's literature as presented in these periodicals to recapitulate the sociology of knowledge in nineteenth-century America. He also observes, mistakenly perhaps, that the field of children's literature is still dominated in authorship and librarianship by the hypocritical ideal of discipline and the premise of a better life. The idea is clever, the title of the book is ironic; but the field of children's literature has been a-changing.

Kemp, Jo, and Farrell, Janet. Carry on Reading: Books for the Child Who Has Just Learned to Read. London: National Book League, 1975. 16p.

The selectors of titles for this traveling exhibition catalog included a primary school headmistress and a media resources officer. Together they have compiled this annotated list of sixty British publications for the inner urban child who enters junior school with certain reading skills but who must carry on before achieving fluency. An A, B, or C notation indicates easy, more difficult, and most difficult books. Criteria for choice included familiar language settings and characters, good illustrations, and suitable length. Individual quality titles have been joined by series and some popular works of less intrinsic merit. Almost all are worth reading aloud. Contents cover fiction and nonfiction (including history), geography and transport, nature, human biology, science, and games.

Kennedy, Mary Lou, ed. Paperbacks in the Elementary School, Their Place, Use and Future: A Handbook for Teachers in the Intermediate Grades. Middletown, Conn.: American Education Pub., 1969. 126p.

The publisher's Weekly Reader staff prepared this publication for the audience of teachers taking part in the magazine's Paperback Book Clubs. The foreword by Eleanor M. Johnson stresses the importance of a "more imaginative approach to literature if we are to have an effective reading program in the elementary school." Designed to encourage a fresh look at teaching goals and responsibilities, contents range from "Bringing Children and Paperbacks Together," through "Reading for Recreation, . . . Information and Understanding, and . . . Literature Appreciation," to "How to Make Best Use of Weekly Reader Paperback Book Clubs." Some selected readings and a bibliography of professional references complement the text. When published, it presented not only a series of ideas but also a list of available paperbacks that librarians could use as a checklist; but taking into account its special purpose, it was of restricted use and did not compare with more thorough analyses of the paperback phenomena, such as Gillespie's Paperback Books for Young People.

Kenworthy, Leonard S. Studying Africa in Elementary and Secondary Schools. World Affairs Guides. 3rd ed. New York: Teachers College Pr., 1970. 74p.

One of a series produced for Teachers College, Columbia University, first published in 1962 and revised in 1965, this selection was designed to help teachers and librarians in elementary and secondary schools meet the rapidly growing interest in Africa. In addition to the unannotated bibliography of all media, arranged on a geographical basis, introductory matter draws on the author's first-hand experience in visiting Africa to combat stereotyping, put forward study concepts, and make curriculum proposals for the various grades. Much has happened over recent years to require updating of this originally well-chosen list.

——. Studying South America in Elementary and Secondary Schools. World Affairs Guides. 2nd ed. New York: Teachers College Pr., 1965. 51p.

One of a series for teachers of grades 1-12, this is similar to the author's Studying Africa . . ., and was first published in 1962.

——. Studying the Middle East in Elementary and Secondary Schools. World Affairs Guides. Rev. ed. New York: Teachers College Pr., 1965. 57p.

First published in 1962 on the same general plan as the author's

Studying Africa . . . in the same series, this work has been outdated by the rapid changes in the area, but the introductory comment for educators on aspects of study about the region for students in grades 1 to 12 retains validity.

——. Studying the U.S.S.R. in Elementary and Secondary Schools. World Affairs Guides. New York: Teachers College Pr., 1969. 58p.

One of a series for teachers of grades 1-12, this bibliography is similar to the author's Studying Africa . . . .

——. Studying the World: Selected Resources. World Affairs Guides. Rev. ed. New York: Teachers College Pr., 1965. 71p.

First published in 1962, this selected unannotated list, suitable for use with grades 1 through 12, is arranged under broad topics: "World Topics and Problems," "World Regions and Countries," and "Teaching Resources." Each is further divided by subject or geography. Books for children receive reading-level designation. The same author's selective list of Free and Inexpensive Materials on World Affairs can supplement this and appeared in its sixth edition in 1965. Much relevant material has been published subsequently.

Kerlan, Irwin. Newbery and Caldecott Awards: A Bibliography of First Editions. Minneapolis: Univ. of Minnesota Pr., 1947. 51p.

Each entry of the bibliography is given a full title-page transcription and collation. Bibliographical points are noted, but there are no descriptions of literary contents. The foreword by Frederic G. Melcher and the author's preface encourage book collecting in the field. More current and detailed information on these famous prizes is now available, but the bibliographical details available here for the books covered may still be useful.

Kiefer, Monica. American Children through Their Books, 1700-1835. Philadelphia: Univ. of Pennsylvania Pr., 1948. 248p.

With the aim of tracing the changing status of the white American child during the colonial and early national periods as it is revealed in juvenile literature, this study analyzes and interprets works written especially for children or intended as an aid in training them. The religion, morals, manners, education, and health and recreation of children, from the age of talking to early adolescence, is examined as revealed in publications between 1700 and 1835. Less emphasis is placed on the contents of the books themselves than on the way in which they illustrate the child's place in the social structure. Illustrations reproduce pages from the books, and there is a short foreword by Dorothy Canfield Fisher.

Kingston, Carolyn T. The Tragic Mode in Children's Literature. New Aims in Children's Literature. New York: Teachers College Pr., 1974. 177p.

This competent presentation is a plea for the importance of tragedy as opposed to escapist literature in children's books. The major argument is that children can comprehend realistic stories with characters who do not find easy solutions to the problems of living. Chapters examine rejection, entrapment, sensitivity, war, and loss, with a concluding view of the hallmarks of the tragic mode for children. Much of the text consists of long analytical reviews of fifty-five highly regarded titles.

Kircher, Clara J. Behavior Patterns in Children's Books: A Bibliography. Washington, D.C.: Catholic Univ. of America Pr., 1966. 132p.

Over 500 fiction and nonfiction titles related to the concept, popular in mid-century, that reading can affect behavior are included here. The selection is designed to replace the author's Character Formation through Books (first published in 1944, with later editions in 1945, 1952, and 1954), by adding new titles and eliminating those out of print. The present selection covers books for preschool through grade 9, but not adult books suitable for young people. The arrangement is by subject categories of interest to the bibliotherapist, and good representation is given to topics such as behavior, psychological themes, and moral values. Very short descriptive annotations are supplemented by indication of grade-level suitability and applicable behavior patterns, which are also accessible through a Behavior Index. An annotated list of recommended readings is added, as well as an author index.

Klemin, Diana. The Art of Art for Children's Books: A Contemporary Survey. New York: Potter, 1966. 128p.

The art director for a New York publisher investigates "the concepts that lie behind the illustrated book for children." The large quarto format complements the anthology of illustrations, mostly line but some color, accompanied by commentary.

Koblitz, Minnie W. The Negro in Schoolroom Literature: Resource Materials for the Teacher of Kindergarten through the Sixth Grade. 2nd ed. New York: Center for Urban Education, 1967. 67p.

An annotated bibliography of books that contribute to "the understanding and appreciation of the Negro-American heritage," this work was designed as a reference tool for elementary school teachers and librarians. The marked increase of titles useful in the primary school curriculum is reflected in this edition covering books published up to September 1966. Over 250 titles carry descriptive annotations and are listed alphabetically by title within subject groups; fiction and biography are divided into reading levels. A brief selection of additional source materials is provided. Reading interest and appropriateness for the age group, rather than literary quality, are the criteria for selection, and many titles are still suitable.

Kujoth, Jean Spealman. Best-Selling Children's Books. Metuchen, N.J.: Scarecrow, 1973. 305p.

A survey of children's trade books from sixty-eight publishers that are currently in print and have sold over 100,000 copies, this work is directed to publishers, authors, librarians, parents, teachers and students. Its primary purpose is to report "what children's books have been of interest to most people." Besides thirty juvenile best sellers cited in Alice Payne Hackett's Seventy Years of Best Sellers, 928 further titles are included, published between 1678 and 1971, the majority after 1940. The elimination of out-of-print titles is explained as due to difficulties experienced by publishers in tracing their records. The basic chapter is an author listing with annotations quoted from selection aids and reviews, and grade levels as recommended by the publishers. Subsequent chapters list entries by title, illustrator, year of publication and type or subject of book with age level.

——, comp. Reading Interests of Children and Young Adults. Metuchen, N.J.: Scarecrow, 1970. 449p.

Over fifty reprints of serial articles intended primarily for teachers, librarians, and students in schools of education and librarianship are found in this anthology. The editor stresses recent research findings and observations by professionals, mostly but not all from the United States. Sections are divided into age groups; the final group is on exceptional children, both retarded and gifted. The selections vary, but by-and-large present limited-scope studies of reading choices by young people, or express the author's personal views based on experience. The collection serves best as a reflection of recent research on reading selection.

Kunitz, Stanley J., and Haycraft, Howard. Junior Book of Authors. 2nd ed. 309p.
Fuller, Muriel. More Junior Authors. 235p.
De Montreville, Doris, and Hill, Donna. Third Book of Junior Authors. 320p. New York: Wilson, 1951, 1963, and 1972.

The first edition of the first volume of this well-known reference trilogy for school and public libraries appeared in 1934, with the subtitle An Introduction to the Lives of Writers and Illustrators for Younger Readers from Lewis Carroll and Louisa Alcott to the Present Day. The second edition of 1951, which eliminated nearly half the entries and added as many again, the second volume of 1963, and the third of 1972, that includes a cumulated index to the whole, emphasized the contemporary, and documented a total of well over eight hundred of the multitude of writers for children and their illustrators during the present century. The original intention, "to answer children's questions in school and out," has broadened, but the method of providing "lively conversation about an author," preferably in his or her own words, has been preserved. Autobiographical statements frequently comment on individual titles, and the latest volume appends a list of selected juvenile titles under each author, with a facsimile signature. Almost a full page of text with a small but informative portrait photograph makes up the average entry. The inclusion of subjects has relied on a consensus of advisory experts, those for the second volume eliminating almost four-fifths of the names considered. Inquirers therefore will not find some minor writers sought, particularly in the increasing borderline area between young people's and adult fiction, but on balance, the overall coverage is impressive. The set can fairly be claimed to be an indispensable tool, combining accuracy and balance with a direct and readable style that will appeal to almost all ages. The Fourth Book of Junior Authors and Illustrators appeared in 1978.

Ladley, Winifred C. Sources of Good Books and Magazines for Children: An Annotated Bibliography. 2nd ed. Newark, Del.: International Reading Assn., 1970. 18p.

This selective bibliography, first compiled in 1965, was intended for anyone choosing materials for children, and specifically for librarians. This revision emphasizes sources published from 1960 through 1969; items prior to 1950 have been eliminated. The explanatory introduction is followed by a general booklist, a list of books about children's literature, a title list of magazines containing annotated lists of current books, and a list of specialized materials--the first and the last of these are the largest. Excluded, perhaps regrettably, are individual periodical articles, and a specialized list of sources for remedial reading is lacking. The citation for entries in each section is accompanied by a descriptive and evaluative annotation; desirable first purchases are indicated by an asterisk. As can be expected from the sponsoring association, this has been a useful tool for source selection for small and larger libraries that cater for children; it is, however, highly selective.

Lanes, Selma G. Down the Rabbit Hole: Adventures and Misadventures in the Realm of Children's Literature. New York: Athenaeum, 1971. 240p.

Personal and introspective value judgments on the worth and direction of the world of children's books are the subjects of this book. Books for the youngest listeners and readers are "viewed not as passing amusements but legitimate contributions to the larger world of literature." Several chapters center on individual authors; others discuss "Children, Grown-Ups and Literature," "America as Fairy Tale," and "Black is Beautiful." Illustrations from modern titles supplement the text. "Voices of Quality: An Idiosyncratic Booklist" forms an appendix, grouping about 125 titles for children from 2 to 7 years of age, "the span when they are at adults' mercy and most receptive to the few that speak to them alone." Arrangement is by ascending age group and in special groupings such as "Sick Bed Specials" and "Superior Books in Series"; most titles receive a sentence or two of comment.

Larrick, Nancy. A Parent's Guide to Children's Reading. 4th ed. Garden City, N.Y.: Doubleday, 1975. 432p.

Publication of this title, intended to serve as a comprehensive handbook for parents on their children's reading, was originally sponsored by the National Book Committee. Consultants from eighteen associated national organizations served as advisors for the first edition in 1958, and the second edition in 1964. The third edition (1969) was completely revised to include new information and books, and this fourth edition was further expanded. The last two editions were also available as paperbacks. Age groups covered are babies to preteens. Three parts discuss "How Parents Can Help Day In Day Out," "How Reading Is Taught Today," and "Getting the Books He Needs." Two concluding sections provide an extensive annotated list of books and magazines for children and recommended reading for parents. Fifty illustrations from children's books are reproduced in the text. As a widely known and frequently printed source, this has been influential on the group for which it has been intended, and librarians, too, will find its list of titles useful for checking.

——. A Teacher's Guide to Children's Books. Columbus, Ohio: Merrill, 1960. 316p.

Written to help teachers become better acquainted with elementary school children and the new books to which they respond eagerly, this guide places a wide range of recent titles of high quality in place in the school reading program, starting with their use with the first grade and beginning readers and proceeding to more extensive reading in the middle grades. The volume continues with a subject approach. Creative activities springing from reading and book selection are also discussed. Besides the annotated bibliographies for each chapter, favorite books for boys and girls are listed in the concluding part with annotations and coding for grade level. A list of recommended further reading for teachers is added. Book illustrations are reproduced in line and half-tone in the text. An abridged edition was published in paperback in 1963 by the same publisher. This was a very useful

aid at the date of publication, although its popularity did not
result in the series of updated editions that the author's better
known Parents Guide . . . has warranted.

Laskey, Harold H.   Red, White and Black (and Brown and Yellow).
   Minorities in America: A Collection of Paperbacks with a Selected List of Bibliographies. Briarcliff Manor, N.Y.: Combined
   Book Exhibit, 1969. 33p.
   Displayed as part of the Combined Paperback Exhibit at the
   American Library Association conference at Atlantic City in
   1969, this collection included nearly 600 items from picture books
   to adult nonfiction, arranged under topical headings. It provided
   an opportunity "to examine the growing volume of paperback
   books and audio-visual materials on all the minorities appropriate
   for classroom, reference or for general reading purposes." Although unannotated, this well-chosen catalog formed a valuable
   checklist for librarians and teachers.

Lathrope, Mary Frost. Children's Books for the Holidays. Urbana, Ill.:
   National Council of Teachers of English, 1964. 20p.
   Addressed to teachers interested in children's reading and
   librarians responsible for children's collections, this bibliographical article on the winter festive season originally appeared in the
   December 1963 issue of Elementary English. Its objective was to
   suggest titles so that "all children will have a chance to partici-
   pate in the joy of the holiday season." Pupils from kindergarten to
   grade 7 are catered to. The text and appended bibliographies
   cover both Hanukkah and Christmas, sections on the latter being
   the larger. Many titles are listed in the text as well as in the lists,
   and careful attention is paid to illustrations and to the quality of
   editions available.

Latimer, Bettye I. et al. Starting Out Right: Choosing Books about
   Black People for Young People, Preschool through Third Grade.
   Madison, Wis.: State Dept. of Public Instruction, 1972. 96p.
   Published as a departmental bulletin, this annotated evaluative bibliography is a tool that can also be used as a role model.
   The compilers, Bettye Latimer, Ann Cosby, Margaret Green,
   Dorothy Holden, Joy Newmann, and Marion Todd, define the
   status of black-inclusive books before analyzing over 300 titles,
   both recommended and not recommended. The criteria they
   established does limit the selection, particularly for very young
   readers, but teachers, librarians, parents, and others can benefit
   by the perceptive evaluations made. Introductory chapters give
   the background rationale. Others examine syndrome patterns,
   give a brief exposé of reviews, and critique in detail Margaret
   de Angeli's Bright April, chosen as a sample with overwhelming

faults. The final chapter is the body of the bibliography, listed by title and largely made up of publications of the late sixties.

Lavender, Ralph. Myths, Legends and Lore. Practical Guides for Teachers. Oxford: Blackwell, 1975. 165p.

This volume regards legendary tales as having special properties for children, and guides teachers toward their effective presentation in the classroom. Lists cover books for children from 4 to 7, 6 to 8, 8 to 10, and over 10. Notes on entries indicate type of story, special appeal, and suitable age. Selected audiovisual material to add dimension to the stories is also listed. There are regional and character indexes.

Lawson, K. S. Children's Reading: A Survey of Reading Material Designed to Assist Teachers and Parents in the Selection of Books Appropriate to the Interests and Abilities of Children. Rev. ed. Leeds, Eng.: Univ. of Leeds Institute of Education, 1971. 26p.

Fictional and nonfictional publishers' series that are currently used in British schools are presented here. The first edition was published in 1968. The aim is to suggest how individual volumes may be combined to form a planned reading program for class or home use. Tabulated, unannotated lists of titles cover reading series, graded reading schemes, and nonfiction series for schools arranged by subject. The sections are divided into primary and secondary. Each title has a reading and interest level indicated. A list of reading texts is added.

Lee, Norman R. Paperbacks for High School: A Guide for School Bookstores and Classroom Libraries. Syracuse, N.Y.: Syracuse Univ. Reading Center, 1962. 31p.

This unannotated listing of 500 paperbacks for high-school readers dates from the first phase of the flood of paperbacks. The objective was to provide judicious selection for teachers, as well as for bookstores and school libraries, and the student's personal library was also kept in mind. Three introductory chapters precede the basic list, which recommends sources, and a supplementary list for teachers, which does not. After twenty years, the selection of titles is outmoded as an acquisitions tool.

Lemieux, Louise. Plein Feux sur la Littérature de Jeunesse au Canada Français. Ottawa: Lemeac, 1972. 337p.

This treatise by a religious at the University of Ottawa seeks to retrace the historic evolution of young people's literature in French Canada, and examine the present French-Canadian publishing scene àpropos of this genre. Equally a guide and a biographical and bibliographical resource, six chapters in two divisions study past and present. The first part covers history from the origins to 1940 and from 1940 to 1965, and examines decisive evolutionary factors. The second describes children's publishing in French Canada, comments on the problem of illustration, and those of distribution and publicity. Appendixes include an "exhaustive preliminary bibliography" listing works of French-Canadian young people's literature, another of books relevant to the topic, a list of illustrators and their books, and a final one of prize-winning titles. The author breaks new ground, makes available much information not available elsewhere, and provides a base for further research in a scarcely documented field.

Lenski, Lois. Adventures in Understanding: Talks to Parents, Teachers and Librarians, 1944-1966. Tallahassee: Friends of Florida State Univ. Library, 1968. 242p.

This collection of the well-known children's artist and author's talks, addresses, and acceptance speeches brings together in book form many of her ideas concerning books and literature in general, young people and the world around them, and, in particular, the creation of books for children and the meaning of her own writing for them. Interspersed are personal anecdotes and a number of poems. Her own decorations adorn the text.

Lepman, Jella A. A Bridge of Children's Books. Translated from the German by Edith McCormick. Leicester, Eng.: Brockhampton; Chicago: American Library Assn., 1969. 155p.

This detailed reminiscence of the author's crusade during the immediate post-World War II years to bring world understanding to future generations through children's books reflects brilliantly the times and her self-appointed goal. In establishing the International Youth Library in Munich and founding the prestigious International Board of Books for Young People, this indomitable woman initiated an interest in international publication for young people and literally elevated juvenile book publishing in Europe and North America. Most useful to students and scholars for the intimate look at both literary and political figures whose names were inextricably bound to the era, the book is also important for the international titles that have been popular with young people and known to children's book fanciers. Unfortunately, there is no index to pick these out with ease.

Lesquereux, J. P., and Mortimer, S. M. The Reluctant Reader. 3rd ed. Reader's Guide, new series, no. 111. London: Library Assn., County Libraries Group, 1969. 36p.

The Youth Libraries Group cooperated in the compilation of this list of books which may be of use to slow or reluctant readers. Selection concentrates on series available in Britain. Symbols indicate age and grade suitability, and outstanding items are annotated. This title was previously published in 1962 and 1965.

Lewis, Naomi. The Best Children's Books of 1963 [-1967]. London:
Hamilton, 1964-1969. Annual.
    An annual selection of the books of the previous year intended
to serve as a record of the year's best in publishing in Britain for
young people, this work includes all types of fiction and nonfiction, except school or educational books. A paragraph of stylish
annotation which is both descriptive and critical is provided for
each item and an age range for readers is suggested. Arrangement
is alphabetical within sections grouped by types of publication for
fiction and an informal classification for nonfiction. Fulfilling its
original purpose as a useful compendium for parents, teachers,
and librarians, this series by an independent critic takes its place
as an annual review of the best of British children's books between
the National Book League's Books for Children, 1955-61, and its
later series edited by Elaine Moss, Children's Books of the Year,
published from 1970 on.

——. Fantasy Books for Children. London: National Book League,
1975. 48p.
    Fantasy is here regarded in the special supernatural sense, and
each of the 168 books has at least a grain of the magical. While in
the main these are twentieth-century publications, some eigh-
teenth- and nineteenth-century works are included in current
editions. The selector provides perceptive, descriptive, and critical annotations for each, as well as an introduction discussing the
value and values of fantasy stories for young people.

Leyland, Eric Arthur. Meet Your Authors. London: Harrap, 1963.
135p.
    The editor, a prolific British writer of books for young people,
describes this as a kind of book week in volume form. Ten "top"
British authors of children's books simulate a personal appearance
before children who find their stories interesting and exciting.
Each author is assigned two pages of biography, a characteristic
extract, and a full-page photograph.

Library Journal. Recommended Children's Books. New York: Bowker,
1951- . Annual.
    "Professionally evaluated by librarians for librarians in the
Junior Libraries section of the Library Journal," the predecessor
of School Library Journal, this annual compilation was edited by
Emily Louise Davis. Arrangement is by grade and subject. A
predecessor, Starred Books from the Library Journal, similarly
chosen and arranged, was edited by Peggy Melcher in 1953. This
included "700 complete reviews of the best books for children of
the last seventeen years." Together these titles form a retrospective reference source for popular children's titles published since
the second world war.

Lickteig, Mary J. Introduction to Children's Books. Columbus, Ohio:
Merrill, 1975. 432p.

An extensive and readable introduction to children's literature,
with a very substantial bibliographical element, this title serves
best as a text for potential teachers and librarians, but has been
written for anyone working with children and anyone who wishes
to be introduced to the field. Besides introducing the variety of
books written for children, objectives include planning the reading
environment of home, school, and library, and promoting reading
among children. Chapters survey broad types of publication, such
as picture books, informational books, traditional literature, fanciful reading, and realistic fiction, as well as practical topics,
such as selecting books, guidance through books, and literature
experiences. Each is accompanied by an extensive list of relevant
titles, the majority publications of the period 1952-72. Useful
appendixes include lists of journals, awards, and thorough indexing. This is a generously illustrated presentation on the large
scale made familiar by Arbuthnot's classic in the field. It functions well as a text for courses and provides a checklist for a core
collection.

Liebert, Robert. A Place to Start: A Graded Bibliography for Children
with Reading Difficulties. Rev. ed. Syracuse, N.Y.: Syracuse
Univ. Press, 1965. 66p.

First compiled by Roy A. Kress in 1963, this unannotated list is
intended as a guide and beginning point for teachers, librarians,
and reading specialists who are trying to locate materials "at
appropriate levels of difficulty." Five sections cover series books,
social studies, science, general works, and Canadian publications.
Paperbacks, serials, and basic texts are excluded. Interest levels
and estimated reading levels according to the Dale-Chall and
Flesch formulas are indicated. The lack of index poses a barrier to
those who wish to use the list as a selection tool.

Lines, Kathleen M. Four to Fourteen: A Library of Books for Children.
Introduction by Walter de la Mare. 2nd ed. Cambridge: Cambridge Univ. Pr., 1956. 351p.

First published in 1950 for the National Book League (also with
an introduction by Walter de la Mare), this annotated list aims to
provide a selection of interesting books from which a child's own
library can be chosen. It is also intended to be useful as a buying
list for school libraries, although the list is not meant to be
exhaustive and represents the compiler's personal choice and
opinion. Arrangement follows traditional types of publication for
children and reading interests. The range of books is for children
from 4 to 15, and the descriptive and critical notes supply, in most
instances, an age guide to be taken in the broadest sense. The
enlarged edition includes new chapters on "The First Bookshelf"

and "Reading Aloud." This fine list still retains its value as the choice of an eminent exponent of British children's literature. The index of both authors and editions in the revised edition makes it doubly advantageous as a checking tool, in spite of a disclaimer about not including books "written for a purpose."

Livsey, Rosemary et al. Notable Children's Books, 1940-1959. Chicago: American Library Assn., 1966. 39p.

Since 1940, the Book Evaluation Committee of the American Library Association's Children's Services Division has annually selected sixty to a hundred books "worth their keep," and listed them as Notable Children's Books in the ALA Bulletin, and published the list as a separate. Since 1950, three book committees have reexamined the original selections to compile five-year revisions which allow "for comparative perspective or the response of children." This list cumulates from the beginning. Arrangement is alphabetically by author, although entry is under title, and a title index is provided. A short paragraph of descriptive and critical annotation is given for each title selected. The official character of this checklist, authorized by a double set of committee decisions, endorses its usefulness as a tool for librarians, parents, and others interested in current children's books of quality. Even for librarians outside the United States, it is an invaluable source for choice. A new edition appeared in 1977 extending coverage to 1970.

Lock, Muriel. Reference Material for Young People. Rev. and enl. ed. London: Clive Bingley; Hamden, Conn.: Linnet, 1971. 532p.

The coverage in this work is confined to works composed entirely or prominently for use by young people. Intended by the author as an excursion among interesting examples, rather than a formal guide to library collections, the presentation is in narrative form with titles identified by bold type within the text. The style is meant to be acceptable to older children as well as teachers, librarians, and parents. Chapter arrangement covers general works, four vaguely defined subject or interest areas, audiovisual material and equipment, and careers. The first edition appeared in the publisher's Readers Guide series in 1967. The change in this revised and enlarged edition to a more objective emphasis places the work in line with other reference tools, but the updated audiovisual coverage fails to give a truly comprehensive list of reference sources in this area. The book is geared to a British audience.

Logasa, Hannah. Book Selection Handbook for Elementary and Secondary School. Boston: Faxon, 1953. 200p.

The views of this well-known teacher and practitioner give a special quality to this guide to book selection for elementary and secondary schools. This is primarily a how-to-do-it tool, not a commentary on children's books. The text is presented in a series of short units arranged alphabetically, each representing a definite topic in the selection process. Included are subject areas, types of material, and areas such as evaluation of the book collection and censorship.

——. Historical Fiction: Guide for Junior and Senior High Schools and Colleges, also for General Reader. 8th ed., rev. and enl. Philadelphia: McKinley, 1964. 368p.

This very extensive list of historical fiction, with a long publication history, goes back to 1927. Editions published after the Second World War were issued in 1949, 1951, 1958, and 1960, a tribute to its continued usefulness. The nonfiction element received special treatment (see below) after 1958. The current edition adds 900 titles and removes a number which are older and less valuable. Arrangement is geographical and then chronological. Annotation is confined to a descriptive phrase or sentence. Symbols identify books of special value, those suitable for junior high, and in-print titles. This is a major and readily available bibliography of historical novels. Its value as an identification tool, rather than a selective one, remains high for all types of libraries.

——. Historical Non-Fiction: An Organized, Annotated, Supplementary Reference Book for the Use of Schools, Libraries, General Reader. McKinley Bibliographies. 7th ed., rev. and enl. Philadelphia: McKinley, 1960. 288p.

One of a series by this author, this edition treats separately an area formerly covered in the previous editions of her Historical Fiction. The list is "designed for pupils in the upper grades of the elementary school, students in high school and college, and the general reader." Arrangement combines geographic and chronological treatment, and annotation on the entries is contained in a single sentence in most cases. Symbols indicate works which are especially valuable or at junior-high level. While this is an extensive assemblage of titles, academically oriented readers at most levels would be better advised to select from academic bibliographies and reviewing journals.

——, ed. Science for Youth: An Annotated Bibliography for Children and Young Adults. Brooklawn, N.J.: McKinley, 1967. 159p.

This is a selection of "recent books on science at the reading and understanding level of children and young adults, designed to arouse their curiosity and interest in the world around them." Pure science is emphasized; invention and technology, as well as textbooks, are excluded. Arrangement is by subject area and annotation is very brief. This work was useful when published to teachers and librarians as a checklist for titles published in the late fifties and early sixties. New publications in this fast-moving field have now eliminated its usefulness as a selection tool.

Lonsdale, Bernard J., and Mackintosh, Helen K. Children Experience Literature. New York: Random, 1973. 540p.

A textbook for college courses in children's literature as well as a source of information for teachers involved in curriculum development, school and children's librarians, and parents, the objectives of this work are to show the panorama of literature for children, both classic and contemporary, and to encourage teachers to read, select, and use books suitable for each stage of children's development. Chapters cover the teachers' and children's joint experience of the literature and the broad types and themes to be found in children's books. Descriptive and critical appreciations of titles, including sample extracts, form a large element of the text. A list of further recommendations with short annotations is added to each chapter, together with questions designed to extend the experiences of the reader and the children. Appendixes include sources for selecting books and other media, and lists of prize-winning children's books.

Looking at London: A Select List of Recent Books and Other Resources for the Primary and Middle School. Oxford: School Library Assn., 1974. 44p.

Compiled by the London branch of the association, this work lists picture books, stories and poems, guides, and environmental studies. Audiovisual materials and music are also included. Interesting descriptive and critical annotations are supplied, and even a folding map that points the way bibliographically to student involvement in local history.

Lorang, Sister Mary Corde. Burning Ice: The Moral and Emotional Effects of Reading. New York: Scribner, 1968. 303p.

This "psychological study of the moral and emotional effect of reading books and magazines" includes a substantial element of bibliographical list of titles read by young people. An appendix of "books read by young adults, rated by judges and young adults" lists over 2,500 titles and 800 periodicals. The panel of twelve judges, including three librarians, graded titles in four categories ranging from "fit for all young adults" to "unfit for young adults." Over 3,000 students in high schools completed the relevant questionnaire forms, and there are also many comments by young adults on individual books cited in the text. The author believes that there is "indisputable evidence that reading material influences young people for good and evil," but the citations will be of considerable interest even to those who disagree with her. Titles familiar in censorship controversies can be identified, and the extent and range of the titles examined are very large.

Lubetski, Edith, and Lubetski, Meir. Writings on Jewish History: A Selected Annotated Bibliography. New York: American Jewish Committee, 1974. 27p.

Originally prepared by Edith Lubetski in 1970, this selected and briefly annotated list is intended "to help social studies teachers bring to their students a better understanding on one minority group, the Jews, through an awareness of Jewish history, culture, personalities and contributions from the biblical period to the present day." Works for younger readers (grades 5 through 12) and those for teenagers and adults are identified. A good checklist for collections, particularly because of the sponsoring organization, its selectivity is such as to need supplementation from other sources; for instance, Isaac Bashevis Singer's A Day of Pleasure is not listed.

Luecke, Fritz J., ed. Children's Books: Views and Values. Middletown, Conn.: Xerox, 1973. 86p.

Eight essays by various contributors selected for teachers from library and education journals such as School Library Journal and Elementary English provide "a cross section of recent professional material [on] the problems, the trends and the future." Emphasizing "how children's books are keeping up with the rapid change taking place in today's world," topics include feminism, realism, violence, death, morals, and values. Children's books that successfully deal with these subjects are identified in the text of the articles, but regrettably not in a separate bibliographical listing.

Lyman, Edna. Storytelling: What to Tell and How to Tell It. Detroit: Singing Tree, 1971. 229p.

Originally published in 1910, this is a facsimile of the third edition of 1911. An added sticker on the title page gives the author's name as Edna Lyman Scott. This elementary guide was intended for the untrained, rather than the professional, storyteller in schools, libraries, and at social gatherings of children. Chapters cover reading aloud, the art of storytelling, and program arrangement. Special emphasis is placed on biographical stories and epic tales, and lengthy extracts are included. A list is given of about seventy books, then in print, which are suggested for the storyteller.

MacCann, Donnarae, and Richard, Olga. The Child's First Books: A Critical Study of Pictures and Texts. New York: Wilson, 1973. 135p.

The full-size reproductions in black-and-white and color of illustrations from contemporary children's books are a prominent feature of this study, the aim of which is to focus attention on aesthetic quality and potential. The books discussed are limited to those where the written narrative is brief and the story largely presented through illustration. Chapters examine the historical perspective, stereotypes in illustration, graphic elements, book design, literary elements, outstanding contemporary illustrators and narrative writers, and the Caldecott award. The 200 works listed are all recommended titles.

——, and Woodard, Gloria, eds. The Black American in Books for Children: Readings in Racism. Metuchen, N.J.: Scarecrow, 1972. 233p.

Over twenty articles relating to blacks, racism, and publishing are here usefully collected into one location and marshalled under five headings: "The Black Perspective, the Basic Criterion," "Racism in Newbery Prize Books," "More Modern Examples," "Some Early Examples," and "Racism and Publishing." Some of those selected, certainly the most interesting, are still controversial; all are worth reading. Many of the books examined and listed in the title index have been reevaluated here and all should be evaluated again. The volume is a valuable point of departure.

McDonough, Irma, ed. Profiles. Rev. ed. Ottawa: Canadian Library Assn., 1975. 159p.

First published in 1971 with twenty biographical and bibliographical sketches of Canadian authors and illustrators of children's books, this expanded edition now includes forty-four, all first published in the Canadian journal of children's literature In Review, and selected by its editor, herself a contributor. The tone is descriptive rather than critical, and there are frequent comments on titles in the text, beside a listing at the end of each biography. Small photographs add to this compendium of information about the current generation of the creators of children's books in Canada.

McGarry, Daniel D., and White, Sarah Harriman. World Historical Fiction Guide: An Annotated Chronological, Geographical and Topical List of Selected Historical Novels. 2nd ed. Metuchen, N.J.: Scarecrow, 1973. 629p.

First published in 1963 as Historical Fiction Guide . . ., this list was designed "especially for use by adults and students in senior high schools, colleges, and universities, but books suitable for junior high school are also included and marked Y.A." Arrangement is first chronological and then geographical, and entries carry a phrase of descriptive annotation. This edition increases the title count from 5,000 to nearly 6,500, which makes it an identificatory rather than a selective tool, and this use is reinforced by the lengthy author-title index.

McGill, Hilda M., ed. Books for Young People. Group I: under 11. Rev. ed. London: Library Assn., 1955. 103p.

First published in 1952, this completely revised new edition formed the first part of a trilogy of classified and annotated lists published by the British Library Association (see also Group II: Eleven to Thirteen Plus, edited by Edgar Osborne, and Group III: Fourteen to Seventeen, by L. M. Harrod). Children's librarians from the North-Western Branch of the association chose titles believed to have some positive value in attracting children to books "by opening windows of imagination and fancy." Catholicity of selection was aimed for from British publications then in print. Nonfiction is arranged in a subject classified order; fiction alphabetically by author. Picture books and picture-story books are starred. Although no claim was made that the selection represented the best books, but rather that it was a working tool, this list acquired a semiofficial character because of the sponsoring association, and in its time was widely utilized in British schools and public libraries.

McGuff, Mary Beth et al. Black is . . . . 3rd ed. Baltimore: Enoch Pratt Free Library, 1972. 57p.

First selected by a committee in 1963 and revised in 1966, this annotated list includes "most of the black-interest books contained in the active collection of children's books in the library." Where a book's central character is white, it has generally been omitted, and only a sampling of books on ethnology and African history have been included. Over 300 titles are given brief descriptive and analytical annotation, and arranged under eight generally chronological topical headings. The handsome printing and illustration of this carefully chosen list enhance its value as a checking tool for librarians and teachers.

McWhirter, Mary Esther, ed. Books for Friendship: A List of Books Recommended for Children. 4th ed. Philadelphia: Society of Friends, American Friends Service Committee, and the Anti-Defamation League of B'nai B'rith, 1968. 46p.

Published initially by the committee in 1953 and again in 1957 under the title Books are Bridges: A List . . ., and jointly in 1962 under the present title, this bibliography is intended to further the cause of "brotherhood and peace as embodied in the Jewish and Christian tradition." The fourth edition covers titles published from 1962 to 1968. The selection represents a committee effort by specialists in children's literature, editors, authors, religious leaders, and others. Among the criteria stated, the first is literary quality. Five sections cover "Neighbors at Home," "Neighbors Abroad," "Belief into Action," "Holidays," and "Holy Days." Each is subdivided by grade level: younger readers 6 to 8; middle years, 8 to 11 or 12; and older boys and girls. Descriptive

annotations include reference to the racial or religious significance of text or illustration. All editions remain valuable checklists for parents, students, teachers, and librarians.

Magaliff, Cecile. The Junior Novel: Its Relationship to Adolescent
Reading. Port Washington, N.Y.: Kennikat, 1964. 116p.
    Published for C. W. Post College of Long Island University, this
study is limited to the junior novel, defined as a story which
explores and perhaps solves the problems of adolescence. The
background of the junior novel and its role in adolescent reading
are examined, and six authors of favorably received titles are
selected for evaluation, with reference to reader-identification,
stimulation of thought, integrity of purpose, interpretation of
life, and credibility and effectiveness of writing. A summary
chart of these qualities is constructed for each author. Intention-
ally a limited study, the six choices are typical of publications
available in the mid-sixties.

Marantz, Kenneth. A Bibliography of Children's Art Literature: An
Annotated Bibliography of Children's Literature Designed to
Stimulate and Enrich the Visual Imagination of the Child. Washington, D.C.: National Art Education Assn., 1965. 18p.
    This is a list of then current titles selected by an art teacher at
the University of Chicago Laboratory School. Over 300 books
were examined, with particular care paid to visual impact, quality
of illustration, and layout. Four sections comprise art history; art
methods, including folk and fantasy tales; anthropology and ar-
cheology; poetry and counting books; and picture books. Entries
carry grade level recommendations from kindergarten to grade
12. Annotations, descriptive and sometimes evaluative, are addressed to teachers and others interested in helping children
develop a more extensive vision through books.

Markey, Lois R. Books Are Vacations: A Horn Book Reading List.
Boston: Horn Book, 1956. 32p.
    Parents, librarians, teachers, or young people themselves can
use this list to supply diversified reading for pleasure over the
summer months. Most books will appeal to grades 4-9. About 150
titles with descriptive annotations are arranged under informal
topical and subject headings. While the familiar classics are
excluded, the high literary quality of the choices indicates that
after twenty-five years many are still worth reading.

Marshall, Margaret R. Each According to His Ability: A List of Books
and Other Visual Materials for Use by and with Mentally Handicapped Children. Oxford: School Library Assn., 1975. 24p.
    This list provides those who work with handicapped children,
institutionalized and otherwise, with an annotated selection of

over 200 items that can be used by or with the children, but does not include material solely to be read to them. Simple wording is a criterion. Other titles by the authors recommended and representative volumes of series are referred to. Some normal children's books and books suitable for handicapped teenagers are represented. Contents include picture and story books, subject interest books, more physically durable books, and nonbook materials.

Marshall, Sybil; Gagg, J. C.; Glynn, Dorothy; and Cass, Joan. Beginning with Books. Oxford: Blackwell, for the School Library Assn., 1971. 106p.

The subject of this title is a survey of the first practical use of books by little children, made with the cooperation of the heads, teachers, and children of sixty-two British schools, and the encouragement of the Primary Schools Subcommittee of the association. After relevant examination of the schools and the children themselves, the study seeks to establish what kind of books are needed and how children can surround themselves with them. Little comment is made on individual titles.

Mason, Bobbie Ann. The Girl Sleuth: A Feminist Guide. Old Westbury, N.Y.: Feminist Pr., 1975. 144p.

A critical analysis of the author's "favorite childhood stories, series books about daring girl detectives," this work examines mystery and adventure series, including Nancy Drew and the Bobbsey Twins, not only as a reflection of popular culture and conventional prejudices, but also to find out what there is in the stories to hold girls from age 9 to 14 spellbound, reflecting and molding real desires and values. Numerous titles are mentioned in the text, some with quotations or illustrations reproduced.

Meade, Richard A., and Small, Robert C. Literature for Adolescents: Selection and Use. Columbus, Ohio: Merrill, 1973. 304p.

This collection of articles and other readings concerned with literature for adolescents was compiled primarily for teachers of English to young adults. Selection has not been limited to educators; librarians and authors are represented. Contributions are grouped in six chapters: "The Literature Classroom"; "The Rise of Literature for the Adolescent"; "Themes in Literature for the Adolescent"; "The Literary Quality of Books for Adolescent Readers"; "Classroom Use of Literature for the Adolescent"; and "Research on Reading Attitudes." Such anthologies run the risk of combining genuine classics with material that is dated in a pejorative sense; but many articles here are interesting and provocative fare, and some are significant and by well-known authorities. Comments on individual books for young people are to be found in the text, but there is no index to make these titles accessible.

Mears, Joyce, and Parker, Anne. Read Aloud: To 7-13 Year Olds. Birmingham, Eng.: Library Assn., Youth Libraries Group, 1974. 25p.

Over 100 stories suitable for reading aloud to children from 7- to 13-years-old, based on British teachers' recommendations, are included in this annotated list intended for teachers, parents, and librarians.

Meeker, Alice M. Enjoying Literature with Children. New York: Odyssey, 1969. 152p.

Aimed at parents and teachers of children up to grade 6, this work is intended to assist parents in introducing good literature during the looking and listening years, and to suggest to teachers sources of enrichment useful as literary tastes develop. Chapters direct attention to culturally deprived children, the library, book reports, storytelling, poetry, holidays, and bulletin boards. At the end of each chapter appropriate titles are listed, each with a paragraph of annotation. In spite of a naiveté about what makes a good librarian in an elementary school, and about the possible effectiveness of schooling in countering adverse environment, the author does try to give helpful hints, references, and titles, albeit these are minimal, standard, and often stereotyped.

Meigs, Cornelia, ed. A Critical History of Children's Literature: A Survey of Children's Books in English from Earliest Times to the Present, Prepared in Four Parts. Rev. ed. New York: Macmillan, 1969. 708p.

This lengthy cooperative work, which first appeared in 1953, studies from a critical point of view what has endured in publications for children in English over the centuries and why. An introduction by Henry Steele Commager summarizes the theme. Divisions are chronological by different authors. The editor covers "Roots in the Past up to 1840"; Ann Eaton, "Widening Horizons, 1840-1890"; Elizabeth Nesbitt, "A Rightful Heritage, 1890-1920"; and Ruth Hill Viguers, "Golden Years and Time of Tumult, 1920-1950." Writing for a general audience that includes teachers, librarians, publishers, and booksellers, the authors have sought for true literary values by tracing a consecutive line of signposts to illustrate basic elements in the development of traditional themes. The text gives descriptive comment about many titles and their authors. Brief bibliographies of further readings are appended to each chapter.

Melcher, Peggy, ed. Starred Books from the Library Journal: 700 Complete Reviews of the Best Books for Children of the Last 17 Years as Evaluated by Children's Librarians. New York: Bowker, 1953. 120p.

These reviews, reprinted as they appeared in Library Journal, represent titles that rated a "double star." "Taken together, they constitute a highly selective list that LJ's reviewers believed to be among the very best books for children . . . ." Each title has full information provided on scope and background, and on age, grade, interest, and reading levels. Authority, uniqueness, curriculum application, and suitability of format are noted. Arrangement is in four age divisions: "For the Youngest," "The Beginning Reader," "Upper Elementary Grades," and "Junior High School Age," each being subdivided into subject areas. A fifth part lists "Books about Books" and an author-title index gives access. Influential with teachers and librarians as a selection tool when it appeared, it was a forerunner of other collected volumes which reprinted periodical reviews of children's books.

Mellor, G. R. A School Library List of History Books for Pupils Aged 11 to 15 Years in Secondary Schools. Teaching of History Leaflet, no. 10. London: The Historical Assn., 1951. 19p.

Textbooks and historical fiction are not included in this annotated list intended for more advanced pupils. Arrangement is by chronological period with a British emphasis in selection.

Mennes, Arthur H., ed. Magazines for Elementary Grades. 3rd ed. Madison, Wis.: Madison Public Schools, 1965. 27p.

Addressed primarily to Wisconsin teachers but appropriate for a wider audience, this committee compilation first appeared in a mimeograph form in 1943, with a printed edition in 1949. Over fifty titles, all suitable for young people, are annotated with comments on their usefulness in the curriculum and appropriate grade level. A number remain in print today.

Mesiano, Lindalee, ed. Paperbound Book Guide for Elementary Schools. New York: Bowker, 1966. 49p.

This "selective subject guide to over 730 inexpensive reprints and originals chosen especially for elementary school use by thirty-five cooper;ting publishers" was designed as a service to the elementary school teacher and librarian. Its preparation was undertaken in response to needs expressed at a Columbia University conference of the previous year on paperbacks in education. Within two main categories, kindergarten to grade 3 and grades 4-6, the entries are arranged in subject areas. Each has a brief descriptive annotation with comment on illustration and typeface where appropriate. This small but select list was influential in heralding the increasing availability and use of paperbacks for elementary classes. For its single year of publication, it served to identify appropriate titles from Bowker's Children's Books in Print but, as with all kinds of paperbacks, the in-print status of its selections rapidly become questionable.

Metzner, Seymour. American History in Juvenile Books: A Chronological Guide. New York: Wilson, 1966. 329p.

All trade books in print during the winter of 1964-65 having
relevance to American history and intended for an audience of
elementary and junior high-school age are included in this unannotated list. The grade level span (3-9) is indicated. More than 2,000
fiction and nonfiction titles are included, but paperback reprints
are generally excluded. Chapters follow a chronological sequence, with topical subheadings, divided by level. A final chapter includes anthologies, collective biographies, and general
histories. Indexing is full. The compilation is intended for school
and public librarians and teachers, particularly those requiring
supplementary material for individualized reading programs.
While many titles have been subsequently published or have become out-of-print, the list retains a reference value, though areas
such as black or American Indian studies are underrepresented in
terms of today's curricular needs.

Millender, Dharathula H. Real Negroes, Honest Settings: Children's
and Young People's Books about Negro Life and History. Curricular Viewpoint series. Chicago: American Federation of Teachers,
AFL-CIO, 1967. 28p.

This selection is intended only as a sampling to show the importance of unbiased books on blacks. Three sections cover books for
the beginning reader, books for the orally independent reader up
to junior high, and those for grades 7 and up. Descriptive and
evaluative annotations for each entry are made based on the text
and illustration, and include reading and interest levels and a
recommendation for remedial reading purposes, if appropriate.
The attractive reproductions of artwork are noteworthy. Useful
to teachers and librarians as a study of role models, the selection,
if used with caution, remains a stimulating one after twenty years
of deep social change.

Miller, Bertha Mahony, and Field, Elinor Whitney. Newbery Medal
Books, 1922-1955: With the Author's Acceptance Papers and
Related Material Chiefly from the Horn Book Magazine. Boston:
Horn Book, 1957. 458p.
Caldecott Medal Books, 1938-1957: With the Artist's Acceptance
Papers . . . . Boston: Horn Book, 1957. 325p.
Kingman, Lee, ed. Newbery and Caldecott Medal Books, 1956-1965:
With Acceptance Papers, Biographies . . . . Boston: Horn Book,
1965. 300p.
Newbery and Caldecott Medal Books, 1966-1975 . . . . Boston: Horn
Book, 1975. 321p.

The Horn Book's continuing series makes available biographical,
autobiographical, and bibliographic information on the winners of
these prestigious awards. The formula for the entries, ten-to-

fifteen pages long and arranged chronologically, consists of a summary of the story, an excerpt from the book, the author's acceptance, and a biographical note by a friend or colleague. Valuable introductory chapters include articles on Frederic G. Melcher and John Newbery in the 1955 volume, Melcher's own article on the "Origin of the Newbery and Caldecott Medals" in the 1965 volume, and John Rowe Townsend's "A Decade of Newbery Books in Perspective" in the 1975 volume. The series presents material significant to all lovers of current literature for the young in a stylish and readable fashion.

——; Latimer, Louise Payson; and Folmsbee, Beulah. Illustrators of Children's Books, 1744-1945. Boston: Horn Book, 1947. 527p.
Viguers, Ruth Hill; Dalphin, Marcia; and Miller, Bertha Mahony. Illustrators of Children's Books, 1946-1956. Boston: Horn Book, 1958. 299p.
Kingman, Lee; Foster, Joanna; and Lontoft, Ruth Giles. Illustrators of Children's Books, 1957-1966. Boston: Horn Book, 1968. 295p.

The original publications, reprinted in 1961 and 1965, together with the two supplements, make this Horn Book series an enormous treasury of information and graphic reproductions for lay people, artists, and librarians. Chapter contributions by distinguished artists and critics supplement the expertise of the team of editors, each responsible for substantial separate sections of these oversize volumes. The basic work falls into three divisions: history and development, with emphasis on Britain and America, but with chapters on foreign picture books and on graphic processes; biographies of living illustrators; and bibliographies. Three major essays in the first supplement and four in the second update the original by twenty-one years. These standard reference works are invaluable to all researchers in the field. A further volume, covering 1967-76, appeared in 1978.

Miller, Margaret H., ed. Book List for Elementary School Libraries. Santa Ana, Calif.: Professional Library Service, 1966. 392p.

An extensive unannotated list of over 5,000 titles for children in grades 1 through 6, this work represents the response of the California Association of School Librarians' Elementary Interest Group (chaired by the editor) to the provision of federal funds for developing elementary school libraries in the state. It was intended for superintendents, teachers, and librarians to use with state approval as an acquisition and processing tool. Dewey classification and subject headings, indication of reading level, and full indexing further this aim. In its time, the list was a good selection tool, useful outside the boundaries of the state.

Mills, Joyce White. The Black World in Literature for Children: A Bibliography of Print and Non-Print Material. Vol. 1. Atlanta, Ga.: Atlanta Univ. School of Library Service, 1975. 42p.

This is an annotated bibliography mainly for juveniles, with book and audiovisual titles interfiled, of material by and about blacks in the United States and Africa. Three divisions cover material for young children (age 3-8), for older children (age 9-13), and for adults. Items are critically evaluated to facilitate selection by parents, teachers, and librarians in school and public libraries. A paragraph of annotation describes each entry and indicates its usefulness. Ratings are provided. Volume 1 covers up to 1974; volume 2 was published in 1976.

Milne, A. A. Books for Children: A Reader's Guide. Cambridge: Cambridge Univ. Pr., 1948. 24p.

Published for the National Book League, this choice of about 120 books is intended as a selected subjective guide. The contribution of the famous English children's author is limited to a short introduction, personal in tone. The bulk of the work consists of the reading list compiled by Miss Kathleen Lines, who has consulted children and their parents. Arranged in informal sections covering age groups, types of publication, and subject themes, entries carry short annotations, critical and descriptive. The selection is mainly concerned with children's classics but includes some then recent favorites with British children. As such, the author and the compiler make a sensitive and informed choice which retains interest in providing a selective access to the limited areas covered. The charming woodcut illustrations by Joan Hassall make this pamphlet a collector's piece.

Montebello, Mary. Children's Literature in the Curriculum. Literature for Children. Dubuque, Ia.: Brown, 1972. 158p.

This introduction to children's literature focuses on the utilitarian function of the literature program for children, with the objective of enriching the elementary curriculum in language arts, the sciences, art, music, and social studies. It discusses and illustrates the contribution made by ordinary trade books, rather than textbooks. Appendixes give criteria for informational books, evaluation suggestions, and a taxonomy of literary understandings and skills. Included is a selected trade book bibliography which lists over 850 titles which supplements this useful guide.

Montgomery County Public Schools (Md.). Negroes in American Life: An Annotated Bibliography of Books for Elementary School. Rockville, Md.: Montgomery Co. Public Schools, 1968. 74p.

Not intended to be confined to the best books on the topic, this alphabetic listing has short critical annotations which indicate positive or negative factors for school use. Outstanding titles are starred. A supplement, . . . An Annotated Bibliography of Nonprint Media was issued in 1971.

Moody, Mildred T., Limper, Hilda K. et al. Biblio-therapy: Methods and Materials. Chicago: American Library Assn., 1971. 161p.

A combined effort by two committees of the Association of Hospital and Institution Libraries, this annotated bibliography seeks to make "practical suggestions on executing a therapeutic program" and to list "books useful for young people facing difficulties and adjustment." "In Part I, the Bibliotherapy Committee has examined broad aspects of the subject . . . . [in] Part II, The Troubled Child Sub-Committee has chosen explicit problem areas and selected specific titles which it hopes will be helpful to those who guide and counsel children with these maladjustments." Problems covered include physical handicaps, sibling and peer relationships, parents with problems, hostility and problems in parent-child relationships, nature books for relief of tension, the drop-out, sex education and behavior, self-discovery, gangs, and youth involved with the law. Lengthy descriptive annotations indicate theme, audience, and grade and interest levels. The majority of titles are from the 1960s; some go back to the 1940s. Titles often reflect the older, more secure, society for young people before Vietnam. Nevertheless, there are entertaining books which will still be read with interest by youngsters in grades 4 to 8. Librarians and therapists will find this a helpful list to check in an area where bibliographical advice is not easy to locate.

Moorachian, Rose, and Lehane, Veronica M. What Is a City? A Multi-Media Guide on Urban Living. Boston: Boston Public Library, 1969. 152p.

Directed to librarians and others who work with young people and to young people themselves, the intent of this annotated listing is to help "to interpret contemporary society to city people." Arranged first by informal topical headings relating to city life, entries are further divided by a wide variety of formats: books, pamphlets, serials, films and filmstrips, slides, recordings, even realia and games. The lively annotations are both descriptive and critical. This unusual bibliography is a genuine multiethnic and multimedia attempt to illustrate living in a city environment to younger citizens.

Moore, Anne Carroll. My Roads to Childhood: Views and Reviews of Children's Books. Boston: Horn Book, 1961. 399p.

This is a book of essays, occasional, personal, and critical, about children's literature by the first Superintendent of Children's Work in the New York Public Library, whose tenure lasted from 1906-41. Introduced by Frances Clarke Sayers, it was first printed in 1939. Reprints followed in 1964 and 1970, but separate parts had been published earlier as Roads to Childhood in 1920, New Roads to Childhood in 1923, and Crossroads to Childhood in 1926.

Many titles of children's classics receive comment in the text and are indexed under author, title, and illustrator. Annotated bibliographic lists include "A List of Books for Middle-Aged Children," "Some Favorite Books of French Children," "A Representative List of Books Published 1926-1938," and others. Moore's essays show her usual keen perception about new talent from 1920 on, and great regard for critical appraisal in the best sense. The pages are filled with the titles of children's books from the nineteenth and early twentieth centuries and make wonderful reading about the life of a famous American children's librarian.

Moore, Vardine. Pre-School Story Hour. 2nd ed. Metuchen, N.J.: Scarecrow, 1972. 174p.

First published in 1966, this account of storytelling procedures is intended for nursery and day schools and recreation programs as well as for libraries. It is book-centered, rather than education-centered. Chapters cover program planning, book selection, the role of parents, and related activities such as group games. A book list of about 200 recommended books, with brief descriptive annotations, is arranged by topic, and is supplemented by short lists of finger plays, game and rhythm books, and recordings.

Morris, Clare E. Selecting Children's Reading. PDK Fastback. Bloomington, Ind.: Phi Delta Kappa, 1973. 30p.

This is a brief resumé sponsored by a professional honorary fraternity in the educational field.

Mortimer, Sheila M. What Shall I Read? A Select List of Quality Books for Children. London: Library Assn., 1973. 163p.

Intended for librarians, teachers, parents, and anyone responsible for recommending books to young people up to age 14 who stop short of maturity in their reading interests, this is a British selection of recreational and informative titles. It is also a guide to desirable titles for children's libraries. In the main, books listed were written specially for children, but adult nonfiction titles that can be appreciated by children are included. The arrangement comprises two large groupings: books of "imagination" arranged alphabetically, and books of "information," following a modified Dewey sequence. Each item is accompanied by a paragraph of descriptive comment. Evaluative annotation is minimal, since quality and the ability to please and satisfy were criteria used by the advisory selection team. The clear arrangement of this carefully chosen British list is enhanced by attractive printing. A new edition appeared in 1978.

Morton, Miriam, ed. A Harvest of Russian Children's Literature. Berkeley, Calif.: Univ. of California Pr., 1967. 474p.

An anthology of Russian tales for children, this work attempts to make available to American children from 5 to 15 "a substantial sampling of Russian children's literature, [to] give American adults who work with children and books and those who teach comparative literature and librarianship an acquaintance with a significant portion, [and to] offer those interested professionally or as concerned laymen, an insight into an important aspect of Russian child culture." The authors of about 100 selections dating from 1825 on receive critical and biographical comment. A generous sampling of the illustrations which are an essential part of this literature makes this a handsome volume.

Moses, Montrose J. Children's Books and Reading. Detroit: Gale, 1975. 272p.
    A photolithographic facsimile of the Mitchell Kennerley edition of 1907, this work sketches the early development of children's literature, with some observations about its qualities in the first years of this century. A list of about 250 titles includes selected publications available at that time. Another reprint was produced by Gryphon in 1971.

Moss, Elaine. Children's Books of the Year 1970- . London: Hamilton, 1971- . Annual.
    Published in association with the National Book League and the British Council, these annual lists of over 300 books are selected from some 2000 British publications (including some titles originating in the United States) submitted by British publishers to the National Book League for its annual touring exhibition. Each volume carries a new introduction by the selector on the children's publishing scene in the preceding year. Items, which receive a paragraph of descriptive annotation, are arranged by type of publication (subdivided by age group) and subject groupings (where symbols are used to indicate age range). For a retrospective view of the best British children's publication, this can be used in conjunction with its predecessor edited by Naomi Lewis.

——. One Hundred Books for Children 1966-7. 2nd ed., with supplement: 25 Books for Children: January-June, 1968. London: National Book League, 1968. 24p.
    An annotated personal choice, first published in 1967, this list of gift books for children emphasizes literary merit and is arranged in four age groups: 3-6; 6-9; 9-11; 11-14.

——. Paperbacks for Children Two to Eleven: A Starter Collection. London: National Book League, 1973. 21p.
    This beginning list of British imprints which includes picture books, folk tales, story collections, stories for 5- to 8-year-olds and for 9- to 11-year-olds, verse, and nonfiction was compiled to help parents and children start building a collection that will bring

repeated pleasure and excitement to the family. Prepared for an NBL traveling exhibition, the 100 items are given brief descriptive annotations.

——. Reading for Enjoyment with 2 to 5 Year Olds. London: Children's Book News, 1975. 32p.

This primary title in the Reading for Enjoyment series was first published in 1970. See also . . . 6-8 Year Olds (1975, Tucker); . . . 8-11 Year Olds (1975, Hill); and . . . 11 Year Olds and Up (1975, Chambers). These are informal guides for parents in selecting books for their children, each based on a National Book League exhibit. The emphasis throughout is on sharing, that is, the mutual appreciation of reading by both parent and child. Mrs. Moss, experienced as a reviewer, teacher, and librarian, selected the titles for the NBL Children's Books of the Year exhibitions. The arrangement divides about 125 books, all British in-print titles, including paperbacks, into broad types of publication: picture books, nursery rhymes and poetry, stories, and "beginning to learn." Each has a lively and graphic descriptive and critical annotation. Indexes are provided for title, author, and illustrator.

Motz, Minnie R., and Johnson, Alice E., eds. University Press Books for Secondary School Libraries. New York: American Univ. Pr. Services, 1975. 89p. Biennial.

Published in association with the American Association of School Librarians of the American Library Association (ALA), this two-year edition succeeds a series of annuals first published in 1966 under the title University Press Books for Young Adults, Selected by High School and Young Adult Librarians, prepared by a committee of the Young Adult Services Division chaired by Opal C. Eagle. The separate title University Press Books for Secondary School Libraries was compiled by a committee chaired by Mary V. Gaver and appeared in 1967. This merged edition presents an annotated selection by a committee of school librarians, arranged by Dewey subject classification. Each entry carries a paragraph of descriptive annotation, supplemented by short quotations from academic review journals. Because of the high quality of titles published by these academic publishers and the careful preparation by members of ALA subdivisions, these lists form a discriminating supplementary source of valuable titles for all libraries dealing with young adults of high school age, and should not be ignored even at the college level.

Muir, Marcie. A Bibliography of Australian Children's Books. Vol. 1. London: Deutsch, 1970. 1038p.

This substantial bibliographical record gives title-page transcriptions and full bibliographical notes for "all children's books relating to Australia irrespective of the nationality of the writer or place of publication," and "all children's books written by Australian authors irrespective of subject matter," up to the end of 1967. Coverage also includes titles relating to Antarctica and, selectively, those relating to the southwest Pacific region, including Papua-New Guinea but excluding New Zealand. Arrangement is alphabetically by author; under each author, titles are listed chronologically. Color, half-tone, and line-block illustrations enhance the record. A second volume published in 1976 contains additional titles and extends coverage to the end of 1972.

Muir, Percy H. Children's Books of Yesterday: A Catalogue of an Exhibition Held at 7 Albermarle Street, London, during May 1946. With a foreword by John Masefield. New ed., rev. and enl. Detroit: Singing Tree, 1970. 211p.

This very large exhibition of examples of historical children's literature, held soon after the end of World War II, had a great influence on literary interest in early children's books and collecting by bibliophiles. The collection, largely formed by F. R. Bussell, was the property of the National Magazine Company and most of it was later sold to Good Housekeeping magazine for exhibition in the United States. The sympathetic foreword by Masefield comments, "Here are the devices which the genius of four centuries has invented to lure some dozen generations of the young into civility." The compiler, a distinguished antiquarian bookseller and historian of the genre, contributes a preface, an introduction to each section, and bibliographical annotations for each title, all of value. Over a thousand items are grouped under instructional material (divided by subject); nursery rhymes and other verse; storybooks (under topic); and illustrated books. The original edition of 1946 was published by the Cambridge University Press for the National Book League, on whose premises the exhibition was staged. The present edition is nothing more than a photolithographic reprint, despite its claim to revision, except for the index. The permanent reference value of the collection has been attested by the 1977 publication by the Children's Books History Society of a full index of authors, illustrators, titles, publishers and printers, and places of publication.

——. English Children's Books, 1600 to 1900. London: Batsford, 1954. 256p.

This historical and bibliographical account by a distinguished antiquarian bookseller avowedly follows in the steps of Harvey Darton's seminal study (see above). Because of the author's wide experience and bibliographical expertise, this account of the classic period of children's literature in England is not likely to be superseded. Six chapters cover the story from "The Prehistoric Age" (before Newbery) to "After Carroll"; two final chapters cover "The Importance of Pictures" and "Nick-Nacks." In addition to the discussion of many titles in the text, checklists and post-scripts at the end of each chapter give detailed bibliographic information in conformity with the author's "firm conviction that all such matters as this should be approached bibliographically." The author's general purpose is to take "a broad sweep within a smaller compass" than his predecessor, "to select certain noble and outstanding specimens" to give "a picture of the wood rather than the trees." The age of Newbery and the romantic period command the author's closest attention, but all is indispensable for historians, students and, in particular, collectors and dealers in rare books. The publisher's characteristic house style of provid-ing many illustrations with color and black-and-white plates and numerous line-blocks in the text help make this a delight to scan as well as an essential work of reference.

Munson, Amelia H. An Ample Field: Books and Young People. Chicago: American Library Assn., 1950. 122p.

A basic account of issues confronting those who work in the field of young people's reading, this work was directly addressed to public librarians but is also appropriate for "all those engaged in bringing together young people and books." The author's intention is to "provide orientation, bring together elusive ideas, vague thoughts, unpublicized activities and unformulated conclusions." She firmly states, "There are no new discoveries here." Her exposition draws upon the experience of twenty-five years of library work in the New York Public Library and Columbia Univer-sity Library School. Chapters reflect three central themes: chal-lenge, general observations on youth and books; resources, includ-ing examining types of the literature such as adventure, romance, and how-to-do-it books; and techniques, such as book selection and book talks. Individual titles discussed are listed at the end of each chapter but there is no attempt to mention all authors acceptable to young people. The popularity of this elementary yet inspirational approach is attested by the numerous unchanged reprints required since the original publication.

Myth, Legend, and Fantasy. Topic Booklists. Tunbridge Wells, Eng.: Fenrose, 1974. 63p.

One of the publisher's series (see Scriptural and Serious), this work includes Greek and Roman gods and heroes, Norse tales, King Arthur, and Robin Hood under such topics as myth and legend and fantasy. All names and places are indexed.

National Aerospace Education Association. Aerospace Bibliography. 6th ed. Washington, D.C.: Govt. Print. Off., 1972. 116p.

Compiled for the National Aeronautics and Space Administra-tion for the use of elementary and secondary schoolteachers, as well as for general adult readers, this annotated bibliography has been constantly revised since its first edition, for elementary schools, in 1961. A second edition appeared in 1963, and succeeding editions under the present title in 1966, 1968, 1970, and 1972. The listing is arranged under four headings: part 1, the subject index, is in broad subdivisions of the topic, such as the general overview, unmanned and manned space exploration, benefits and social impacts of the space program, space science, career opportunities, and curriculum and resource materials and other aids to teachers; part 2 is a bibliography of materials alphabetically listed by author, each item with a paragraph of descriptive annotation and designated reading level; part 3 presents reference materials under specific types; and part 4, periodicals listed by title. A title index and a list of addresses for source material is added. Copyright dates for entries in this edition range from 1969 to 1971 and indicate the fast-changing nature of the field. Over the years this careful and thorough selection has proved extremely useful to practitioners in schools and libraries, as well as to the public.

National Association for the Advancement of Colored People. Education Dept. Integrated School Books: A Descriptive Bibliography of 399 Pre-School and Elementary School Texts and Story Books. New York: The Association, 1967. 55p.

This beginning list was prepared as a model for parents, school officials, and concerned citizens. Entries, with brief descriptive annotations, are arranged in subject and type of publication divisions that are applicable to curricular areas in elementary school. One of the earlier lists in this area, it reflects the time of publication and the moderate position of the association; consequently, it is of some historic and sociological interest, although superseded from a selection viewpoint.

National Association of Independent Schools. Junior Booklist: Current Books. Milton, Mass.: The Association, 1964-67. Annual.

Under variant titles, predecessors of this annotated list for students from preschool to grade 9 go back as far as 1937, with the imprint of the association's former names, the Independent Schools Education Board and the Secondary Education Board. It is a companion to the Senior Booklist. Selection is by a committee of teachers and librarians with a working knowledge of what boys and girls like to read, and the quality of titles chosen reflects their interests, besides information value and literary quality. About 450 titles annually are arranged alphabetically within six groups by grade and age: grades 6-9, 4-6, 2-4, K-2, "For the Youngest," and "For the Family Bookshelf." Annotations are critical as well as descriptive, and are written for young people, rather than teachers and librarians. The list has been widely used by both private and public schools, and by others interested in offerings that tend to reflect an eclectic measure of evaluating with some emphasis on literary quality. The annual selection represents a small collection of titles, which, it can be assumed, young readers will find stimulating and worthwhile. However, it offers little for the many who find reading, for whatever reason, difficult. The last editions achieved popularity as a buying list for libraries in and out of the private-school sector.

——. Senior Booklist: Current Books. Milton, Mass.: The Association, 1964-67. Annual.
    Predecessors of this annotated list appeared under variant titles with the imprint of the association's former name, the Independent Schools Education Board. It is a companion to the Junior Booklist. Titles are selected for interest and entertainment, as well as educational value, by a committee made up of teachers and librarians "who have had years of experience in knowing what students like to read." They are arranged alphabetically within twelve groups by literary form or broad topic. Annotations are written "for students, not for teachers or adults." Literary quality is primary for each selection and popularity alone is not a factor. It includes adult as well as young people's books, and has been praised and especially recommended for use with advanced or gifted students. Libraries in public as well as private schools have used the list liberally as a buying tool for titles that bright young people could and would read.

——. Library Committee. Books for Secondary School Libraries. 4th ed. New York: Bowker, 1971. 308p.
    This work was first published in 1955 as 1000 Books for Independent School Libraries, and the titles of the succeeding editions reflected the concern of the Independent Schools Education Board for the library support of all secondary schools. The second edition, 3000 Books for Secondary School Libraries, appeared in 1961, the third, 4000 Books . . . in 1968. The purpose of this extensive but unannotated listing is to provide a guide on the college-bound level for school librarians, teachers, and mature students working on class assignments and independent projects. Arranged by Dewey decimal classification, with Library of Congress subject headings supplied, it is also designed to be a foundation for a basic new library collection. A combined index of author, title, and subject entries and a list of professional tools are provided. The fourth edition reflects an expansion of interest in areas relating to current problems, such as ecology. This well-established and carefully selected source will perform as a valuable checklist for all secondary school libraries. A fifth edition was published in 1976.

National Congress of Parents and Teachers and Children's Services Division of the American Library Association. Special Committee. <u>Let's Read Together</u>. 3rd ed. Chicago: American Library Assn., 1969. 103p.

First published in 1960 and revised in 1964, this selection by a joint committee of two major organizations interested in family reading lists titles which will appeal to parents and children from early years up to the teens. Suitability for joint participation is the criterion, and emphasis is placed on books that can form part of a personal library. About 550 books are arranged under traditional subject-interest categories, such as mystery, adventure, and hobbies. Titles are also grouped by age levels. Annotations are descriptive and to the point. The bibliography is a basic one for parents interested in children's reading, and is a sound source for librarians to use with inquiring parents, and for teachers. The fourth edition was published in 1981.

National Recreation and Park Association. Committee. <u>For the Storyteller</u>. Rev. ed. New York: The Association, 1961. 32p.

First compiled in 1938 by Mary J. Breen, with a second edition in 1957, this introductory booklet is a classified list of stories and books for the storyteller suitable for use in a park or playground environment.

Neesam, Malcolm. <u>Into Space</u>. YLG Storylines, no. 2. Birmingham, Eng.: Library Assn., Youth Libraries Group, 1972. 16p.

Listing space stories, to the exclusion of other science fiction and fantasy, the compiler briefly annotates about fifty items which constitute a healthy body of good children's literature. Some adult titles for the older child and background reference books are included.

<u>Negro History and Literature: A Selected Annotated Bibliography</u>. New York: American Jewish Committee, Anti-Defamation League of B'nai B'rith, and National Federation of Settlement and Neighborhood Centers, 1968. 29p.

This jointly sponsored bibliography of titles selected from publishers' catalogs is intended to correct distortions and remedy omissions in the teaching of American history and life. Books by sensitive authors dealing with what might be termed the black experience have been chosen so that this experience "may be brought into the classrooms, the settlement house, the scout troop, the library and the home." The first section on resource materials lists over fifty books for teachers, youth leaders, parents, and high-school students. Some eighty-five books are cited in the following sections, graded for ages 5 to 8, 9 to 12, and 13 to 15. The titles include autobiography, nonfiction, fiction, and poetry, each with a sentence or brief paragraph of descriptive annotation. Although only a representative sampling, and lacking later publications, the careful selection makes this valuable as a checklist for librarians and teachers.

Neil, Alexander. Books for Reluctant Readers in Secondary Schools. Arbroath, Scotland: School Library Assn. in Scotland, 1973. 85p.
Titles in this work were selected on the basis of practical experience by a Scottish school librarian for students of varying ability who are competent to read but show little interest in doing so. Books include hardbound and paperbound British publications and are listed, with brief descriptive notes, in two parts: school library books and class library books, each divided into fiction and nonfiction and then classified into genre or subject groups.

——. Fiction and Non-Fiction Books: For Use by the Least Able Pupils in Secondary Schools. London: School Library Assn., 1971. 69p.
British books found useful in work with "least able" pupils make up this annotated list, chosen by a school librarian with the assistance of Scottish teachers. Fiction and nonfiction titles, with brief notes, are arranged by fields of interest.

Nettlefold, Mary, ed. Scotland. YLG Storylines, no. 5. Birmingham, Eng.: Library Assn., Youth Libraries Group, 1974. 22p.
This list of children's fiction set in Scotland--but not necessarily by Scottish authors--was compiled by Scottish children's librarians to give children an authentic insight into Scottish life. Over fifty items covering contemporary and historical fiction, folklore, fantasy, and background reading are briefly annotated. Age interest is indicated.

New York Library Association. Children's and Young Adult Services Section. Children's Booklist for Small Public Libraries. 2nd ed. Albany, N.Y.: The Association, 1964. 98p.
First published in 1955 as a brief Basic Children's Booklist . . ., this second edition, compiled by a committee of the association and cooperatively sponsored by the State University of New York, the State Education Department, and the New York State Library's Extension Division, makes "an attempt . . . to cover a cross section of children's literature" by using both lasting value and popularity as criteria. Over 700 entries are arranged under the traditional categories of children's publications, such as serial books, stories for younger children, and for older boys and girls. Titles that are not self-explanatory receive brief annotation and in this edition carry a notation indicating reading level. Publication dates range from the 1940s through the 1960s, the majority falling in the late 1950s; consequently, the sound and often standard selections will require substantial supplementation.

——. Children's and Young Adult Services Section. <u>Young Adult</u> <u>Booklist for Small Public Libraries</u>. 2nd ed. Albany, N.Y.: The Association, 1964. 31p.

First published in 1958 as a brief <u>Basic Young Adult Booklist ...</u>, this revised and expanded edition lists over 250 titles "as a sampling of broad-ranging interests" to serve as a buying guide to libraries in selection for the teenager, mature and immature. Only titles proven to be of interest to the reluctant and the avid reader have been included. Adult titles are not excluded but brief annotations indicate titles judged mature. Entries are arranged within broad subject headings. A "transitional titles" section is provided for younger readers. Minimal checklists are useful tools for small libraries, and this careful selection by a state association remains a suggestive one for libraries outside the area but will require substantial updating.

New York Public Library. Countee Cullen Regional Branch. <u>A Touch</u> <u>of Soul</u>. 3rd ed. New York: The Library, 1972. 16p.

The third edition of a selective list with variant titles and contents was published by the branch as a buying guide. The 1966 edition, <u>Books by and about American Negroes</u>, was augmented in 1968 to include films and recordings, and was further supplemented in 1970 as <u>Black America: Books, Films and Recordings</u>. Films included were tested with young audiences, and the records comprise jazz and soul music and other contributions by blacks. This 1972 publication selects books only by and about Africans and Afro-Americans recommended for children from preschool through grade 8. About 130 titles, chosen from the James Weldon Johnson Memorial Collection at the branch, are given brief descriptive annotations, and grouped under eight broad topical categories. The 1972 edition retains value as a highly selective list for book acquisition, but will require updating for later publications in this active area.

——. Office of Children's Services. <u>Children's Books and Recordings</u> <u>Suggested as Holiday Gifts</u>. New York: The Library, 1911- . Annual.

Since 1911, an annual selection of books chosen by the library's children's librarians and subject specialists has been exhibited in the two closing months of the year. Librarians, students of children's literature, parents, and children themselves may inspect and form their own preferences. Since 1972, a small group of recordings have been included with an appropriate change in the title of the catalog. By 1975, this list contained some 450 items, briefly annotated and arranged by title under informal topics, such as Christmas stories, sports, and native Americans. Topics appeal to the varied communities in New York. New editions and reprints are noted as well as new publications. Over the years this high-quality professional selection has furnished an instructive sampling of the best of American children's publishing, useful for current buying and as a retrospective checklist for students. A retrospective list, Children's Books 1910-1960, appeared in 1960.

——. Office of Children's Services. The Chinese in Children's Books. New York: The Library, 1973. 30p.

A library committee compiled this annotated list of books mostly in English but with some in Chinese, for the branch library serving the Chinatown area. Selection criteria were accurate representation and literary quality. Topical divisions include books about China, including picture books, stories for younger children, stories for older children, folktales, people and places, art and culture, and the Chinese in the United States. Most Chinese titles are Taiwan publications; the selectors note the scarcity of appropriate material available from the People's Republic and also about Chinese in the United States. A useful starting checklist for other libraries with a clientele interested in China and the Chinese.

——. Office of Children's Services. Japanese Children's Books on Exhibition in the Central Children's Room. New York: The Library, 1972. 30p.

A display for International Book Year, 1972, exhibited at the library's Donnell Center, this annotated catalog of about 250 works is divided into two sections covering publications before 1969 and after. The majority are picture books and stories for younger readers; nonfiction receives more cursory treatment. Japanese titles are translated into English. Graded lists are provided of picture books, stories for young readers, and stories for older children. A supplement covers 1971-72 titles. This is a useful checklist of hard-to-find information.

——. Office of Young Adult Services. Books for the Teen Age. New York: The Library, 1955- . Annual.

Revised annually and published every February, this well-known list is comprised of books on subjects of special interest and appeal to teenagers from the eighth grade and up. All titles have been read and selected by the Committee on Books for Young Adults, made up of librarians who work in the New York Public Library and chaired in 1975 by Lillian Morrison. The titles are constantly tested and tried with teenage readers. Selection is not confined to books written for young people; in fact, a high proportion are adult publications in paperback and hard cover. Writing is required that is "clear, vivid, appealing [and] imaginative." Some 1,250 titles in the 1975 edition were arranged under 90 topical headings that emphasize current interests. A special bicentennial feature represented American themes and social problems. The brief critical annotations are well expressed, often just a cogent phrase. The clear presentation will aid use by young people themselves, but parents, teachers, librarians, and other professionals concerned with young adult reading will all benefit from this outstanding annual selection. Current issues are indispensable acquisition tools for school and public libraries. Previous editions, prepared by committees chaired by Margaret C. Scoggin, furnish significant background material for sociological as well as literary research.

New York (State) University. Educational Resources Center. <u>Discovering India: A Guide to Indian Books for Use in American Schools.</u> 2nd ed. Thompson, Conn.: Interculture Associates, 1970. 34p.

   This annotated bibliography of about 100 books by Indian authors about India stemmed from a project at the center to develop materials for teaching and studying about India in American schools and colleges, and was first published in 1969. Part 1 lists titles selected for suitability in elementary and secondary schools. Descriptive annotation often includes comment on the physical quality of the volume, often unsatisfactory in Indian publications. The second part describes possible instructional uses in different grades from primary to junior high. A supplementary section lists aids for the teacher. The stress laid on nonstereotyped materials and its recommendation of Indian publications little known in North American libraries make this list an original contribution. It is also available as an ERIC document (ED 055 943).

Newton, Mary Griffin. <u>Books for Deaf Children: A Graded Annotated Bibliography.</u> Washington, D.C.: Alexander Graham Bell Assn. for the Deaf, 1962. 173p.

   "Prepared to help parents, teachers and librarians find appropriate reading materials for children handicapped by loss of hearing," this work of over 1,000 titles is arranged in sections from nursery school to grade 9. Grading has the profoundly deaf in mind who may necessarily be reading one or two grade levels lower than ordinary children. Brief annotations stress usefulness as well as describe each entry. Selection was made after analysis of the books for vocabulary, language, content, and format. Simplified adaptations are cited as well as originals of favorite titles, because deaf children may lack the necessary experiential language or conceptualization to appreciate many works. For those deaf readerͻ profoundly hard of hearing or retarded, there are few bibliographical aids available. The careful editing of this list, with its striving to provide a wide representative range, ensures its continued value.

Nicholsen, Margaret E. People in Books: A Selective Guide to Biographical Literature Arranged by Vocation and Other Fields of Reader Interest. New York: Wilson, 1969. 498p.

Originally conceived to answer high-school requests and endorsed by the ALA's Young Adult Services Division, this reference tool was expanded to serve the needs of elementary-school children and adults. It identifies "by vocation or field of activity, by country and by century" the subjects of biographies and other biographical writings that are recommended for libraries serving these groups. This standard aid provides indispensable information within the limitation of its included titles. A supplementary volume was issued in 1977.

Noonan, Eileen. A Basic Book Collection for High Schools. 7th ed. Chicago: American Library Assn., 1968. 184p.

An annotated book list for high schools, with a long-standing reputation, editions appeared under variant titles in 1924, 1930, 1935, 1942, and under the above title in 1950 edited by D. Dawson and 1957 edited by M. K. McAllister. The current editor received the assistance of consultants from the ALA and five other national educational organizations. The selection, covering grades 9 through 12, was "designed primarily to serve as an authoritative buying guide for high schools and public libraries and be particularly useful in establishing a new collection . . . ." 1,400 books are arranged by the abridged Dewey Decimal Classification, with subject headings supplied from Sears. A short fiction section and seventy magazines for high schools complete the list. A brief descriptive paragraph of annotation for each title is addressed to librarians and teachers. Excellent and essential as this tool was for school libraries when published, it would probably be impossible for current high school media centers, with their greater and more sophisticated demands for material, to rely on any relatively brief basic selection, however authoritative.

Norvell, George W. The Reading Interests of Young People. Boston: Heath, 1950. 262p.

Directed to classroom teachers and librarians, this study is based largely on statistical research over a twelve-year period by the supervisor of English in the New York state educational system. "More than 50,000 young people and 625 teachers in all types of communities and all sizes of schools in New York State participated." 1,700 titles used in the secondary schools were examined. The conclusion is that more popular titles should replace others of comparable quality for school use. Many books cited seem to have been out-of-date at the time of compilation, and are less applicable today. The study is of some retrospective interest as an early example of the application of scientific observation to readers' habits.

——. What Boys and Girls Like to Read. Morristown, N.J.: Silver, 1958. 30p.

A follow-up to the author's The Reading Interests of Young People (1950), directed to school superintendents, teachers, and others concerned with children's reading, this work investigates children's actual preferences vis-à-vis "authoritarian" selections which prescribe what they like to read. Chapters examine the collection and interpretation of the data, age and sex in reading preferences, bright children, children's interest in poetry and in prose, the effect of media and mass communication, and the formulation of a successful literature program in the school. The second part gives a tabular presentation of titles in order of popularity by sex and grade. The basic message is that scientific investigation should preclude divination in assessing children's reading interests. The study has been widely quoted over the years, though conclusions considered novel in 1958 seem almost old-fashioned today.

Ogden, John A. High Interest, Low Vocabulary Books: A Bibliography. Rev. ed. Denver: Colorado State Dept. of Education, 1965. 45p.

First published in 1962, this unannotated list of over 2,000 books for retarded and reluctant readers was prepared by a consultant in the department of education for the use of teachers and others working with young people who have difficulty reading at their grade level, or who have retarded mental development. Reading levels from primary to grade 9 are covered, and a vocabulary level and student interest level are provided for each title. Arrangement is by vocabulary levels, P through 7, and where necessary is subdivided by month of schooling.

An attempt was made to be comprehensive up to the time of preparation; and while this has not been fully realized, a substantial number of titles have been provided. A proportion will still be in print, but the age of the publication will require the list to be used with care.

The One Hundred Best Books for Children: A Special Sunday Times Survey. London: Sunday Times, 1960. 16p.

Those books considered best for children in point of illustration and format as well as textually are represented by in-print editions. Titles were selected in close association with Miss Kathleen Lines, arranged by type of publication, and annotated with a full paragraph of descriptive and critical comment.

Ontario (Province). Dept. of Education. Multi-Media Resource List: Eskimos and Indians. Toronto: The Department, 1969. 50p.
——. Supplement, 1970. 16p.

Compiled to assist Ontario teachers to become aware of teaching aids in the area, this compendium lists some books and most types of audiovisual material, from maps and prints to slide sets and film loops, together with information on museums and art collections. Emphasis is placed on Canadian material and the list is still useful in identifying hard-to-locate items.

Opie, Iona, and Opie, Peter. Three Centuries of Nursery Rhymes and Poetry for Children: An Exhibition Held at the National Book League, May 1973. London: National Book League, 1973. 70p.

This assemblage of 829 publications for the young and very young, in which traditional nursery rhymes in English are to be found, is claimed to be a greater assortment than previously exhibited. American imprints are represented alongside the British. The examples form a section of the compilers' own collection documenting child life and literature. Full bibliographical entries are given, and annotations are chiefly bibliographical in nature. They are supplemented by line and half-tone reproductions of title pages and illustrations. Arrangement is, as far as possible, chronological in each grouping within the two divisions: "Nursery Rhymes," comprising first books, classic collections, popular and period collections, illustrious illustrators, and celebrated characters; and "Poetry for Children" representing first and early appearances of well-known poems. A second edition was published in 1977.

Osborne, Charles Humfrey C. A List of General Reference Books Suitable for Secondary School Libraries. 4th ed. [with] Some Suggestions for Primary Schools [and] A List of Books on Librarianship and Library Techniques of Interest to School Librarians. 3rd ed. London: School Library Assn., 1954. 62p.

A standard list, intended for British secondary schools, replaced by the association's Books of Reference for School Libraries (1961), compiled by Peggy Heeks. The definition of general reference excludes works on specific subject fields. The 381 annotated entries include 45 for primary schools first listed in this edition. The previous edition appeared in 1950. Two editions by C. W. Morris had appeared in periodical form in 1937 and 1939. All are now dated.

——. Primary School Library Books: An Annotated List. London: School Library Assn., 1960. 85p.

Intended to help British primary school teachers select essential books for their school library, part 1 of this work includes books for recreational reading--picture books and traditional divisions of children's literature--arranged into three age levels: for younger children; for eight- to ten-year-olds and slower readers; and for nine-to-eleven plus. The second part includes books for study and reference divided in large subjects and subdivided into smaller areas. Short descriptive and critical notes on each title indicate tentative appeal and appropriate age level. Many titles are now superseded or out of print.

Osborne, Edgar, ed. Books for Young People. Group II: Eleven to Thirteen Plus. 3rd ed. London: Library Assn., 1960. 239p.

First published in 1953, with a second edition in 1954 and a supplement in 1955, this annotated and classified list complements Group I: under 11, edited by Hilda M. McGill, and Group III: Fourteen to Seventeen, edited by L. M. Harrod. It was compiled by librarians in the North Midland Branch of the association. Much enlarged in this edition, it became a standard list in British school and public libraries, but is now substantially outdated.

Owen, Betty M. A Smorgasbord of Books: Titles Junior High Readers Relish. New York: Citation, 1974. 87p.

A personal choice by the editor of the Teen Age Book Club sponsored by Scholastic, Inc., the New York educational publishers and suppliers, almost all titles in this list were selections for this reading club. The compiler points out that "many lists recommended for youngsters weren't very useful for teenagers," and popularity with young people has been the principal criterion for inclusion, with no special attention paid to "quality" or "classic" titles. Four sections cover teen fiction, teen nonfiction, anthologies and collections, and adult books. Paragraphs of descriptive annotation have been directed mainly to young readers, but titles containing profanity or rough language are pointed out. Mysteries and science-fiction titles are identified, and recommended grade levels are given. As a guide to encourage reading, this provided lively and interesting suggestions to librarians and teachers, with the caveat that popular appeal to teenagers had moved fast over half-a-dozen years.

Palmer, Julia Reed. Read for Your Life: Two Successful Efforts to Help People Read, and An Annotated List of the Books That Made Them Want to. Metuchen, N.J.: Scarecrow, 1974. 501p.

A New York City school volunteer describes her contribution to the widespread problem of lack of reading ability among minority adolescents, and comments on library techniques suitable in disadvantaged areas, including a bookmobile project. A list of books to interest young blacks, Chicanos, Orientals, American Indians, and Puerto Ricans takes up most of the volume. Some titles likely to lower morale in these groups have been excluded on the advice of bookmobile staff. Arranged in broad subject areas in Dewey sequence, each item has brief descriptive annotations that often include personal comment. Reading levels and interest levels according to grade are indicated, and a symbol distinguishes books appropriate for private and suburban schools to foster understanding of minority groups.

Parrott, Phyllis. <u>Books for Children: A Selection</u>. London: National Book League, 1955. 26p.

A personal selection by an English children's librarian lists over 125 then current books that children will enjoy reading and want to possess. Arrangement is by type of publication with a few brief annotations.

Pascoe, T. W., ed. <u>A Second Survey of Books for Backward Readers, Compiled by a Committee of Teachers of Backward Children</u>. London: Univ. of London Pr., 1962. 171p.

This publication of the University of Bristol Institute of Education succeeds <u>A Survey of Books for Backward Readers</u> (1956), compiled by members of the Bristol Teacher's Backwardness Research Group and edited by D. H. Stott. In the revision as well as in the original publication, most titles commented on were British monographs and series. The passage of time has inevitably superannuated selections useful at the time of publication.

Patterson, Sylvia W. <u>Rousseau's Emile and Early Children's Literature</u>. Metuchen, N.J.: Scarecrow, 1971. 185p.

This study was based on a Ph.D. thesis on the influence of the French philosophical novel on some well-known English writers for children at the end of the eighteenth century and the beginning of the nineteenth.

Pellowski, Anne. <u>The World of Children's Literature</u>. New York: Bowker, 1968. 538p.

An annotated bibliography of books and some articles about all phases of literature for children throughout the world is presented here, together with supplementary commentary. The direct outgrowth of a questionnaire and survey made for the International Board of Books for Young People and the International Youth Library, it seeks to spread knowledge and understanding by making available an accurate picture of development in newly independent nations, as well as those with a longer history of writing for children. Nearly 4,500 items are arranged geographically and then subdivided nationally to bring together linguistically and culturally related countries. Introductory essays for each section and country give a brief general survey of the development of children's literature and libraries. Library locations for each entry are given. A first attempt to bring together a worldwide approach to children's literature and a major contribution to the study of the field, which is also a delight to consult.

Penn, Joseph L.; Wells, Elaine Brooks; and Berch, Mollie L. <u>The Negro American in Paperback: A Selected List of Paperbound Books, Compiled and Annotated for Secondary School Students</u>. Rev. ed. Washington, D.C.: National Education Assn., 1968. 49p.

Compiled under the auspices of the association's Center for Human Relations, with the cooperation of the National Commission on Professional Rights and Responsibilities' Committee on Civil and Human Rights, this revision includes 300 titles, an increase of 140 over the first edition of 1967. The list "is intended as an aid and reference guide to teachers and students who may have a limited background of information on the role and contributions of Negro Americans to the American way of life." Family and community group use is also kept in mind. Entries are arranged alphabetically by author and carry brief descriptive annotations, with a graded symbol for junior or senior high-school use. Items range from grade 7 through grade 12 and college preparatory, with wide subject coverage from current problems to fiction. Many seminal works of the black American movement are included and remain in print in paperback format. Consequently, this carefully chosen selection remains valuable.

Perkins, Flossie L. Book and Non-Book Media: Annotated Guide to Selection Aids for Educational Materials. Urbana, Ill.: National Council of Teachers of English, 1972. 298p.

Intended "for all persons who need to choose from among the current profusion of books and educational materials," this work revises Book Selection Media (1967) by Ralph Perkins. The title as well as the scope, enlarged to include nonbook media, indicates a stronger educational direction to serve the needs of the school-age clientele, though there is much college and university and adult material here that may also be useful for high schools. This edition reflects changing interests and current needs.

Peterson, Carolyn Sue. Reference Books for Elementary and Junior High School Libraries. 2nd ed. Metuchen, N.J.: Scarecrow, 1975. 314p.

A thorough and complete revision of the first edition of 1970, with much additional recent material, this list of nearly 900 titles is useful for work with children from preschool to grade 9. It also functions as a buying guide for elementary and junior high-school libraries. Directed to school reference librarians and teachers, the requirements of education and library school students have also been kept in mind. The intention is to "list and evaluate various types of reference books from general encyclopedias to hobby dictionaries. While few schools will need or want all of the material described, most will find a growing need to include much of it in their reference collection." The subject arrangement is in sixteen chapters, each with an introductory passage on the basic criteria for the type of book and suggestions on use. Annotations are substantial and include organizational and historical features as well as a critical assessment. While not exhaustive, this evaluative guide does a more than adequate job, and provides a quality selection with a broad scope, covering all major areas of the curriculum, special interests, and current needs for different levels of students.

Pickard, Phyllis M., ed. British Comics: An Appraisal. London: Comics Campaign Council, n.d. 32p.

This assessment of the social and educational significance of crime, horror, and other types of comics is intended to be studied by teachers, parents, and others concerned with the mental health and happiness of young people. Opinions are contributed by a panel that includes an editor, a librarian, a headmistress, a psychologist, a magistrate, and two priests. Sixteen crime and horror comics and thirteen other comics are examined.

——. I Could a Tale Unfold: Violence, Horror and Sensationalism in Stories for Children. London: Tavistock, 1961. 228p.

In this not unbiased study of an unwelcome element in children's reading with a long history, earlier classics such as Hans Christian Andersen are analyzed, but current comics receive the most attention, prompted by observations made at English primary schools. Published in New York by Humanities Press in the same year.

Picture Books and Story Books for Primary Schools. Hull, Eng.: School Library Assn., Hull and East Riding Branch, 1966. 24p.

An unannotated list of books available in Britain, intended as a guide for teachers, this work covers books for infants, books for lower juniors, and books for upper juniors in three sections.

Pilgrim, Geneva Hanna, and McAllister, Mariana K. Books, Young People, and Reading Guidance. 2nd ed. New York: Harper, 1968. 241p.

First published in 1960, this volume is designed for those concerned with the reading of young people of junior and senior high-school age--teachers, librarians, parents--and also as a text for college courses. The objective is to guide young people into increased maturity by fostering enthusiastic reading. Chapters cover types of literature for young people, characteristics of adolescents, reading interests and needs of youth, book selection and reading guidance. Titles of interest and appeal illustrate points under discussion, and there is a list of recommended books at the end of the book, together with a selected bibliography of classified reading lists and sources for selection and evaluation. Each chapter carries references to additional readings.

Pitz, Henry C. Illustrating Children's Books: History-Technique-Production. New York: Watson-Guptill, 1963. 207p.

The author provides historical and critical comment on individual illustrated editions, mostly but not all from the twentieth century, as well as giving technical production details.

Platt, Peter. A Guide to Book Lists and Bibliographies for the Use of Schools. 4th ed. Oxford: School Library Assn., 1975. 33p.

This listing for British school libraries of nearly 400 subject bibliographies, in book, pamphlet, and periodical article form, can be helpful in book selection and the provision of bibliographical information to students. Originally published in 1956, it was revised in 1961 and 1969.

Pledger, Keith, ed. Reading Lists for Parents and Children. Ace Educational Booklet. Cambridge, Eng.: Advisory Centre for Education, 1968. 38p.

This is an unannotated British selection arranged by subject, subdivided by age group, with a preface entitled "Why Have a Booklist?".

Potvin, Claude. La Littérature de Jeunesse au Canada Français. Montreal: Assn. Canadienne des Bibliothêcaires de Langue Française, 1972. 110p.

A historical account and comprehensive bibliography of French-Canadian children's books make up the two parts of this book. The perceptive introductory essay by Claude Aubry is followed by a lengthy critical and historical review, with a briefly annotated bibliography of source material. The entries for the children's titles are unannotated and arranged chronologically in groups: before 1920; 1920-29; 1930-39; 1940-49; 1950-59; 1960-69. This title constitutes a thorough and essential aid to the appreciation of this little-documented field.

Pullen, Alan. Words of Persuasion: Reference Books for Retarded Readers. An Analysis and Evaluation of More than 150 Books, Suitable for Those Unskilled at Reading. Birmingham, Eng.: C. Combridge, 1962. 128p.

Choice of entries in this guide to nonfiction books suitable for consultation by semi-illiterate and unskilled readers has been based predominantly on practical experience and current availability of the books in Britain. Titles are arranged to conform approximately to the main classes of the Dewey classification, subdivided by the age level of reading achievement. Notes indicate vocabulary level, readability, physical suitability of the format, and an evaluation.

Pumphrey, George H. Comics and Your Children. London: Comics Campaign Council, 1955. 24p.

Written by a parent and teacher for parents and teachers, this is a harsh criticism of a wide range of comics then available in Britain.

Quayle, Eric. The Collector's Book of Children's Books. London: Studio Vista, 1971. 144p.

Largely an account of English publications, this is a delightful volume by an enthusiastic collector of early juveniles that offers both sage advice and a full measure of anecdotal, descriptive, and bibliographical information calculated to warm the cockles of all incipient book-collectors' hearts. The lively prose engages the reader, and the credibility of the text is enhanced by the many illustrations from the author's own collection. The general treatment is chronological, with the nineteenth century receiving most emphasis, and attention is paid to the development of types and genres in children's books, such as fairy and folk tales and adventure stories.

Quebec (Province). Ministère de l'Education. Choix de Consultation en Langues Française et Anglaise pour les Bibliothèques d'Écoles Secondaires. Quebec: The Department, 1964. 30p.

Prepared for French-speaking high-school students by the department's Service des Bibliothèques Scolaires, this is a basic, briefly annotated list of eighty-seven reference books in both languages arranged by Dewey.

Quimby, Harriet B.; Jackson, Clara O.; and Weber, Rosemary. Building a Children's Literature Collection. Middleton, Conn.: Choice, 1975. 34p.

These two articles reprinted from 1974 issues of Choice, the book-selection review for college libraries, deal with issues in acquiring children's books for academic collections where children's literature has become a subject of scholarly attention. Quimby and Jackson propose A Suggested Basic Reference Collection for Academic Libraries; Weber recommends A Suggested Basic Reference Collection of Children's Books. Both selected listings will be useful for other libraries.

Quinnan, Barbara. Fables from Incunabula to Modern Picture Books: A Selected Bibliography. Washington, D.C.: Library of Congress, 1966. 85p.

An exhibition catalog of fables for adults as well as children, compiled by a specialist in the Children's Book Section, Virginia Haviland who contributes the foreword, the purpose of this title is to acquaint students of literature and folklorists with the rich holdings of the library, including items not on exhibition. Citations of titles include some in other libraries. Five sections with explanatory introductions cover general studies, Indian fables, Aesop, La Fontaine, and Krylov. Annotations are descriptive and interpretative. Particular attention is given to the illustrations, and excellent reproductions provide a full historical range of the editions exhibited. An attractive and informative publication, valuable to collectors and libraries as a bibliographical checklist.

Rabban, Elana. Books from Other Countries, 1968-1971. Chicago: American Library Assn., 1972. 48p.

This annotated bibliography was sponsored by the American Association of School Librarians as a contribution to International Book Year. About 200 translations available in the United States are listed under twenty-three countries of origin. The selection "is designed for use by children, and young people, parents, teachers, and library media specialists when focusing on any phase of international or intercultural relations." The compiler hopes that "translations of good books may help to promote understanding by giving new insight into international values." Descriptive annotations note authors' other works and are supplemented by symbols for reading range and a categorization based on social studies concepts, such as partnership with nature and living with others. A similarly titled list covering 1972 to 1976 was published in 1978.

Racist and Sexist Images in Children's Books. Papers on Children's Literature. London: Writers and Readers Pub. Cooperative, 1975. 49p.

Ten critical articles, which were originally published from 1968 to 1974 by the Council on Interracial Books for Children in their bulletin of the same name, are included.

Ramsey, Eloise. Folklore for Children and Young People: A Critical and Descriptive Bibliography for Use in the Elementary and Intermediate School. Philadelphia: American Folklore Society, 1952. 110p.

Prepared under the auspices of a committee of the society to help teachers in selecting folklore material, both in its authentic form and literary adaptation, this bibliography is for students from kindergarten through grade 9. The first part lists books for young people's reading, including folktales, rhymes and songs, and legends and myths, as well as poetry, biography, and fiction, that reflect the literary use of folklore. The second part contains sources for teachers categorized under folktales, folk rhymes, legends, folklore, storytelling, folk arts and crafts, and periodicals. Annotations are mainly descriptive for the first part and evaluative for the second part. Because it draws on expert scholarship in the field, this listing remains a standard for researchers and others interested in folklore study, as well as for teachers.

Rankin, Marie. Children's Interests in Library Books of Fiction. New York: AMS Pr., 1972. 146p.

A photolithographic reprint of the original 1944 edition published by Teachers College of Columbia University as one of their Contributions to Education series, this book was originally the author's thesis. Intended to probe characteristics in books of contemporary fiction which appeal to near and early adolescents, the research investigates how far changes in contemporary culture are reflected in children's literature, particularly highly popular books. The reception of Newbery prize books by readers in various libraries is examined and compared with other popular titles, with a view to identifying the features that cause them to be selected by young readers. Original for the time of publication in identifying the interest of the young themselves as a predominant factor in book choice, the study marks a change of professional attitude among librarians. The limited number of titles investigated highlights seven authors, some of whom are now considered controversial. For comparative purposes, this study retains value and interest to students of the recent history of children's literature.

Ray, Colin. Background to Children's Books. 3rd ed. London: National Book League, 1975. 21p.

A very useful select list of books about children's books and reading, this work is directed to teachers, student-teachers, and parents, as well as to scholars and researchers in the development of children's literature. Confined to "more useful" books and including British and American publications currently available, each item is annotated. The first edition appeared in 1971, and the second in 1974.

Ray, Sheila G. Children's Fiction: A Handbook for Librarians. 2nd ed., rev. London: Brockhampton, 1972. 239p.

This handbook, first published in 1970, was written for students preparing to become qualified librarians through professional examinations in Britain, Australia, and New Zealand. It is not intended to be a guide to the best children's books, though many examples (where possible in print) are described in the text. Chapters discuss traditional subject types of publication. Further readings are recommended. Fiction for immigrants is given special treatment. As an account of fiction written for children, it affords a straightforward treatment and can be a useful guide at a fairly elementary level.

——, and Ray, Colin. Attitudes and Adventure. 4th ed. Reader's Guide, no. 134. London: Library Assn., County Libraries Group, 1974. 32p.

The 300 selected titles in this work aimed at catching young

people's attention and encouraging their reading. Books on attitudes explore relationships characteristic of adolescence; books
on adventure are chiefly good stories. Controversial and critical
books are marked with a C̲. Some items are briefly annotated.
Previous editions appeared in 1965, 1968, and 1971.

Reid, Virginia M., ed. Children's Literature: Old and New. Champaign, Ill.: National Council of Teachers of English, 1964. 66p.
  A series of articles first published in the May 1963 issue of
Elementary English make up this work. The authors were members of the NCTE Committee on Children's Literature-Old and
New, which was set up in 1960 to explore new developments and
make recommendations concerning the nature of the educational
program in children's literature. Chapters answer these questions: "What Is the Role of Children's Literature in the Elementary School?"; "What Is Children's Literature?"; "What are Some
Meaningful Experiences with Literature?"; and "What are Some
Resources for the Teacher of Children's Literature?"

——, et al. Reading Ladders for Human Relations. 5th ed. Washington,
  D.C.: American Council on Education, 1972. 346p.
  This greatly expanded edition of a well-established guide, designed for teachers but also valuable for others interested in
young people's reading, was prepared under the direction of the
Committee on Reading Ladders for Human Relations of the National Council of Teachers of English. The project, which has over
the years depended on the cooperation of several groups and a
team of specialists in human relations and children's literature,
goes back as far as 1947, when the first edition, edited by Hilda
Tabb, appeared as a report in a series on intergroup relations in
the public schools. Revised and enlarged editions appeared in
1949 and 1955, edited by Margaret Heaton and Helen B. Lewis.
The reorganized and updated 1962 edition, edited by Muriel
Crosby, was sponsored by the National Council of Teachers of
English, the American Council on Education, and the National
Conference of Christians and Jews. This fifth edition carries on
the mission to extend sensitivity towards people and their values,
and thereby to better human relations through the appreciation of
books by young people. The primary criterion has been "most
pertinent content," even though some choices are not of superior
literary merit. The titles with comprehensive annotations are
organized around four principal themes, with their own subdivisions: "Creating a Positive Self-Image"; "Living with Others";
"Appreciating Different Cultures"; "Coping with Change." Each
is introduced by a bibliographical essay, and James Baldwin's
stimulating essay Understanding One's Self precedes the whole.
Within each subdivision titles are grouped academically by level.
Choice of titles and treatment give primary consideration to the

needs of the English teacher, and the listed sources of selection show adherence to the conventional works available to librarians and teachers. There is some defensiveness about certain titles, but the work well serves its objectives in approach and high level of coverage of all levels of publishing. Its long tradition of usefulness confirms its value as an important tool for librarians and parents as well as teachers.

Robertson, Catherine C., ed. Books for Youth: A Guide for Teen-Age Readers. 3rd ed. Toronto: Toronto Public Libraries, 1966. 154p.
 First published in 1940, with a second edition in 1956, this annotated selection, "much enlarged" by a group of young people's librarians on the staff of the Toronto Public Library, parallels the library's Books for Boys and Girls, edited by Marguerite Bagshaw. It is not confined to Canadian books, but is a general aid to book selection with a balance of new and old. The compilers aimed to select books that "bring challenges, widen horizons, stimulate thought, and encourage reading for enjoyment." Out-of-print titles and textbooks were excluded. Arranged in twenty conventional types of literature or subject interest categories, titles carry a sentence of annotation which "attempts to give succinctly the thesis or plot." Occasional notations indicate "senior" or "junior" suitability. There are some black-and-white illustrations. When last published, this was a sound working list for young people's librarians, who could rely on selected titles as being both worth reading and popular with young adults.

Robinson, Evelyn Rose, ed. Readings About Children's Literature. New York: McKay, 1966. 431p.
 Selected articles and extracts from books by writers on children's literature were chosen primarily for students. They are grouped in nine categories, covering the child and his reading, evaluation and selection, history and trends, illustration, the young child, imaginative tales, fiction, and nonfiction. The coverage of this anthology is competent and the selection useful. The articles comment on many appropriate titles.

Rogers, Margaret. English for Immigrant Children. 2nd ed. London: National Book League, 1969. 44p.
 Catering to the needs of children of immigrant groups in Britain who are entering the school system, this list of 500 items includes material for teachers and readers and other useful books in easy English for student use. First published in 1966; both editions accompanied NBL traveling exhibits.

Rollins, Charlemae, ed. We Build Together: A Reader's Guide to Negro Life and Literature for Elementary and High School Use.

3rd ed., rev. Champaign, Ill.: National Council of Teachers of English, 1967. 71p.

First published in 1941, and enlarged in 1948, this work seeks to provide a list of good books for young people that would present Negroes as human beings and not as stereotypes. This edition, compiled with the assistance of Augusta Baker and others, has been completely rewritten as a result of the vast changes that have occurred in the role of the Negro socially and in children's literature. The chairman of the revision committee, herself a biographer and anthologist, comments on these changes in the introduction. Over 200 titles, each with a carefully written descriptive and critical annotation, are arranged in large subject groups, with an opening section on picture books and easy-to-read books.

Rollock, Barbara. The Black Experience in Children's Books. New York: New York Public Library, 1974. 122p.

Designed to make known books that show an unbiased view of life for blacks, this list compiled by the staff of the New York Public Library was one of the very first bibliographies of its kind for children. The titles listed have grown along with the rapid increase of publication in this area since the first edition of 1949, which was entitled Books about Negro Life for Children. Further editions under that title appeared in 1957, 1961, 1963, 1965, and in 1971 with a new title and edited by Augusta Baker. Over 300 titles, each with a paragraph of descriptive annotation, are arranged by subject, topic, or by geographical area. This selection not only has served well its intended younger audience from kindergarten to age 12, but also constitutes an excellent selection source for librarians, as well as supplying valuable material for sociological study. Another edition appeared in 1979. A companion volume, The Black Experience in Children's Audiovisual Materials, was published in 1973 and reissued in 1979.

Roos, Jean Carolyn. Patterns in Reading: An Annotated Book List for Young Adults. 2nd ed. Chicago: American Library Assn., 1961. 172p.

The aim of this book is to stimulate and develop the reading of young people. A predecessor of this volume appeared in 1938, and a revised edition in 1947 under the title By Way of Introduction: A Book List for Young People. The present title, subtitled . . . For Young People, appeared in 1954. Published under the joint sponsorship of the American Library Association, the National Education Association, and the National Council of Teachers of English, it was prepared by a committee chaired by the present author and edited by Frances M. Grim. This enlarged edition caters to young adults and those who work with them. 1,600 titles are listed with brief descriptive notes under seventy-five informally designated categories that represent adolescent interests. Within these, books which are easier to read are placed first and the progressively more difficult later in the listing. This "step approach," which was also employed in the earlier editions, made the book very influential among teachers and librarians catering for adolescents. Its selections and ratings, which include traditional titles, remain of interest; though, after twenty additional years of publishing for young people, caution will dictate many substitutions and additions.

Root, Betty, and Brownhill, Sue. Starting Point: Books for the Illiterate Adult and Older Reluctant Reader. London: National Book League, 1975. 37p.
 Intended for teachers of adult illiterates, this title is useful too for adolescents, because inevitably this list has had to be selected from books written for teenagers and young adults. Presupposing a reading age of at least seven years, the selector has provided a reading age notation. The emphasis is on series, each of which has an introductory annotation.

Root, Shelton L., ed. Adventuring with Books: 2,400 Titles for Pre-K-Grade 8. 3rd ed. New York: Citation, 1973. 395p.
 This annotated bibliography is "intended to serve as a guide to any adult, be he teacher, layman, or librarian, or parent, who is interested in selecting books for children of preschool age through 8th grade." It was preceded by editions in 1950, edited by Margaret M. Clark, and 1966, edited by Elizabeth Guilfoile and published by the New American Library, both limited to elementary grades. Each was prepared by committees of the National Council of Teachers of English for the council, which cooperated with commercial publishers beginning with the second edition. Contents are arranged in twelve broad subject topics. Descriptive annotations prepared by English teachers on the committee are in a readable style and specify the appropriate age span. Out-of-print titles are excluded. Because of the good balance, the emphasis on books written for children which children will enjoy, and thorough indexing, the selection fulfills its objective as a helpful tool in bringing children and books together. Due to the prestigious sponsorship and wide distribution, the list has proved an influential one with teachers. A new edition appeared in 1977.

Roscoe, Sydney. John Newbery and His Successors, 1740-1814: A Bibliography. Wormley, Hertfordshire, Eng.: Five Owls Pr., 1973. 461p.
 This is an alphabetical listing, with title-page transcriptions and collations of children's books published by the famous eighteenth-century bookseller and the members of his family who succeeded him. There is a long introduction about the Newbery

family and business. Appended is a chronological list of dated and datable books and a note on bindings. Location symbols of copies are given. Illustrations reproduce pages and pictures from the books.

Rosenbach, Abraham S. W. Early American Children's Books: With Bibliographical Descriptions of the Books in His Private Collection. New York: Kraus, 1966. 354p.

A photofacsimile of the original Southworth Anthoensen Press edition of 1933, describing 816 books in the famous antiquarian bookseller's private collection ranging in date from 1682 to 1836, this scholarly bibliography is one of the classic collections in the field. Now in the Free Library of Philadelphia, it forms a valuable reference source. Entries are arranged chronologically with full bibliographical descriptions and collations, and many items have title pages and illustrations reproduced. The delightful introduction by "Rosy" gives an informative account of the history and character of early American publication for children, with observations about his own collecting activities. There is also an entertaining foreword by A. Edward Newton. Another reprint in paperback was published by Dover in 1971.

Rosenberg, Judith K., and Rosenberg, Kenyon C. Young People's Literature in Series: Fiction: An Annotated Bibliographical Guide. Littleton, Colo.: Libraries Unlimited, 1972. 176p.

Intended as a book selection tool to aid in guiding young people's reading, over 1,400 titles are evaluated in terms of plot, depth and believability of characterization, reading level, style, and format. The vast majority are specifically for young people, although a few suitable adult titles are included. Books for kindergarten through grade 2 have been excluded, and series of "consistently low quality" are omitted. The definition is generous enough to include some sequels, and it is claimed all existing series that are relevant are covered. Out-of-print titles are included, but only up to 1955. Arrangement is alphabetical, series and title access being provided through indexes. A combined new edition of this and the author's similar nonfiction guide appeared in 1977.

——. Young People's Literature in Series: Publishers' and Non-Fiction Series: An Annotated Bibliographical Guide. Littleton, Colo.: Libraries Unlimited, 1973. 280p.

Publishers' series that comprise more than one author, share a basic theme, and are produced in a common format, as well as nonfiction, are included. Coverage ranges from grades 3 to 12, and includes publications through 1972. A combined edition of this and the authors' fiction guide appeared in 1977, and it furnishes very useful bibliographical information for school and young people's libraries, as well as providing genuinely critical annotations for selection purposes.

Ross, Eulalie Steinmetz. The Spirited Life: Bertha Mahoney Miller and Children's Books. Boston: Horn Book, 1973. 274p.
   This inspirational biography relates Miller's life story to her seminal activity with children's literature as a writer and bookseller and, above all, with her contributions to The Horn Book, with its crucial role from the twenties onward in the development of national appreciation of the value of children's books. The bibliographical list of her selected writings was contributed by Virginia Haviland.

Rue, Eloise et al. America Past and Present: An Annotated Bibliography of Children's Stories for Students, Teachers, and Librarians. New York: Wilson, 1948. 80p.
   Compiled thirty years ago by a class of teacher-librarians at Chicago Teachers College under the direction of Eloise Rue, this selection retains some historic interest, as well as including a few titles still appropriate and available for young readers.

St. John, Judith. The Osborne Collection of Early Children's Books, 1566-1910: A Catalogue. 2 vols. Toronto: Univ. of Toronto Pr., 1966, 1975. 1138p.
   Prepared at Boys and Girls House, part of the Toronto Public Library, with the aid of many members of its staff, the first volume forms a bibliographical record of some 3,000 volumes of the Osborne Collection of early English-language children's books housed there. It was reprinted photolithographically with minor corrections in 1966 and 1975. The introduction by the donor, Edgar Osborne, describes how the collection developed, his standards of collecting, and the reasons for his gift to Toronto. He also comments on the principal types of publishing for children until the end of the Edwardian era. The preface by Jean Thomson, Head of the Boys and Girls Division, explains its scope, "representing all types and phases of writing for children of the English-speaking world," and its arrangement, alphabetically within subject or "reading interest" groups. These correspond approximately to the traditional areas of publishing for children in a broadly chronological sequence; fiction being divided into two groups at 1850. All entries transcribe from the wording of the title page; the earliest items receiving the fullest transcription. Collations and description of illustrations are provided, with a paragraph of historical and bibliographical annotation. Appendix and index material includes biographies of publishers, booksellers and printers, a list of illustrators and engravers, and a chronological list of imprints before 1800, besides a full general index. The carefully selected illustrations, including color and

black-and-white plates and line blocks in the text, are excellent in quality.

The second volume, prepared by the compiler with the assistance of Dana Tenny and Hazel I. MacTaggart, reflects the high level of new acquisitions, only recording titles not represented in volume 1. A third volume is planned to cover boys' periodicals and "penny dreadfuls." Because of the quality and quantity of the collection and the meticulous scholarship of the catalog, this must remain a major bibliographical source for rare book libraries, collectors, dealers, and all students of the history of children's literature.

Salvatore, Dominic, ed. The Paperback Goes to School. New York: Bureau of Independent Publishers and Distributors, 1965-72. Annual.

Paperback wholesalers made this unannotated catalog available free since the late 1940s, with the subtitle "A Selected List of High and Junior High School Titles." It achieved increased value as a selection tool with the 1964-65 edition that was edited by a joint committee of the National Education Committee and the American Association of School Librarians. This increased the volume count to 3,500, in an arrangement by subject, author, and title, within separate sections for elementary and high-school use. Succeeding editions were popular with teachers and school librarians, but they ceased with the 1972 issue.

Saretsky, Augusta, and Schulman, Elias. A Guide to Jewish Juvenile Literature. Rev. ed. New York: Jewish Education Committee Pr., 1968. 70p.

First published in 1964, this guide "for parents who have an appreciation of Jewish cultural values and a desire for their children to read Jewish books" is also intended for use by librarians of congregations, schools, and centers. It will also be suggestive to those choosing books for other types of young people's libraries. One or two sentences describe each of the titles, which are arranged alphabetically within age groups, 2-5, 5-8, 8-11, 11-13, and 13+.

Saxby, Henry Maurice. A History of Australian Children's Literature 1841-1941. Sydney: Wentworth, 1969. 212p.

Confined in the main to works of fiction written specifically for children and young people, this is a first attempt to compile a detailed history of Australian children's books. The term Australian is interpreted fairly widely. Three periods are identified: up to 1900; from 1900 to 1918; and from 1918 to 1941. Books and authors are examined against the social background and the publishing scene. A select bibliography of Australian children's books published from 1841 to 1941 is added. Half-tone plates supplement the text with reproductions of book illustrations. The story is continued in the author's A History of Australian Children's Literature 1941-1970 (1971).

——. A History of Australian Children's Literature 1941-1970. With supplementary chapters by Marjorie Cotton. Sydney: Wentworth, 1971. 316p.

This brings up to date the record in the author's earlier volume, and provides a guide to those discovering that there is a considerable body of Australian literature for children. The pattern of development in relation to the literary and educational background is examined under types of publication, such as adventure, family stories, fantasy, birds and beasts, and aborigines. The supplement covers books for the very young child, and "in-between" books. Half-tone plates reproduce illustrations in the books.

Sayers, Frances Clarke. Summoned by Books: Essays and Speeches. New York: Viking, 1965. 173p.

This collection of occasional pieces by a library school faculty member was compiled by a student, Marjeanne Jensen Blinn, and carries a foreword by a colleague, Lawrence Clark Powell. Themes include children's librarians, the telling and writing of tales for children, and the appeal of children's literature. It provides good reading and some valuable insights.

Schaaf, William L. The High School Mathematics Library. 5th ed. Reston, Va.: National Council of Teachers of Mathematics, 1973. 74p.

First published in 1960, with enlarged and updated editions in 1963, 1967, and 1970, this selective subject bibliography is prepared as a guide for high-school librarians, educational administrators, teachers and students, and parents. Some 950 mathematical items are arranged in subject groups and most carry brief annotation. "The present edition remains devoted to the needs of students of average ability, but its scope has been enlarged to cater to mathematically talented and mature students." As did the previous edition, this lays greater emphasis on modern topics such as computers. Material on vocational mathematics has been eliminated; highly specialized, out-of-print, and earlier publications are minimally represented. Other features include a section on professional books for teachers, and a starring system applied to 200 priority items for schools with limited budgets. The determination of the council to publish frequent revisions makes this a reliable and invaluable tool for school libraries, and even college and public libraries can often profit by the insight offered in this difficult area for the layman. The sixth edition appeared in 1976.

Schatzki, Walter. <u>Children's Books, Old and Rare: Catalogue Number One</u>. Detroit: Gale, 1974. 46p.

This is a facsimile reprint of the now-famous antiquarian catalog of early children's books issued in 1941. A new foreword by the author of the original foreword, Leslie Shepard, gives biographical anecdotes of some notable dealers in juvenilia, and the original foreword by this famous bookseller and specialist in the field stimulates the collecting interest in parents, educators, librarians, and even uncles and aunts. Over 200 items in five languages dating from the fifteenth century to 1937 are listed chronologically with scrupulous bibliographical detail and observant notes. Although the individual copies have long since gone to institutional or private buyers, the richness and selectivity of the group make the catalogue a valuable reference source today, and the forty illustrations add to its usefulness.

Schechter, Ilene R., and Bogart, Gary L., eds. <u>Junior High School Library Catalog</u>. 3rd ed. New York: Wilson, 1975. 991p. Supplements, 1976-79.

This title is a classified and annotated index of book titles that has been designed for grades 7 through 9. Mention is made in the preface that two titles in the publisher's Standard Catalog series, the <u>Children's Catalog</u> and the <u>Senior High School Library Catalog</u>, will also be useful in providing a basic collection of print materials for a junior high or middle school. The first edition under the editorship of Rachel Shor and Estelle A. Fidell was published in 1965 in response to the many educational pressures of the era. Since its companion volume, renamed the <u>Senior High School Library Catalog</u>, contained many of the same titles, duplication was one of the first apparent problems. This problem was addressed in the second edition of 1970 by the editors, Estelle A. Fidell and Gary L. Bogart, and by the advisory committee. As all who are familiar with reading and the young recognize, some duplication is inevitable as well as desirable among elementary, junior, and senior high-school grades. The advisory committee, comprised of librarians from various parts of the country, helped to choose the titles that the consultants representing prestigious organizations such as the American Library Association/AASL (American Association of School Librarians) then voted on. This procedure has been standard practice for the titles in the Standard Catalog series over the years. As is also customary, there are no out-of-print titles included. A new edition appears every fifth year (quinquennially) and is kept up-to-date by the publication of annual supplements. These annual supplements are included in the initial purchase price.

There are 3,791 titles and 10,673 analytics in the third edition. Approximately 2,000 books were added in the supplements. Like the publisher's other titles in this series, this newest member title is divided into three sections. Section 1, the classified catalog, uses the abridged Dewey decimal system and cites the book by author under the appropriate class number and Sears's subject headings. This is followed by a brief descriptive evaluation taken from a selection source such as The Horn Book. More than one of these is generally given. Section 2, the analytic key, is the author, title, subject, and analytic single alphabetical listing, which makes this volume especially useful as a reference aid. Section 3 contains a directory of publishers and distributors of materials that appear in the volume.

This aid is valuable for selection and acquisition, for checking, and for reference. As stated by the publisher, this title represents only the core collection and should be supplemented by all but the smallest library. Although some attention has been given to titles that reflect social concerns, the number of inclusions is necessarily tiny in a basic collection as small as this one. In spite of this, the catalog is an important consideration for everyone who deals with or is interested in reading and young people. The fourth edition was published in 1980 under the editorship of Gary L. Bogart and Richard H. Isaacson.

Scherf, Walter. The Best of the Best. New York: Bowker, 1971. 187p.

A bilingual publication of the International Youth Library in Munich, this compilation of the best picture books, children's books and books written for young adults in fifty-seven countries and languages was simultaneously published there under a German title. Books are listed alphabetically by author under each country and, while there are no annotations, illustrator information and appropriate age levels from 3 to 16 are indicated. Highly selective, it is inevitable that there is occasional unevenness of quality and that some countries, particularly those of the Third World and socialist bloc, are underrepresented. But the provision of this wealth of titles makes great strides towards the accessibility of other countries and cultures. Some have been translated; more are fit for translation. Teachers and librarians can use this as a valuable tool for fostering international understanding.

——. Preisgekrönte Kinderbücher. Children's Prize Books. 3rd ed. New York: Bowker, 1969. 238p.

A publication of the International Youth Library in Munich, the third edition of this bilingual international list of literary prizes for children's books was simultaneously published there. Previous editions appeared in 1959 and 1964. The objective is "to foster international comparison in the field of children's literature." Prefaced by the editor's introductory remarks on book prizes, sixty-seven awards, including six international ones, represent twenty-four countries and are listed chronologically in the original language for each country. There are historical notes on the prizes but no annotations for the books. There is no mention of honorary citations. This is a selective listing with many omissions, some obsolete, some not, such as Britain's Carnegie Medal. As far as it goes, the information is valuable for reference and can furnish to the selector the titles of some fine children's books from all over the world.

Schmidt, Nancy J. Children's Books on Africa and Their Authors: An Annotated Bibliography. New York: Africana, 1975. 290p.

An experienced anthropologist here makes an evaluation of children's books about Africa, in terms of the validity of the perspective of Africa which they present. "Only the African content of the books is evaluated here, not whether the books are interesting, attractive or well-written." The definition of children's books is fairly liberal, and serious nonfiction is included. Information about the authors is provided, particularly about their familiarity with Africa. Titles are arranged alphabetically by author with a descriptive and critical assessment that is personal and perceptive. A collection of indexes by series, subject, title, geographic and tribal names enhances the value of this original and significant list.

School Library Books: Non-Fiction. 2nd ed. London: National Book League, 1969. 351p.

A major British list for schools, intended to provide a guide for teachers and librarians buying basic titles for a new school or updating an existing school library, this book was first published in 1965. It accompanied the largest-ever NBL traveling exhibit, and was designed to illustrate the range and quality necessary for a sound nonfiction library for children 7 to 15. Over 2,000 items are arranged by subject according to Dewey. Each entry carries a brief descriptive annotation, a Dewey number, and a number and letter code which indicates reading ability required and interest age. Books for sixth-forms were beyond the scope of selection. Most are British publications, and some out-of-print books are included. The basis for this edition was books remaining in print from the previous edition, but more than half the items appeared in 1966 or later. The fiction complement to the first edition was published in parts in 1966 as School Library Fiction.

School Library Exhibition. 3rd ed. London: National Book League, 1960. 59p.
Additions to Your School Library (supplements), 1962, 1964. 51p., 70p.

Previous similar exhibitions were provided with catalogs in 1956, 1958, and 1959. This edition lists 2,500 books for children of all ages selected from titles submitted by English publishers. All were recommended for use in schools. The first supplement catalogs 664 additional titles published from January 1960 to May

1962; the second includes 785 published for children from age 5 to 15 from June 1962 to December 1963.

School Library Fiction. Part I. Historical Fiction. Part II. Children and Adults. Part III. Mystery and Adventure. Part IV. Fantasy. London: National Book League, 1966. 35p., 39p., 33p., 44p.

The fiction complement to the NBL's School Library Books: Non-Fiction was planned to appear in seven parts, each based on a special exhibition. Three parts, Children of Other Lands, Animal Stories, and After Thirteen: Fiction for Young People are not recorded as having been published. Each part lists between 160 and 220 books selected by a panel of teachers and librarians. The selections provide a wide range of fiction titles published in England for children aged 7-13, who are beyond the picture book stage but who are not ready for adult literature. Each entry carries a short descriptive and evaluative note. As a way of accessing good British writing for this age group, the lists can still be informative.

School Library Journal Book Review, 1968-69 [-1969-70]. New York: Bowker, 1969, 1970. Annual.

Covering the period from the preceding June 1 through May 31, this annual selection from over 2,000 book reviews published each year in School Library Journal provided convenient access to critical assessments of significant children's titles. Within three divisions, picture books, fiction and nonfiction, entries are arranged alphabetically by author in general reading levels from preschool through junior high. A star symbol indicates a book is "excellent in relation to other books of its kind." Many reviews are signed, and correspondence generated by them is reprinted. Books listed in the periodical's round-up columns on beginning books, mysteries, and sports titles, and in the monthly adult-books-for-young-adults section are rearranged in subject categories. As SLJ gives a comprehensive and widely read reviewing service for young people's books, whose reviewers frequently reach a high critical standard, an extended series of these annual compilations would have formed a valuable resource for reference and selection.

Scobbie, H. C. Y., and Neil, Alex. Historical Novels for Use in Schools. Edinburgh: School Library Assn. in Scotland, 1970. 59p.

In-print British publications, but not confined to British history, these titles were found by teachers and librarians to be useful in Scottish schools. Most are intended for pupils from 11 to 16 years, but some are identified as being for younger or older readers. The list is divided into periods and short descriptive annotations are provided.

Scott, Margaret B., ed. Aids to the Selection of Materials for Canadian
     School Libraries. Ottawa: Canadian Library Assn., 1971. 16p.
        This short list was compiled by the Selection Aids Committee of
     the Canadian School Library Association. Titles published outside
     Canada are not excluded, and adult aids useful for Canadian
     schools are also listed. Items with brief descriptive annotations
     are arranged alphabetically within sections that include general
     lists, subject and specialist lists, current reviewing periodicals,
     and acquisition tools.

Scott, Marian H. Periodicals for School Libraries: A Guide to Maga-
     zines, Newspapers and Periodical Indexes. Rev. ed. Chicago:
     American Library Assn., 1973. 269p.
        First published under this title in 1969, this work is the succes-
     sor to Laura K. Martin's similar work published by Wilson in 1941,
     Magazines for High Schools, and in 1946 and 1950 as Magazines for
     School Libraries. Intended as a buying guide to periodicals and
     newspapers for school libraries, it is designed to serve the need of
     school librarians and teachers and covers all grade levels from
     kindergarten through grade 12. The basic criteria for selection
     were curricular usefulness and appeal to young people. Out of
     approximately 1,500 periodicals available in the United States
     that were examined, 429 titles were chosen. Introductory mate-
     rial explains the methodology (very specialized journals are ex-
     cluded from its scope) and advises on the use of the list and the use
     of periodicals in schools. Entries are arranged alphabetically,
     with a generous paragraph of descriptive and evaluative informa-
     tion. Appropriate grade level and full publication details are
     given. A listing of periodical indexes, some defunct titles, and a
     subject index is provided. Because of the thorough, practical, and
     liberal approach that includes periodicals like Ramparts and Roll-
     ing Stone that have a following among young adults, this has been
     an extremely useful list for both school libraries and public li-
     braries. A new edition appeared in 1978.

Scriptural and Serious. Topic Booklists. Tunbridge Wells, Eng.: Fen-
     rose, 1974. 59p.
        This title is one of the publisher's series planned to simplify
     research on the children's literature available on given themes.
     Titles, selected from publications then available in Britain, usual-
     ly carry a brief descriptive note. This number arranges Biblical
     stories written for children by character, including novels touch-
     ing on Biblical themes and about saints and missionaries.

Sebasta, Sam Leaton, ed. Ivory, Apes, and Peacocks; The Literature
     Point of View. Newark, Del.: International Reading Assn., 1968.
     148p.
        These proceedings of the association's 1967 annual conference

bring together for the benefit of educators and lay people "the opinions and evidence" of sixteen specialists on the writing, selection, and role of literature in reading instruction. The papers, grouped under "Appreciation and Selection," "Techniques and Types," and "Programs and Projects," include interesting articles by well-known names in the education and children's literature fields. Authors and educators such as May Hill Arbuthnot, Charlotte Huck, and Marjorie Smiley state their viewpoints on fiction and nonfiction for young people and generally discuss titles to illustrate points in their texts. One of the articles by the librarian Sara Fenwick appends additional titles for the use of the reader. Though designed for reading teachers, the book has been read, enjoyed, and used as a book list by others interested in literature for youngsters. Popular at the time of publication, many titles mentioned have withstood the test of time uncommonly well.

——, and Iverson, William J. Literature for Thursday's Child. Chicago: Science Research Associates, 1975. 565p.

Intended to be a practical guide to using books with youngsters in the classroom, this book aims "to present literary teaching techniques while identifying literary types and examples." The author's method is "never to present a theory without also presenting its tested outcome in practice." In so doing, many chapter references to individual titles are related to their use with children of three age groups: early, from early childhood to 8 years; intermediate, 8 to 11; and upper, 11 to young adult. Three parts explore choosing, surveying, and exploring literature. Book qualities sought for include tone, suspense, and values. The illustrations, though liberally provided, are disappointing in quality. This fully indexed, systematic and current presentation contains many suggestions for school librarians, as well as for teachers.

Segal, Stanley S. Help in Reading. 6th ed. London: National Book League, 1975. 41p.

First published in 1962, with subsequent editions in 1964, 1966, 1969, and 1972, this annotated guide to books for backward readers concentrates largely on specially written series publications available in Britain. The criterion for selection was that the content or interest age would be at least two years higher than the reading age, for which a ceiling of nine was adopted. The books are grouped first by reading age and, within that, by interest age. Short annotations provide a basis for teachers' individual choice. In addition to reading schemes and graded series, selected books for the teacher for testing reading and about reading backwardness are included. All editions were included in NBL traveling exhibitions. This complete revision by the author, assisted by Tom Pascoe, includes nearly 600 items.

Selections: Federal Government and International Publications for
    Educators. Ottawa: Information Canada, 1975. 215p.
    Originally published in 1973, after discussions with the Canadi-
    an School Library Association, as Federal Government Publica-
    tions Selected for High School Libraries, and revised and expanded
    in 1974, this selection of Canadian Federal Government publica-
    tions covers the period from January 1967 to April 1975 and
    includes some international publications.   Choice is based on
    school curricula. Titles are annotated to indicate content, gener-
    al format, and depth of treatment. Suggested grade levels are
    indicated in the subject index, which is organized under broad
    curriculum topics.   Because of the large number of Canadian
    Government publications of general interest to Canadians young
    and old, as well as to outsiders, in fields such as sports, health,
    film, zoology, and sociology, the demise of this significant pallia-
    tive to the foreign-produced titles used in Canadian schools is
    regrettable. A French edition was simultaneously published as
    Titres: Choix de Publications Fedérales et Internationales à
    l'Usage des Educateurs.

Sell, Violet; Smith, Dorothy B. Frizzell; O'Hoyt, Ardis Sarff; and
    Bakke, Mildred. Subject Index to Poetry for Children and Young
    People. Chicago: American Library Assn., 1957. 582p.
    This index to poetry printed in collective volumes is intended
    primarily for librarians who deal with children and young people
    from kindergarten through high school, but will also help teachers,
    students, and the general public. About 150 volumes in print at
    the time of publication, with some out-of-print titles found in
    libraries, are included with grade or interest levels noted. Titles
    in Wilson's Children's Catalog and Standard Catalog are coded.
    The subject index to the poems forms the main part of the book,
    headings being adapted from Eloise Rue's Subject Index to Books
    for Intermediate Grades to cover specific topics, universal con-
    cepts, special occasions, and programs, beside persons, places,
    and things. A supplementary volume covering collective volumes
    published from 1957 to 1975 appeared in 1977.

Shaw, Spencer et al. For Storytellers and Storytelling: Bibliographies,
    Materials, and Resource Aids. Chicago: American Library Assn.,
    1968. 30p.
    Prepared by the Storytelling Materials Survey Committee of
    the ALA's Children's Services Division, this booklet had the objec-
    tive of determining availability, assessing quality, and surveying
    needs relating to materials for storytellers in the school, the
    library, or the home. The unannotated entries, covering a wide
    range of media, are arranged in four chapters: "The Storyteller
    Explores His Art in Books," "The Storyteller Discovers His Art in
    Pamphlets and Periodicals," "The Storyteller Interprets His Art

with Multi-Media Aids," and "The Storyteller Pursues His Art in Studies." Eulalie S. Ross's introduction is a practical and literary short course on the general principles of storytelling. Although responsibility for inclusiveness is disclaimed, the very many references that remain useful make this a fundamental bibliographic guide for storytellers. Regrettably, accessibility is impaired by the lack of indexing.

Shedlock, Marie L. The Art of the Storyteller. 2nd ed., reprinted. New York: Dover, 1951. 290p.

This inspirational account of storytelling, originally published in 1915, merited many reprintings and a second edition in 1936. The author wishes to share her vision with others, and reveal the intimate relations between children's instincts and the dramatic presentation of the storytelling art. Arrangement is in three parts: "The Art of Storytelling" essentially gives practical suggestions from the author's point of view; "The Stories" retell eighteen famous stories as examples; and the final bibliography is a list of stories, new to this reissue, prepared by Eulalie Steinmetz, sometime supervisor of storytelling at the New York Public Library. These are arranged within informal genre categories, with citation to the collected volume in which they appear, along with a sentence of evaluative annotation.

Shelley, Hugh. French from Five to Fifteen: A List of French Books and Books on France for School Libraries. London: School Library Assn., 1962. 30p.

French and English publications written for or particularly suitable for young people up to the age of 15 make up this list. About 250 items carry short descriptive and critical annotations, and include dictionaries and grammars, picture books, fiction (divided into age groups), and books on subjects and topics.

Sherrard-Smith, Barbara. Read and Find Out: Information Books, 6-9. London: National Book League, 1975. 23p.

This selection concentrates on works of nonfiction likely to give information and pleasure to this age group, open new horizons, and provide new interests. The needs of children varying from tentative beginners to fluent connoisseurs are taken into account. Over a hundred British in-print items cover the arts, hobbies and sports, people and places, science, natural history, and technology. Dictionaries, encyclopedias, and textbooks are omitted. The brief but lively annotations are critical as well as descriptive. A revised edition was published in 1976.

Shields, Agnes, and Hill, Marcia. Challenge: Background Readings for and about the Physically Handicapped, Adults and Children. Reading for Background. New York: Wilson, 1946. 18p.

A pamphlet prepared to provide practical material both for handicapped individuals and for those interested in their welfare, this list includes juvenile books for upper elementary to adult levels. Titles are arranged, with brief descriptive annotation, in four sections: "It's How You Take It," "The Road Back," biography, and fiction. The selections are inspirational and reflect the period's treatment of the handicapped. This has changed significantly over the years; newer publications have effectively superseded those recommended here.

Shute, Nerina. Favourite Books for Boys and Girls: A Book Guide for Parents, Teachers and Children. London: Jarrolds, 1955. 176p.
This guide for parents and teachers is organized into chapters by the type of school in England for which the books are appropriate and the level, from kindergarten to secondary school, including backward readers and advanced students. Appended to each chapter is a lengthy book list divided by topic with descriptive annotations on each of the titles, usually English publications. The text is chatty and anecdotal in style.

Silverman, Judith. Index to Young Readers' Collective Biographies: Elementary and Junior High School Level. 2nd ed. New York: Bowker, 1975. 322p.
To solve "the constant need which faces all librarians working with students to provide short biographical material about specific people or about people in specific fields of work" is the aim of this work. The first edition, published in 1970, had its origin in the author's personal file compiled over years as a children's librarian in a public library and as a junior high-school librarian. The present edition is expanded and updated, adding almost 1,250 biographies and 250 titles, for a total of more than 5,800 biographees and over 700 collective biographies. Listing is inclusive rather than selective, predicating the librarian's own choice from books in their own collections, and some titles are out of print. All are claimed to be suitable for elementary level reading. Two main sections list biographees alphabetically and by subject. The alphabetic section provides dates, nationality, subject field, and a symbol for the collective biography. The subject section lists persons by occupation and nationality, using headings from Sears and Library of Congress lists. Detailed indexing includes collective biographies by title and symbol, subject headings, and publishers. Invaluable for classwork, reading guidance, and personal study, this compilation is an extremely useful aid for public as well as school libraries. An enlarged third edition was published in 1979.

Simmons, Beatrice et al. Paperback Books for Children. New York: Citation, 1972. 130p.

Prepared by a committee on paperback books for elementary schools for the American Association of School Librarians, this bibliography of almost 700 titles with brief descriptive annotations is part of a continuing effort by the AASL to foster the liberal use of paperbacks. While committee members did review titles personally, favorable recommendations were culled from half-a-dozen well-known selection aids such as the Children's Catalog and School Library Journal. Titles were required to have essentially the same content as their hard-bound equivalents. The author arrangement is subdivided under the traditional categories of publishing: picture books, fiction, nonfiction, myths, and poetry, with some guides for adults. While this orthodox selection presented the pick of the crop at the time of compilation, the out-of-print syndrome so prevalent in paperbacks has inevitably reduced its value as a standard buying list for elementary schools today.

Simms, T. H. Citizenship: A Select Book List for the Use of Teachers and School Librarians in Secondary Schools, and for Non-Specialist Students. London: School Library Assn., 1953. 24p.
Intended for the guidance of teachers in all types of British secondary schools, the selection offered in this booklet ranges from very simple introductory books for the use of younger children in the library to advanced works for sixth-form study. Textbooks are excluded. The 225 items are very briefly annotated and arranged in sections by subject.

Sloane, William. Children's Books in England and America in the Seventeenth Century: A History and a Checklist, together with the Young Christian's Library, the First Printed Catalogue of Books for Children. New York: King's Crown Pr., Columbia Univ., 1955. 251p.
This scholarly work documents the lengthy, interesting, and neglected history of children's literature in England and America before its much better-known development in the eighteenth century. Religious, instructional, traditional, and entertaining books are covered, but only if specifically written for children. Two parts provide a history of the literature and its place in the manners and mores of the age, and a chronological checklist of 261 titles from 1557 to 1710, with descriptive annotations, bibliographic references, and locations, but no collations. A facsimile of The Young Christian's Library, the first English catalog of children's books, is reproduced from the Bodleian Library copy. Based on research for a thesis, this readable account is of interest to the social historian as well as the bibliographer.

Smaridge, Norah. Famous Author-Illustrators for Young People. Famous Biographies for Young People. New York: Dodd, 1973. 160p.

The nineteen brief biographies found here include such well-known figures as Roger Duvoisin, Dr. Seuss, Kate Greenaway, Lois Lenski, and Tomi Ungerer. Three are of the last century, the rest of this century. Written in a simple style, information is mainly biographical, but includes critical comment and itemizes titles in the text. A half-tone portrait of each subject is provided. A companion volume in the same series is Laura Benét's Famous Storytellers for Young People.

———. Famous Modern Storytellers for Young People. Famous Biographies for Young People. New York: Dodd, 1969. 121p.
Supplementary to Laura Benét's similar title for earlier authors, this collection of seventeen biographies is actually one of twentieth-century authors, rather than storytellers in the restrictive sense. A number are adult authors whose books are of interest to young people, in addition to children's authors such as A. A. Milne and Hugh Lofting. Half-tone portraits are provided.

Smith, Dora V. Fifty Years of Children's Books, 1910-1960: Trends, Backgrounds, Influences. Champaign, Ill.: National Council of Teachers of English, 1963. 149p.
This is a personal portrayal of outstanding children's literature over a period of changing living, learning, and publishing concepts, based on many years' experience. Five chronological sections cover The Children's Book World of 1910; The Period of Transition, 1910-1925; The Golden Age of Children's Books, 1925-1940; Children's Books in World War II and Beyond, 1940-1949; and Children's Books in a Bursting World, 1950-1960. Many titles are described in the text or referred to in the notes. A list of Significant Books of 1910-1959, arranged by theme and chronologically, gives bibliographical details and grade levels. A supplementary bibliography of other books mentioned, including earlier ones, indicates original and recommended editions. Reproductions of illustrations from the books enhance an attractive format. This helpful account has almost become a standard text, and is especially good for the earlier years.

Smith, Irene. A History of the Newbery and Caldecott Medals. New York: Viking, 1957. 143p.
An account of the two most prestigious American annual prizes in children's literature, based on the recollections of many people, is offered here. Although an official and definitive biography of the originator, Frederic G. Melcher, postdates this slim volume, it cannot compare in relating the bookman to children's books any more faithfully or engagingly. For this alone, the volume must stand. In its annual listing of awards and prizes, the Children's Book Council has superseded the book lists appended here of winners and runners-up.

Smith, James Steel. <u>A Critical Approach to Children's Literature.</u>
New York: McGraw, 1967. 442p.

A state college professor of English literature, who is also a
poet, has written this consideration of children's literature as
literature, stating it to be "susceptible of serious critical analysis
and understanding." An objective is to apply a series of critical
questions as an exercise in method to assess the sense and sensibil-
ity of children's books. A long, personal treatment that also
covers much of the ground of more conventional textbooks, the
volume has been criticized as not fulfilling the promise implied in
its title. However, the treatment of some of the topics examined,
such as children's poetry, is helpful, and interesting comparisons
are made between adult and children's literature. Bibliographical
and other references are plentiful.

Smith, Janet Adam. <u>Children's Illustrated Books.</u> Britain in Pictures.
London: Collins, 1948. 49p.

One in a publisher's series notable for reproductions of early
paintings and prints in black and white and color, this volume
reprints pages from early children's books and modern illustrations. This descriptive and perceptive historical survey, from an
aesthetic standpoint, ranges from the seventeenth to the twentieth century.

Smith, Lillian Helena. <u>The Unreluctant Years: A Critical Approach to
Children's Literature.</u> Chicago: American Library Assn., 1953.
193p.

Not intended as an exhaustive guide to book selection, this
overview considers children's books as literature and indicates the
signposts that point to recognition of those qualities that are basic
in good writing for children. The works chosen for analysis in the
text are a personal choice from many titles judged of permanent
quality, and are not intended as a recommended listing of suitable
books. Contents include "The Case for Children's Literature,"
"The Lineage of Children's Literature," and "An Approach to
Criticism," as well as chapters dealing with traditional themes
and types. Each chapter is followed by a brief listing of supplementary reading. The author's long experience at the head of the
Toronto Public Library's Boys' and Girls' House, with its outstanding collections of children's books, both early and more recent,
gives a special quality to the erudition, as well as the charm, that
has made this a favorite text for library schools.

Snow, Kathleen M., and Hauck, Philomena. <u>Canadian Materials for
Schools.</u> Toronto: McClelland, 1970. 200p.

This description of material useful for Canadian teachers and
school librarians is presented in chapter form. Many titles are
cited in the text. Chapters cover newspapers and periodicals,

government publications, Canadian literature and elementary materials, and audiovisual materials. Canadian publishing is also treated. A decade of active publication will require substantial updating.

Southall, Ivan. A Journey of Discovery on Writing for Children. Kestrel Books. Harmondsworth, Middlesex, Eng.: Penguin, 1975. 102p.

The author of many children's books and works of popular fiction has here collected six of his lectures, written over a period of years as a personal expression rather than as a handbook or manual. Topics include the book-creation process, the theme of adventure, and the debatable existence of a boundary between literature for children and for adults.

Spache, George Daniel. Good Reading for Poor Readers. 9th ed., rev. Champaign, Ill.: Garrard, 1974. 303p.

This standard list of books for children experiencing reading difficulties was compiled by the originator of the Spache readability formula. The genesis of its long publication history goes back to a 1941 pamphlet, Books for Youth Who Dislike Reading, by Russell Slater. Increasingly enlarged listings under the present title appeared in 1954, 1960, 1964, 1966, 1968, 1970, and 1972, demonstrating its acceptance by educators. Representing "an effort to go beyond the general prescriptions of lists of good books" that points out many factors which influence children's reaction to books, its objective is to aid reading teachers to select more effectively for children experiencing reading difficulties. This edition adds several hundred books for poor readers not noted before and aims to keep abreast of the materials explosion. Introductory chapters indicate many factors which influence children's reactions to books, and include discussions of "The Right Book for the Right Child"; "Choosing the Right Type of Book"; "Using Books to Help Solve Children's Problems"; and "Estimating Readability." Following chapters list materials, including trade books, textbooks, serials and series, as well as programmed materials, indexes, reading lists, and resources for teachers of the disadvantaged, including new instructional tools. Brief annotations are supplemented by recommendations of grade, reading, and interest levels. While, inevitably perhaps, some series and adaptations listed are mediocre, the standard of selectivity of the trade books, categorized in type and topical groupings, provides a valuable checklist for librarians. An appendix explains in detail the Spache readability formula, which has been completely revised in terms of current vocabulary usage by primary pupils, with new tables for computation. As this extensive and comprehensive listing has been refined over a long period, it remains a valuable and practical tool for all who deal with this difficult group of readers. A new edition appeared in 1978.

——. Good Reading for the Disadvantaged Reader: Multi-Ethnic Resources. Rev. ed. Champaign, Ill.: Garrard, 1975. 311p.
Previously published in 1970, this book is concerned with ways of improving reading instruction among disadvantaged minority groups, and is addressed to reading specialists. Selection priority is placed on "true, realistic, integrated stories that these groups can identify with." Chapters cover black Americans, American Indians, Eskimos, Mexican Americans, Orientals, and Puerto Ricans, as well as the inner city and migrant workers. These include extensive listings of titles with short descriptive annotations.

Spain, Frances Lander. The Contents of the Basket, and Other Papers on Children's Books and Reading. New York: New York Public Library, 1960. 83p.
A collection of lectures given at the New York Public Library from 1954 to 1960, edited by the coordinator of Children's Services, these were addressed to an adult audience generally or professionally interested in children's literature or library work for children. In addition to the five lectures by children's librarians, authors, and editors, four similar addresses are included for the further clarification they bring the subject of children's books and reading.

Spain, Frances Lander, ed. Reading without Boundaries: Essays Presented to Anne Carroll Moore on the Occasion of the 50th Anniversary of the Inauguration of Library Service to Children at the New York Public Library. New York: New York Public Library, 1956. 104p.
This compilation of sixteen articles written by friends of Anne Carroll Moore and dedicated to the first supervisor of Children's Work at the New York Public Library provides profitable reading to all interested in children and the books they read. Many titles of children's books, past and present, receive comment in the text. Those contributing included editors and illustrators, as well as librarians, and their articles attest the inspiration given by her work. A bibliography of her own publications, mainly articles and book lists, is appended. Each contributor receives a brief biographical sketch in conclusion.

Spengler, Margaret V. A Basic Book Collection for Junior High School. 3rd ed. Chicago: American Library Assn., 1960. 136p.
First published in 1950 and revised in 1956, both editions being compiled by Elsa R. Berner, this standard recommended list was "prepared to serve as an authoritative buying list for first purchases in small- and medium-sized junior high-school libraries."

The intended audience includes librarians and teachers, students in librarianship and teacher-training institutions, and anyone purchasing books for children in grades 7-9. It is suggested that it be supplemented when necessary by the ALA's other two Basic Book Collection tools for elementary and for high schools (see above). Over 1,000 titles are arranged by subject under Dewey decimal number, with subject headings provided. Fiction, short story collections, and periodicals follow. Descriptive annotations indicate, where appropriate, other titles by the authors and notes on physical format. Used as a standard list in its time, it has now been superseded due to changes in school media centers, the tastes of students in this age group, and the titles published for them. But there are many sound recommendations here, especially in fiction, that are still available.

Spieseke, Alice W. World History Book List for High Schools: A Selection for Supplementary Reading. Washington, D.C.: National Council for the Social Studies, 1962. 145p.

A revised and enlarged edition of a bulletin first prepared in 1959 by the council's World History Bibliography Committee, this book was intended primarily for social studies teachers but also for librarians and school administrators. Nearly 500 titles published up to 1962 are annotated in a style suitable for high-school students. Part 1 is arranged alphabetically by author, with the descriptive, sometimes didactic, annotation supplemented by a code identifying fiction, easy reading, or adult reading. Part 2 lists the books according to time period, topic, and geographic area. A title index gives access and provides a useful checking tool. While some titles appeared as far back as the 1930s, the selection remains a valid reading list, if supplemented with later publications.

Sprague, Audrey M. Fiction for the Slow Reader. 2nd ed. London: National Book League, 1973. 24p.

Drawing on the experience of teachers of backward readers, the compiler has in mind a fiction section of a library that will attract reluctant readers, who might be mentally retarded but more usually are hindered by absence from school. Criteria for selection include interesting reading matter, identifiable situations, and an element of magic adventure, combined with short paragraphs and lots of conversation. Attention is also paid to clear print, good illustration, and reasonable cost. Entries, which are available British publications, are divided into three groups: junior (up to 11 years), overlap (between 9 and 13), and secondary (over 11), and are then arranged alphabetically with brief descriptive annotations. First published in 1970, this edition increases the number of items from 86 to 205, and a few more expensive books are included.

Standen, John. <u>The Victorian Age</u>. London: National Book League, 1967. 36p.

A selection of almost 200 items with short annotations, this title is intended to give some idea of the books available to children and teachers on the Victorian age, particularly those relevant to social history. Three divisions comprise Victorian children's books, books for children about Victoria's reign, and books for teachers and sixth-formers. Textbooks and out-of-print items are excluded.

Stanius, Ellen J. <u>Index to Short Biographies for Elementary and Junior High Grades</u>. Metuchen, N.J.: Scarecrow, 1971. 348p.

Over 450 collective biographies, some out of print, are analyzed to assist public and school librarians and teachers in search of short biographies for students in grades 3-5 and 6-8. Part 1 arranges the book titles alphabetically by author and recommends grade level; part 2 lists alphabetically between three and four thousand recent and historical biographees in all fields, with descriptive comments and page references to the collective works. A separate section covers saints. Because of the extensive coverage, this compilation is a useful tool for school and other libraries.

Stensland, Anna Lee. <u>Literature by and about the American Indian: An Annotated Bibliography for Junior and Senior High-School Students</u>. Urbana, Ill.: National Council of Teachers of English, 1973. 208p.

Several hundred appropriate books intended to help English teachers in the classroom are included in this annotated list. Adult and more mature titles are added to those for younger students, stress being placed on myths and legends, poetry, fiction, and biography. Arrangement is by topic, and annotations are critical and descriptive. Information about American Indian authors in included. A number of titles selected as specially suitable for class use carry a full study guide. An essay on stereotypes of Indians and Indian life gives further guidance. This selection forms a valuable introduction to the field.

Sturt, Felicity, ed. <u>Primary School Library Books: An Annotated List</u>. 2nd ed. London: School Library Assn., 1965. 106p.

The Primary Schools Sub-Committee of the School Library Association first compiled this annotated list in 1960. It aims to help primary school teachers select essential books for their school libraries, but is also appropriate for teacher-training colleges, children's librarians, and parents. Selections were made on teachers' recommendations from British titles in print at the beginning of 1964. Part 1 includes imaginative titles for infants, younger juniors, and other juniors; part 2 is a subject breakdown of factual titles. An appendix covers books of simple format produced in series. There are concise descriptive and critical notes on each title, and a full subject and other indexes.

Sullivan, Helen Blair, and Tolman, Lorraine. High Interest-Low Vocabulary Reading Materials: A Selected Booklist. Boston: Boston Univ. School of Education, 1956. 132p.

Reprinted without alteration in 1961 and 1964 from the school's Journal of Education (vol. 139, no. 2, Dec. 1956), this annotated listing is "designed to help teachers, administrators, and librarians to select books for the youngsters who have difficulty reading at one grade level." It is divided into grade levels from one through five, six, and seven; there is a subject arrangement within each division. Brief descriptive annotations suggest curricular use. As most titles date from the forties and fifties, the usefulness of the selection today is limited.

Sutherland, Zena. The Best in Children's Books: The University of Chicago Guide to Children's Literature, 1966-1972. Chicago: Univ. of Chicago Pr., 1973. 484p.

The expertise of the university's prestigious Center for Children's Books has been drawn on for this annotated selection, which achieves its goal of listing the best books for children published between 1966 and 1972. The editor has selected from reviews already published in the Bulletin of the Center for Children's Books, availing herself of the judgmental skills of the members of the Bulletin's advisory committee, comprised of teachers and librarians in public and private schools and libraries. The result is a highly pedigreed list, selected primarily on the basis of literary quality, of 1,400 fiction and nonfiction trade titles written for children, with an occasional adult book of particular interest to adolescents--all furnished with substantial descriptive and critical reviews, and all recommended, with a few titles coded as additional or for the special reader. The arrangement is alphabetical by author, with titles sequentially numbered to facilitate the use of the six indexes provided: title, developmental values, curricular use, reading level, subject and type of literature. The book has not been planned as a balanced list in respect of grade or age group, or of coverage of subject and genre. The introduction includes a discussion of why it is important to select children's books with discrimination. An appendix gives addresses for the American and British publishers of listed books. Constituting a veritable mine of American and some British publications that appeared during the period, the volume has exactly the same tone as its parent periodical, well expressed and balanced, with a full nod to developmental values and literary aspects. However, it is just this sense of balance that makes it mandatory for the user to check other more biased sources. Nevertheless, this can be relied on as one of the best comprehensive lists for its coverage. A supplementary volume covering 1973-78 was published in 1980.

——. History in Children's Books: An Annotated Bibliography for Schools and Libraries. McKinley Bibliographies. Brooklawn, N.J.: McKinley, 1967. 248p.

This annotated list is intended to assist social studies teachers and librarians. Arrangement is by countries and regions of the earth with chronological sub-arrangement, each group being divided into titles for the lower grades (up to 5) and for the upper grades (6, 7, and 8). Brief annotations include coding for biographies, fiction, and easy-to-read books; out-of-print status is noted. This extensive collection still remains a valuable checklist.

Tanyzer, Harold, and Karl, Jean, eds. Reading, Children's Books and Our Pluralistic Society. Perspectives in Reading, no. 16. Newark, Del.: International Reading Assn., 1972. 89p.

These conference papers, prepared by a joint committee of the association and the Children's Book Council, show how children's literature can supply fresh insights into the heritage of minority groups in American society. All cultures receive consideration here, particularly those of blacks and the Spanish-speaking. Nineteen notable contributors from different backgrounds and professions, ranging from psychology to librarianship and including two Newbery award winners, focus on a wide range of minority experiences. The two editors respectively supply an introductory overview and a summation. Dramatic changes have been taking place in this field but these papers, often urgent and eloquent, retain their significance.

Tappaan, Beth. Children's Books around the Year: A Handbook of Practical Suggestions for Teachers, Librarians and Booksellers. New York: Children's Book Council, 1945. 128p.

This manual from a book-trade organization aimed to stimulate children's reading and the sale of books to schools, libraries, and homes. Many suggestions cover topics such as Book Week, book fairs, exhibits and displays, and library and school activities such as parades, projects, and storytelling. Although its themes are still familiar, this presentation is now to be read almost as a period piece.

Targ, William, ed. Bibliophile in the Nursery: A Bookman's Treasury of Collector's Lore on Old and Rare Children's Books. Metuchen, N.J.: Scarecrow, 1969. 503p.

This reprints without change the original 1957 edition, published by World. The collectors' classic "attempts to provide a broad range of material--factual and entertaining--relating to the

whole field of children's books of other days and in many places."
Twenty-three essays, mainly on children's literature of the eighteenth and nineteenth centuries, but including a few on the twentieth, are contributed by such well-known figures as Paul Hazard,
Harvey Darton, the Opies, John T. Winterich, Frederic G.
Melcher, Jacob Blanck, and W. H. Bond. An introduction by the
editor addresses book-collecting issues in the field.

Thomison, Dennis, ed. Readings about Adolescent Literature. Metuchen, N.J.: Scarecrow, 1970. 222p.
   The editor of this collection of articles, a library school faculty
member, denies attempting to cover a typical course on literature
for adolescents, but does indicate the problem of providing suffi-
cient text material for that purpose. The selection is intended to
act as a supplement of meaningful articles that will assist in
providing an informational foundation about the field (regarding
adolescence as covering the 7th to the 12th grades). Five parts
cover the adolescent and his reading, fiction, nonfiction, problems
in adolescent literature, and giving a book talk.

Thompson, Elizabeth, ed. Resources for Teaching about the United
Nations. Washington, D.C.: National Education Assn., 1962. 90p.
   Prepared for the association's Committee on International Relations to be of practical help to classroom teachers, this guide
replaces a 1958 edition with a variant title. Chapters in the first
part include background information on the United Nations system and what it does, and material on its specialized agencies.
The second part comprises the annotated bibliography, divided
into categories of publication, including books, pamphlets and
audiovisual materials. As a resource guide with suggestions for
classroom use, this title proved popular when the United Nations
became a frequent curriculum topic, but world events have now
dated the selections.

Thwaite, Mary F. et al. Books for All Time: A Guide to Current
Editions of Classics for Young People. Birmingham, Eng.: Combridge Jackson, 1973. 122p.
   The classics have here been widely interpreted to cover popular
and enduring favorites, but no books first published after 1922
have been included in this list compiled by the North West Branch,
Youth Libraries Group of the Library Association. This selection
lists nearly 600 editions currently available in Britain, with occasional bibliographic and descriptive notes.

——, ed. Children's Books of This Century: A First List of Books
Covering the Years 1899-1956, Chosen for the Library of Chil-
dren's Literature Now Being Formed at Chaucer House. London:
Library Assn., Youth Libraries Section, 1958. 36p.

This listing of over 100 titles in 150 editions, with several periodicals, was the initial choice of a committee forming a study collection to record more important books and trends in publication for children during the current century. A paragraph of annotation is given for each item, and the editor adds an interesting critical introduction.

——. From Primer to Pleasure in Reading: An Introduction to the History of Children's Books in England from the Invention of Printing to 1914, with an Outline of Some Developments in Other Countries. 2nd ed. London: Library Assn., 1972. 338p.

This work is a general survey of the historical development of children's literature in England up to the beginning of the twentieth century. The second edition substantially revises the first, which appeared in 1963 and was reprinted with corrections in 1966. That was concerned with the needs of British students studying for Library Association examinations, and was designed to serve as an introduction to more scholarly and detailed studies. This edition is a substantial and well-produced volume which provides a fuller account for librarians and others seeking enlightenment about the origins and background of early books for children. Broad historical divisions cover the earliest sources in the fifteenth to seventeenth centuries, the "dawn of imagination" in the early Victorian period, and the "flood tide" of later Victorian and Edwardian times. From the beginning of the nineteenth century, attention is paid to the development of themes and the forms of publication for children, rather than to chronological sequence. The revision pushes the chronological limit from 1900 to 1914, although the earlier twentieth century is not treated as fully as the preceding period. The final part, which gives a geographical account of children's books abroad, has been completely rewritten and considerably extended. Half-tone plates and linecuts supplement the text with reproductions of early illustrations and title pages. Appendixes include a chronological list of significant and important works in children's literature from Caxton to the end of the eighteenth century, and a bibliography of works referred to with annotations. This edition was also published in the United States by Horn Book in 1972.

Today's World: An Annotated List. London: National Book League, 1967. 32p.

Published in conjunction with the British Society for International Understanding, to accompany an exhibition designed for school children and teachers interested in recent history and developments all over the world, this pamphlet includes almost two-hundred items, selected as simple and informative, that cover international institutions, history, economics, geography, ideas, religions, science and technology.

Tooze, Ruth. <u>Storytelling</u>. New York: Prentice-Hall, 1959. 268p.

This manual for storytellers contains, in addition to material on the traditions of storytelling and practical techniques and a selection of actual stories and narrative poems, an extensive annotated bibliography of ancient and modern stories for the telling. Traditional stories are arranged by country; modern ones by age level. Sections also cover holidays and special occasions, and a supplementary list of outstanding series of children's classics.

——. <u>Your Children Want to Read: A Guide for Teachers and Parents.</u> Englewood Cliffs, N.J.: Prentice-Hall, 1957. 222p.

An informal treatment of many aspects of the problem of reading from the child's point of view, this work is not a study of children's literature or intended as a textbook for teachers, though much of it is concerned with schools. Chapters discuss the nature and purpose of reading, changing concepts in meeting needs, and books to help children understand and adjust to the physical and social world and to meet emotional needs. Relevant titles are noted in the text, but not indexed. Primarily useful for teachers who were interested in a "good read," today it retains some interest as a sociological discussion of the titles of a previous generation.

Townsend, John Rowe. <u>A Sense of Story: Essays on Contemporary Writers for Children</u>. London: Longmans, 1971. 216p.

The English doyen of children's literature introduces the work of nineteen well-known writers for children in the English language--British, American, and Australian. While biographical and bibliographical details are given with comments by the authors themselves about their books, primarily these essays treat their work in literary terms. This edition was published in the United States by Lippincott in the same year.

——. <u>Written for Children: An Outline of English-Language Children's Literature</u>. Rev. ed. Kestrel Books. Harmondsworth, Middlesex, Eng.: Penguin, 1974. 368p.

Designed to provide a brief and readable account of prose fiction for children from its beginnings to the present day, this is a revised and expanded version of the original 1965 edition, which now includes other English-language works of imagination, not only fiction and not only British. The author makes clear that he has kept to the highways and not strayed in the byways, and has preferred selection to compression. Studying literature, not reading matter, the treatment is proportionately weighed towards current authors and in-print books. Four chronological divisions cover before 1840, 1840-1915, 1915-1945, and after 1945. Within these periods, chapters follow genres and types of reader appeal. Realism receives special treatment, and the differences between

American and British styles of writing are explained. Illustrations, a select bibliography, and a thorough index supplement this personal but authoritative assessment of a wide field.

Tozier, Virginia, ed. The Reading of Youth. Frontiers of Librarianship. Syracuse, N.Y.: Syracuse Univ. Pr., 1960. 28p.
One of the School of Library Science's publication series, this reprints three lectures designed to "contribute to better understanding of the reading of youth," given by guest lecturers to the school. E. Preston Sharp comments on "Reading and the Delinquent Child"; Richard L. Carner on "Reading and the Gifted Youth"; and Julia Losinski on the "Reading of Normal Youth." Observations are principally psychological and sociological; little attention is paid to the qualities of children's literature as such.

Translated Children's Books Offered by Publishers in the U.S.A. 2nd ed. Locust Valley, N.Y.: Storybooks Internatl., 1968. 83p.
A publishers' service for children's books first prepared this list in 1963 for librarians, teachers, students, and the public, as well as publishers and their agents. The catalog lists "all children's books which have been translated from a foreign language and are currently available from publishers in the United States." Adaptations, folk and fairy tales, and paperbacks are excluded. Fifteen languages are covered. Citations mention details of illustration and translation, appropriate age level, and Library of Congress number. The descriptive annotations include references to reviews, but the list is not an evaluative one. The extensive coverage at the time of writing makes it a still valuable source for research or reference.

Trease, Geoffrey. Tales Out of School. 2nd ed. London: Heinemann, 1964. 181p.
This edition of a "personal survey" of literature for young people by a prolific British writer for children has been drastically rewritten since the first publication in 1949, exploring new territory and bringing coverage up to date. Concentrating on twentieth-century British publications, the author seeks to identify general tendencies "as they are discoverable by a single critic." Popular stereotypes and types of publication are shrewdly analyzed from an original standpoint.

Tucker, Joan, and Tucker, Allan. Reading for Enjoyment for 6 to 8 Year Olds. 2nd ed. London: Children's Book News, 1975. 30p.
The second in the series--see Moss, . . . 2 to 5 Year Olds--the purpose of this list is to find the right book to encourage reading by children who are just beginning to read, as well as look at picture books. Emphasis is on narrative and on books the family

would like to own. About 125 items are arranged alphabetically with annotations. This work was first compiled by Brian Alderson in 1970. A third edition was published in 1977.

Tuer, Andrew White. Pages and Pictures from Forgotten Children's Books. Detroit: Singing Tree, 1969. 510p.
   This photolithographic reissue of the original Leadenhall Press edition, published in London in 1898-99, presents a collection of half-tone reproductions of illustrations and type-facsimiles of pages from British children's books of the early nineteenth century, chosen for their quaintness or unconscious humor. A similar reprint was published in New York by Benjamin Blom in 1968.

Turner, Ernest Sackville. Boys Will Be Boys: The Story of Sweeney Todd, Deadwood Dick, Sexton Blake, Billy Bunter, Dick Barton, et al. 3rd ed. London: Joseph, 1975. 280p.
   Described as a backward plunge into the new mythology of boyhood idols from Dick Turpin on, this refresher course for the sentimental reader is a detailed historical and critical account of a socially significant branch of nineteenth- and twentieth-century literature for boys. Popular rather than scholarly in tone, it handles a largely British content, but there are substantial American references. First published in 1948 and enlarged in 1957, this third edition has been revised and updated.

Ullom, Judith C. Folklore of the North American Indians: An Annotated Bibliography. Washington: Library of Congress, 1969. 126p.
   Not restricted to materials for young people, this select list includes "much that is important to children for their reading and to storytellers for their repertoires." The foreword is by Virginia Haviland, head of the library's Children's Book Section. Coverage, which is not intended to be fully comprehensive, includes North America north of Mexico, and entries are grouped under eleven culture areas including the Eskimo. Library of Congress call numbers and bibliographical references are provided. The section on general background includes "the primitive folktale," children's anthologies, and bibliographies besides other studies not specifically oriented to one area. The extensive annotation for each entry is both descriptive and evaluative. Many illustrations add to the attraction of this valuable source for scholars, teachers, librarians, and interested lay people.

United States. Library of Congress. Children's Book Section. Americana in Children's Books: Rarities from the 18th and 19th Centuries. Washington, D.C.: Library of Congress, 1974. 28p.
   The catalog of an exhibition held in the rare book room of the Library of Congress, the forty-nine items included were chosen and annotated by the Children's Book Section, whose head, Virgin-

ia Haviland, contributed a preface. They show a "small sampling of such riches published up to 1900" drawn chiefly from the large juvenilia collection in the Library of Congress's rare book holdings. The selection illustrates the early ties to English publishing, the growth of American publishers, and the contribution of nineteenth-century American magazines for girls and boys. Sections include: "Instructive and Improving Works"; "Early Rhymes and Curiosities"; "Later Songs and Verses"; and "Famous Fiction in First Editions." The paragraphs of descriptive and historical annotation give this attractive illustrated booklet reference value to collectors and historians of children's literature.

——. Rare Book Division. Children's Books in the Rare Book Division of the Library of Congress; Author/Title and Chronological Catalogs. Totowa, N.J.: Rowman, 1975. 2 vols. 890p., 493p.
   For the historian of children's literature, a complete record of titles must, of course, remain a bibliographical dream, and even for American publications in the national library, cataloging practices past and present are technically incapable of isolating the genre and demonstrating its holdings in the area comprehensively. This listing of 15,000 titles, American and foreign, only includes those in the rare book division's special collection of children's books, with the very important addition of 1,000 more from other collections in the division. Therefore, it cannot represent all American children's books, or all early children's books, or all important children's books from the literary or artistic standpoint. But it is a mine for the researcher to start with, approachable from the main entry standpoint in one volume, and a year-by-year arrangement in the other. The collection is strongest for American imprints of the latter half of the nineteenth century, has important but proportionately less significant early holdings, English and European as well as American, and a more selective approach to twentieth-century output. In spite of these deficiencies, this massive list remains indispensable for the scholar and the student, as well as the collector and the book dealer. The researcher can supplement its inclusions with the Free Library of Philadelphia's typescript Checklist of Children's Books 1837-1876 (1975), regrettably again only a partial list of that library's distinguished holdings in the field.

University of Chicago. Library. Science in Nineteenth Century Children's Books: An Exhibition Based on the Encyclopaedia Britannica Historical Collection of Books for Children. Chicago: The Library, 1966. 19p.
   This is an annotated catalog of 100 books on display in the Harper Memorial Library during the university's seventy-fifth anniversary year. The exhibit was arranged to demonstrate the relationship of children's books published in America and England

to contemporaneous scientific and technical developments. Titles are arranged chronologically within five topics: The beginning of science books for children, science as a source of salvation and moral behavior, science as a source of knowledge about the world, science as a source of progress, and science as a source of conflict.

University of Minnesota. Library Services Institute for Minnesota Indians. American Indians: An Annotated Bibliography of Selected Library Resources. Minneapolis: Univ. of Minnesota, 1970. 171p.

An annotated bibliography, with a special but not exclusive emphasis on Minnesota Indians, prepared by participants in the institute, including twenty-eight librarians. Five hundred entries were selected for reader appeal and artistic quality as well as for potential contribution to the study of American Indians. Descriptive annotation often quotes from review sources. A graded arrangement from elementary through senior high school is provided. Besides books in the university's Kerlan collection, pamphlets, periodicals, pictorial, and audiovisual materials are included. Supplementary lists cover local arts and crafts and Indian organizations in the United States. The general nature of this substantial checklist makes it of more than local interest, and it identifies much hard-to-find material.

University Press Books for Secondary School Libraries. New York: Assn. of American Univ. Presses, 1967- . Annual.

The original edition of this briefly annotated selection for young people from the publications of the about seventy North American university presses appeared in 1966 under the title University Press Books for Young Adults Selected by High School and Young Adult Librarians. The revised title represents the selections of a committee of five from the members' annual output reviewed in the journal Scholarly Books in America. These choices include books which should find a place on the shelves of high-school libraries as being of interest to high-school faculty, gifted readers, or students delving with some depth into special subjects. Some are interpretations for the intelligent young adult--or adult--of the fruits of scholarly and scientific research.

Van Orden, Phyllis, ed., assisted by Mary V. Gaver. The Elementary School Library Collection: A Guide to Books and Other Media, Phases 1-2-3. 9th ed. New Brunswick, N.J.: Brodart, 1974. 778p. Supplement, 1975, 139p.

The titles in this well-recognized catalog represent those that should be in a media center. Phase 1 titles indicate the media that should be available for an opening day collection: priority purchase items. Phases 2 and 3 list titles that are considered important in the order in which subsequent monies allow. The work is designed to make it easier for librarians and teachers in K-6 schools to know which media to choose.

Under the general editorship of Mary Virginia Gaver from its inception in 1965 to the eighth edition in 1973, this title has been an annual, accompanied by supplements for some volumes. There were supplements issued in 1966, 1967, and 1968 (issued as the 1969 annual issue). In 1970, with the publication of the fifth edition, the editors were listed as Mary V. Gaver and Dorothy Fix and remained through the eighth edition at which time the present editor took over. Mary V. Gaver, who had retired, contributed guidance and direction.

The ninth edition was issued in 1974 and its supplement appeared in 1975. It is based, as were its predecessors, on the work of an extensive advisory committee who set the selection policy, as well as a selection committee who implemented that policy by writing the brief annotations after evaluating and reevaluating former works for description on a systematic basis. Overall, the classified catalog arrangement permits the option of in-house cataloging for small institutions, while annotations that are useful are given. A notation that indicates whether the item should be considered for Phase 1, 2, or 3 is listed together with an interest level symbol and a reading level symbol, based on the Fry readability scale. Prices are also included.

This large work has an extensive preface that explains the policies; credits the many individuals who were members of the committees and otherwise involved; states clearly and in detail the selection policy which pays particular attention to curricular interests, new social developments, and specific areas in the collection. The gold-star list which consists of special Phase 1 recommendations also appears here. This is a unique feature of ESLC and is considered both basic and essential by the editor. To complete this preface, a directory of publishers, producers, and distributors whose materials appear in the volume and an explanation of the classification principles that are used appear.

Three sections follow the preface. Section 1 is the classified catalog containing the citations and annotations. These entries appear by author under the headings: reference, nonfiction; fiction; easy; periodicals; and professional tools. Audiovisual materials are integrated with books and other material. This section makes up the body of the work. Section 2 contains three indexes: author, title, and subject. These indexes make it easy to find a specific item under the appropriate number in the DDC number in the classified listing in Section 1. Section 3 contains the appendixes: media for preschool children; books; and books for independent reading. The first edition listed approximately 5,000 titles; this ninth edition lists about 10,000.

The ninth edition supplement, published in 1975, is in effect the annual volume of ESLC for 1975 and noteworthy for several reasons. The changeover of editors and the amount of work no doubt interfered with the usual orderly annual issue of editions since 1965. In addition, this supplement explains that it would be impractical, if not impossible, to go back prior to the fifth edition (1970) when the revised Spache readability formula was used, to make the adjustment of lowering the readability of each entry by one or two grade levels according to the newly used Fry formula. Also, no Spanish-language material is included, on the assumption that there are many dialects used throughout various parts of the country. Although only thirty-seven gold-star items appear, one must remember that this volume is a hybrid issue: a supplement that has assumed annual status. The rest of the volume is similar to the ninth edition in format.

This aid met almost immediate universal acceptance. It has attained this position because of its realistic three phase project to get materials into a media center and because it integrates many media during the selection process. Its concern with school curriculum has also served it and its users well. Unfortunately it is not as perfect as the practicing librarian would like, e.g., it doesn't cover all media. However, it is indispensable for those who deal with grades K-6 and is highly recommended to teachers and librarians as a selection aid.

The tenth edition was published in 1976 under the editorship of Lois Winkel and continues to date. In 1977, with the publication of the eleventh edition, ESLC became a biennial.

Victoria and Albert Museum. Library. Victorian Children's Books: Selected from the Library of the Victoria and Albert Museum, London. An Exhibition at the Bibliothèque Royale, Brussels, 29 September-13 November 1973. London: National Book League, 1973. 107p.

This is an exhibition catalog of selected items from a famous collection assembled over the last century to illustrate the artistic and technical qualities of children's publication. Entries are annotated to reflect those aspects of the books. Pages of many of these are reproduced on a large scale. The introduction by the compiler, Irene Whalley, is a brief survey of the field.

Viguers, Ruth Hill. Margin for Surprise: About Books, Children and Librarians. Boston: Little, 1964. 175p.

Several times reprinted, including an English publication (London: Constable, 1966), this collection of nine essays by a veteran's librarian and editor of The Horn Book magazine is organized under three themes: The Books; The Librarians; and The Children. Most originated as talks delivered to librarians; some appeared in The Horn Book. The title essay, first given as the Anne Carroll Moore

lecture at the New York Public Library, has as a subtitle, "Reflections on the Pursuit of Excellence in Books for Children," which
sums up the whole. Comments on children's titles are found
throughout the text, and a list of references and an author-title
index make these accessible. Experience and inspiration blend in
making this a stimulating volume to other lovers of children's
literature, as well as librarians.

Vita, Susan H. Books on Conservation and Environment for Youth
   Libraries. Washington, D.C.: Govt. Print. Off., 1971. 27p.
      This unannotated buying guide for librarians serving young
   adults from 15 to 18 years of age was compiled for the Office of
   Library Services in the U.S. Department of the Interior. Over one
   hundred nonfiction entries are arranged under subjects such as
   conservation, environmental science, pollution, ecology, and the
   natural history of the United States. Costly and out-of-print
   items have been omitted; paperbacks are preferred. Items to be
   considered for first purchase are starred. More titles on these
   topics will now be available to add to the still appropriate ones
   recommended in this useful list.

Voysey, A. Farming and Kindred Subjects: An Annotated List of Books
   for Readers of Eleven to Fifteen Years. London: School Library
   Assn., 1951. 24p.
      Over twenty subject subdivisions on topics relevant to British
   agriculture are included in this regionalized list. Although now
   outdated, it remains an example for similar current bibliographical contributions for other areas in the world.

Wagner, Joseph Anthony. Children's Literature through Storytelling.
   Dubuque, Ia.: Brown, 1970. 118p.
      Planned to fulfill a need in the area of speech instruction, this
   material has been prepared to assist teachers and others tell
   stories more effectively. Contents include sections on types of
   stories, choosing stories, their preparation and presentation,
   story-acting, the child as storyteller and listener, and visual aids
   such as puppets. A story index is provided of books arranged by
   grade.

Waite, Clifford A. Periodicals for Schools: An Annotated List.
   London: School Library Assn., 1969. 45p.
      A selection of magazines, not exclusively British, for use in
   schools, including those produced specifically for children, those
   suitable for adoption by teachers for classroom use or general
   reading, and adult magazines judged enjoyable by and beneficial
   to children. Newspapers are excluded and free publications are
   stressed. Entries are in an orderly arrangement of informed
   interest groupings, rather than strictly by subject. Annotations

include an indication of age suitability. Designed for British schools, this selection will repay examination by North American librarians for comparative purposes.

Wakevainen, Alden. Reading for the Reluctant Reader. Harrisburg, Pa.: Pennsylvania State Library, 1963. 20p.

Designed as a buying guide or checklist for those working with the school age or adult problem reader, this is a list of books of high interest combined with low reading level, briefly annotated with assessment of reading interest and grade levels. Most titles date from the late fifties and early sixties, and consequently this brief collection's usefulness has now been superseded.

Walker, Elinor. Book Bait: Detailed Notes on Adult Books Popular with Young People. 2nd ed.: Chicago: American Library Assn., 1969. 129p.

Compiled for the Association of Young People's Librarians and first published in 1957, this list consists of adult books that are popular with teenagers and which librarians and other interested adults can recommend without reservation. The criteria of selection were to include books which give lasting pleasure and contribute to growth and understanding. These easier adult books would be used as stepping-stones to mature reading. Lengthy descriptive annotations give a good idea of the contents of each book. Further titles to follow up are mentioned briefly under each entry. The second edition adds fifty-six new titles and retains forty-four from the first; out-of-print books are eliminated. Extremely popular with librarians and teachers, this title was the forerunner of books that introduce or reintroduce the plot and give ideas on book talks for young adults who are reading adult books. As such, it has proven extremely useful both for the long plot summaries and the title index. A third edition appeared in 1979.

Walker, Jerry L., ed. Your Reading: A Booklist for Junior High Students. 5th ed. Urbana, Ill.: National Council of Teachers of English, 1975. 440p.

In the introduction to the student, the editorial chairman of the council's Committee on the Junior High School Booklist states positively: "This book was written for you. Teachers and librarians can use it of course but they are not the audience we had in mind." Notwithstanding a long history as an official selection list of this prestigious group of educators, with editions in 1946, 1950, 1959, supplemented in 1963, and 1966, the presentation of this substantial selection is designed to be a pupil's personal aid. The two-thirds devoted to fiction is arranged in informal interest topics, such as: "Here and Now," "On Being Free," "On Being in Love," "On Being a Member of a Minority," "On Growing Up Male," "On Growing Up Female," and "On Solving a Mystery." The remainder covers nonfiction arranged in broad subject areas. Generous annotations avoid grade and age recommendations and are written "to tempt your curiosity," providing for fiction "a sketch of the story and a glimpse of the characters" and for nonfiction notes on scope and aims. The over-1,500 titles are mostly recent, though "well-written older books" are included; consequently, the previous editions by Mark Neville and Charles B. Willard retain retrospective interest. A short list of classic titles includes many candidates for class discussion.

Wallace, Viola. Books for Adult Beginners, Grades I to VII. Chicago: American Library Assn., 1954. 66p.

This graded and annotated listing was first compiled by staff of the Cincinnati Public Library in 1939 and reissued in 1946. Ostensibly for adult learners (presumably, a large proportion of these would be young adults), many of the books and pamphlets chosen are useful in work with retarded and slow-learning children. Criteria for inclusion were uncomplicated sentence structure, simplicity of concept, and meaningful illustration, in addition to content and attractiveness of format. After listing books on adult education, including literacy and citizenship, textbooks and workbooks, entries are arranged in supplementary reading groups for grades 1-2, 3, 4, 5, 6, and 7, each subdivided by subject and interest topics. Descriptive annotations are brief, and readability is indicated, using the Flesch formula for higher grades, and the Dale formula for lower grades. Useful when published, few titles listed are now available.

Walls, Esther J., ed. African Encounter: A Selected Bibliography of Books, Films, and Other Materials for Promoting an Understanding of Africa among Young Adults. Chicago: American Library Assn., 1963. 69p.

Prepared by a committee of the Young Adult Services Division of the ALA, this annotated bibliography is designed as a selective guide to materials for librarians, teachers, and other adults working with those in eighth grade through high school. It is planned to be useful for book talks, teachers' reading, course planning, or for organizations having African programs. Recreational and informational materials are arranged side by side within informal groupings that take note of current problems, such as "African Voices," "Africa A-Z," "Animals in Africa," "The Man Next to Me" and "Naught for Comfort," as well as art, folktales, and music. Annotations are lengthy and evaluative. Most titles are suitable for adults, those suitable for the beginner or the mature young adult being noted, though grade levels are not recommended. This eclectic selection appeared when interest in Africa by and with young adults was beginning to increase sharply. Because of careful choice and wide variety, more recent developments have not invalidated the usefulness of this pleasant and appealing pamphlet, though of course much must be added to update the coverage of this fast-changing area.

Walsh, Frances, ed. That Eager Zest: First Discoveries in the Magic World of Books. Philadelphia: Lippincott, 1961. 252p.
    An anthology of reminiscent articles about their childhood reading by well-known literary figures of the first half of the twentieth century, including Ogden Nash, E. E. Cummings, and Eudora Welty, these contributions are grouped into informal sections such as "Secret Devouring" and "Great Big Wonderful Words." Children's and adults' books do receive comment in the text, but the lack of an index precludes use as any kind of checklist. Consequently, its usefulness is confined to pleasurable browsing, with occasionally original insights into children's literature.

Ward, Martha E., and Marquardt, Dorothy A. Authors of Books for Young People. 2nd ed. Metuchen, N.J.: Scarecrow, 1971. 579p.
    First published in 1964, with a supplement in 1967, this edition contains over 2,100 short paragraphs of biographical information, doubling the count of the first edition. The authors' emphasis is on difficult-to-locate contemporary authors of all countries. All Newbery and Caldecott winners are included. The compilers' basic source is their author file in the children's department of the Quincy, Illinois, Public Library. References are made to Wilson's Junior Book of Authors and its successors, and to Gale's Contemporary Authors. This on-going compilation (a supplement appeared in 1979) is useful for research precisely because of its limitations; for criticism and for famous figures, look elsewhere.

——. Illustrators of Books for Young People. 2nd ed. Metuchen, N.J.: Scarecrow, 1975. 223p.
    First published in 1970, this edition of the companion to the compilers' Authors of Books for Young People increases the number of short biographies from 370 to 750. Based on files maintained in the Quincy, Illinois, Public Library, its usefulness to researchers lies in its providing biographical facts about lesser known illustrators, American and international, most of them contemporary. All recipients of Caldecott Medals are listed. References are made to entries in the Horn Book series, Illustrators of Children's Books.

Warren, Dorothea, and Barton, Griselda. Fiction, Verse and Legend: A Guide to the Selection of Imaginative Literature for the Middle and Secondary School Years. London: School Library Assn., 1972. 68p.
    Intended as a guide for teachers and librarians rather than as a

definitive collection for a British school library, the 368 titles included here, in the experience of the compilers and their colleagues, elicit a positive response from young people. Modern adult fiction is excluded and selection is not confined to best books or class readings. Divisions include general stories and adventure, historical, family, school, animal stories, science fiction, fantasy, myths and poetry. Some American titles are included with the mainly British selections, but translations from other languages are well represented. Brief annotations are descriptive, but occasionally comment on audience suitability.

Watt, Lois B., ed. Bibliography of Books for Children. Washington, D.C.: Assn. for Childhood Education Internatl., 1974. Triennial.
      Parents and educators are the primary audience for this selected and annotated listing sponsored by this influential association. Predecessors, each prepared by a special committee under a different chairperson, go back as far as 1937, first as an annual, since 1950 as a biennial, and as a triennial since 1965. Reviewing is a joint team effort; many titles having been noted in the association journal, Childhood Education. A high degree of selectivity is aimed at, with commonly accepted literary standards as criteria: plot, style, and believability in fiction, and accuracy and pertinency for age level in nonfiction. The ideal set is that "every book here could bring help to some child." The listing is fairly comprehensive in covering school curricula, and pays particular attention to elementary grades. Arrangement is in broad general subject areas (editions up to 1965 favored Dewey) within main groups, such as for early childhood and middle and older children. Brief annotations include age level and a "content symbol." A new edition appeared in 1977.

——. Literature for Disadvantaged Children: A Bibliography. Washington, D.C.: U.S. Office of Education, 1968. 16p.
      A brief annotated bibliography prepared for teachers, librarians, and others by the head of the Educational Materials Center. There is a general interpretation of the word disadvantaged-- through poverty, cultural deprivation, and intercultural inexperience or other handicaps, including mental retardation. Titles, arranged by subject topics, are a sampling selected from about 5000 juvenile titles found in standard library reviewing sources, each receiving a short descriptive annotation and a grade recommendation. Inclusion does not necessarily indicate endorsement. Originally compiled in 1966 and made available for a conference in the same year, this balanced list can be supplemented from that date.

——, and Stanley, Caroline. Books Related to the Social Studies in Elementary and Secondary Schools: A Bibliography from the

Educational Material Center. Washington, D.C.: Govt. Print.
Off., 1969. 27p.

Issued by the Bureau of Research in the U.S. Office of Education, this brief annotated bibliography is intended for elementary
and secondary school teachers in the social studies field and
librarians. Juvenile literature and textbooks are arranged in two
parts appropriate to the two levels of education, and each subdivided into subject and geographical topics. Annotations are readable in style and descriptive in nature, indicating recommended
grade level. A representative rather than comprehensive selection, it will now require supplementation with more recent
publications.

Webb, Flora, ed. College Preparatory Reading List. Rev. ed. New
York: New York Library Assn., 1968. 23p.

Compiled by the Editorial Committee of the Children's and
Young Adults' Services Section, this is a revised edition of a list
prepared by the same editor for the Nioga, N.Y., Library System
in 1964. The selection is aimed at students and those who help
prepare them for college. The list, drawn from all fields, is
arranged in ten groups according to informal themes related to
looking at life as a whole and not necessarily in subject sequence.
Well-written annotations are critical, as well as descriptive, and
mention other titles which the authors have written. Because
titles of high literary quality by first-rate authors have been
preferred, the compilation still fulfills its purpose of providing a
checklist of books that form a necessary reading background for
the student with college ambitions.

Webb, Shelagh. Paperbacks for Nursery School. London: National
Book League, 1975. 18p.

Covering the best of the paperback readers and picture books
for very young children available in Britain, this is a consumer's
guide to ninety titles, with short descriptive and critical annotations. Included are fables and fantasies, stories and nursery
rhymes and books for "learning and laughing and living with."
References are made to series and to hardbound British editions.

Weber, Olga S., ed. Annual Paperbound Book Guide for High Schools; A
Selective Subject Guide to Approximately 5,500 Inexpensive Reprints and Originals Chosen Especially for Secondary School Use
by 143 Co-operating Publishers . . . . New York: Bowker, 1963-
1970.

This guide was "produced as a service to secondary school
teachers," in the belief that "the involvement of youth today in
reappraisals of his environment . . . and his need to know more
about the now of his concerns make the paperbound the perfect
complement to the standard school textbooks." First issued in

1963 from the office of Paperbound Books in Print as a biennial, it became annual in 1966 until its demise with the 1970 edition. Selection was limited to "those of greatest interest" to the high-school student and his teacher. Four major sections cover the language arts, social studies, science and mathematics, and arts and crafts, sports and humor; each has close topical subdivisions. There are occasional short descriptive annotations and indication of grade levels where available. Because of the wide distribution at a nominal price, this became a handy interim guide for those who dealt with young people during an explosive phase of the paperback revolution, influencing choice in book stores as well as libraries.

Welch, James d'Alté Aldridge. A Bibliography of American Children's Books Printed prior to 1821. Worcester, Mass.: American Antiquarian Society, 1972. 516p.

A life-long collector of children's books has compiled this bibliography, based on but not confined to the largest collection of early American children's books, that of the American Antiquarian Society, in whose Proceedings this list originally appeared. The book is dedicated to a former director, Clarence S. Brigham, and has a preface by the present director, Marcus A. McCorison. Coverage is limited to narrative books written in English which were designed for children under fifteen to read at leisure for pleasure, though some exceptions to this rule are described. Broadsides, sermons, catechisms, and school books are omitted. Nearly fifteen hundred entries arranged alphabetically by author, where known, and title, include title-page transcriptions, collations, locations, and bibliographical references. An introductory essay by the compiler, "A Chronological History of American Children's Books," gives useful information, in particular a description of major collections in the field. In spite of an index, all but dedicated scholars will find the compiler's unique listing scheme difficult. For the serious student, it nevertheless is an invaluable historical bibliography.

Welsh, Charles. A Bookseller of the Last Century: Being Some Account of the Life of John Newbery, and of the Books He Published, with a Notice of the Later Newberys. New York: Kelley, 1972. 373p.

This being a photolithographic facsimile of the original edition printed in London in 1885, the last century of the title is the eighteenth, and the bookseller the most famous children's publisher of that age. The text retains its value as an entertaining blend of anecdote and factual information; and the appendix, over half the volume, consists of a list of the firm's publications with extensive quotations and notes that has been a basis for later bibliographies.

Whalley, Joyce Irene. Cobwebs to Catch Flies: Illustrated Books for
the Nursery and Schoolroom, 1700-1900. London: Elek, 1974.
163p.
    The emphasis of this historical study of illustrated educational
books used over a two-hundred-year period to instruct young
children in the home, rather than at school, is on aspects of the
books themselves, with many illustrations. English and American
publications are compared to their continental contemporaries
where appropriate. Select bibliographies list English and foreign-
language books on the history of juvenile literature and children's
books noted in the text, arranged by type of publication. There is
also a list of selected collections of children's books. An American reissue was published by the University of California Press in
1975.

White, Dorothy Neal. About Books for Children. Wellington, New
Zealand: New Zealand Council for Educational Research, 1946.
222p.
    Published in conjunction with the New Zealand Library Associa-
tion, this elementary approach to the criticism of children's literature was intended for beginning librarians and parents. The
material was originally gathered for a correspondence course.
Children's books then current are discussed by type of publication;
however, New Zealand titles are given no special prominence over
others from the English-speaking world.

White, Marian, ed. High Interest-Easy Reading for Junior and Senior
High-School Students. 2nd ed. New York: Citation, 1972. 140p.
    Compiled by a committee of the National Council of Teachers
of English, this annotated booklist for students considered
reluctant--not retarded--readers was first published by the NCTE
in 1965, with Raymond C. Emery and Margaret B. Househower as
compilers. Intended to persuade pupils to like to read, the criteria
for selection included attractive format and in-print status, as
well as high-interest and easy reading. Books are listed within
eighteen informal thematic groups. Short descriptive annotations
are accompanied by a symbol for junior or senior high-school use.
This substantial checklist includes many titles valid for basic
collections. A further edition appeared in 1979.

Whitehead, Robert. Children's Literature: Strategies of Teaching.
Modern Elementary Methods Series. Englewood Cliffs, N.J.:
Prentice-Hall, 1968. 234p.
    This work is a textbook for teachers who wish to create a
successful literature program in a classroom setting. The objective is to develop a children's literary appreciation and instill a
love for literature as a basic part of the educational process; the
method of achieving this is for inspired and knowledgeable teach-

ers to sustain a well-defined literary program. Carefully sec-
tioned chapters with numbered paragraphs cover all aspects (even
the furniture required), and each provides selected references to
books and materials. Topics include planning, personal reading,
teaching literature through group activities, oral interpretation,
experiencing and appreciating literature, and literary games and
puzzles. Appendixes cover the evaluation of a program in children's literature and provide a general bibliography. Although a
how-to-do-it book, the ideas are imaginative. Many titles about
and for children are cited in the text. These need updating as
some are aged, and occasionally stereotypical or miscast.

Wiese, M. Bernice, ed. Asia: A Guide to Books for Children: Selected
and Annotated. New York: Asia Society, 1966. 54p.
    A companion volume to a similar list of adult titles published by
the Asia Society, this selection of children's books was made by a
committee drawn from the American Library Association's Children's Services Division. Designed for use by teachers, librarians,
and youth leaders, the titles serve as an introduction to a country,
its people, or an aspect of its culture. Criteria for choice include
appropriate contents, illustrations, and format for children
through grade 12. Titles, with brief descriptive annotations, are
grouped within an alphabetical arrangement by country (selections for each are chosen by individual committee members), and
further subdivided into fiction, nonfiction, and folklore. This
listing is noteworthy as an early attempt in selecting books for
children about Asian countries, but it suffers the fate of all
selective bibliographies that reflect a political situation: patterns of national change have invalidated the choice and outmoded the factual content of the books themselves.

Wighton, Rosemary. Early Australian Children's Literature. Australian Writers and their Work. Melbourne: Lansdowne, 1963. 40p.
    Concerned with the molding of the juvenile myth of Australian
life, this coverage of children's literature in Australia during the
nineteenth century treats themes and subjects rather than making
a chronological review.

Williams, Gladys. Children and Their Books. London: Duckworth,
1970. 158p.
    A book for parents that teachers, librarians, and social workers
may find useful, this work was written to enable them to help their
children develop their own choice in an atmosphere of freedom.
Issues concerned with the reading of various age groups are
discussed. Although a few books are mentioned in the text, it is
the twelve-page bibliography of authors and titles arranged by age
level and genre that makes this small volume a basic resource list
for parents. The selection is British with a full complement of
American authors.

Williams, Tom. <u>Prehistory</u>. YLG Storylines, no. 6. Birmingham, Eng.:
  Library Assn., Youth Libraries Group, 1975. 12p.
    Covering prehistorical novels written for children between age
  7-8 and their early teens, this pamphlet includes miscellaneous
  related works, picture books, and background reading. The compiler adds descriptive and critical notes, since the standard of
  quality varies.

Wilson, Jean A., ed. <u>Books for You: A Reading List for Senior High
  School Students</u>. 5th ed. New York: Washington Square, 1971.
  335p.
    Also published as a paperback by Pocket Books, this enlarged
  fifth edition, selected by a special committee of the National
  Council of Teachers of English for students' leisure reading, follows predecessors in 1945, 1951 (edited by Mark Neville and
  supplemented in 1954), and 1964, edited by Richard S. Alm. The
  foreword by G. Robert Carlsen is addressed to the student, and
  personal appeal is enhanced by humorous line drawings. Over
  2,000 titles, each with a short paragraph of descriptive annotation, are arranged under forty-five topical themes and geographical groupings. The thoroughness and balance of this selection
  have maintained its good reputation as an authoritative checklist
  for teachers and librarians. Many of the titles will still be avidly
  read; however a further edition in 1977 has remedied inevitable
  out-of-dateness in this changing field.

Wiltz, John E., ed. <u>Books in American History: A Basic List for High
  Schools</u>. Bloomington: Indiana Univ. Pr., 1964. 150p.
    This annotated bibliography of books about American history
  for junior and senior high-school students is based on a mimeographed list of basic books compiled in 1961. The present work
  aims to advance the use of books in the teaching of high-school
  American history. It is written for teachers and librarians on the
  assumption that reading includes the study of history. After a
  preface by the editor, the work is divided into eight chapters from
  reference works to paperbacks. Each chapter is introduced by
  approximately a page of text, followed by the book, listed by
  author alphabetically with a paragraph of annotation. The annotations include cross references and comparisons with other
  titles. A section entitled "100 Selected Titles" cites the author,
  title, and page number on which the book appears. There is also an
  author index which lists every title cited in the book. This is a
  good checklist for a core collection up to 1964.

Wintle, Justin, and Fisher, Emma. <u>The Pied Pipers: Interviews with
  the Influential Creators of Children's Literature</u>. New York: Two
  Continents, 1974. 320p.
    Twenty-four famous authors and illustrators, from Maurice

Sendak and Edward Ardizzone to Rumer Godden and Judy Blume, give personal interviews. Questions are asked and answers given about their lives, opinions, and writings. Certainly all children's librarians will want to read this British and American tour-de-force. The interviewers provide absorbing and informative reading, as well as skillfully drawing forth the characters of these well-known figures in today's children's literature. The book was simultaneously issued in London by Paddington.

Withrow, Dorothy E.; Carey, Helen B.; and Hirzel, Bertha M. Gateways to Readable Books. 5th ed. New York: Wilson, 1975. 299p.
　　Subtitled "an annotated, graded list of books in many fields for adolescents who are reluctant to read or who find reading difficult," this frequently revised guide was first compiled in 1944 by Ruth M. Strang, who prepared the second edition of 1952 with collaborators Christine B. Gilbert and Margaret C. Scoggin, and the third edition of 1958 and the fourth of 1966 with Ethylene Phelps and Dorothy Withrow. More than one thousand titles of special interest to this group of young people were chosen with the assistance of high-school teachers, librarians, and reading specialists according to an extensive catalog of criteria. Each book carries a symbol for grade level of difficulty and a brief annotation to indicate its nature and to give clues to interest and motives for reading. The list is arranged by subject and interest areas which combine fiction and nonfiction. It lays stress on categories such as community problems, family life and problems, and racial minorities. Hardback and paperback editions are noted. Supplementary lists cite reading texts and workbooks, books in series, and magazines and newspapers. Separate indexes cover authors, titles, and grade level of reading difficulty ranging from pre-primer to adult. Although there has been a tendency to enlarge each edition--this one consisting 85 percent of new titles--the increase truly represents the increase in publication of appropriate books. The present introduction continues to describe what makes a book easy to read, and dependence on the Lorge formula has been replaced by the use of an average of readability formulas. The annotations are informative and readable enough for the young adults who are the intended beneficiaries. This well-known resource continues to be a helpful source for librarians, teachers, and students.

Witucke, Virginia. Poetry in the Elementary School. Literature for Children. Dubuque, Ia.: Brown, 1970. 115p.
　　Designed for adults working with children, this title attempts to give a taste of and feeling for poetry for children and some information about it. Suggestions for using poetry with children are an important part of the book. Three groupings of related chapters examine "What Is Poetry?," "Finding Poetry," and "Poets

and Pedagogues." Each part has selected references appended, the most extensive being a list of books about poetry. Titles cited in the text are indexed by author, title, and subject, making it useful as a checklist by practitioners.

Wolfe, Ann G. About One Hundred Books: A Gateway to Better Intergroup Understanding. 7th ed. New York: American Jewish Committee, Institute of Human Relations, 1972. 47p.

First published in 1948, with succeeding editions in 1956, 1959, 1962, 1965, and 1969, the compiler has continuously reevaluated the selection according to the thematic values of intercultural education and the promotion of human understanding in changing times. Addressed generally to all who care about books, this work is intended specifically to "help Jewish children understand the emotional scars of their parents and grandparents" while they learn about other groups. The list is divided into three age groupings: "Five to Nine--Just Beginning"; "Eight to Thirteen--The World Is Big"; and "Eleven to Sixteen--These Teen Years." The choice of titles is competent while eclectic, and the parent-directed annotations have a personal flavor. The selection makes up a stimulating and suggestive checklist for librarians and teachers of all religious persuasions.

Wood, Anne. Children and Books. Billericay, Eng.: Home and School Council, 1973. 24p.

This annotated list includes about 175 titles arranged by age group for children from under 5 to 12, with an introduction which stresses the parents' role in children's reading.

Wood, Kenneth A. Buy, Beg or Borrow: A Choice of Books for Children. YLG Pamphlet. Birmingham, Eng.: Library Assn., Youth Libraries Group, 1969. 16p.

Intended as a guide for discriminating parents and others, this lists, with brief annotations, one hundred books considered good sources of interest and pleasure to young children. Each was chosen for strong individual qualities that should make a lasting impression. Arrangement is under informal interest topics, and age suitability is indicated, with some illustrations.

Woodhams, Mary P. The Middle Ages, 1066-1485. YLG Storylines, no. 1. London: National Book League, 1972. 16p.

The first publication in the Library Association Youth Libraries Group series aims to satisfy the needs of teachers, storytellers, and others who are looking for a well-written story to hold a child's imagination that does not conflict with historical facts. About sixty items currently in print include stories set in the Middle Ages, tales and legends, and some background reference material.

The World in Children's Picture Books. Washington, D.C.: Assn. for
    Childhood Education Internatl., 1968. 16p.
        Compiled by a committee from the early childhood program at
    Towson State College for the twelfth world assembly of the World
    Organization for Early Childhood Education, this is a list of
    distinguished and appealing picture books from and about other
    countries for a readership under eight years of age. This minimal
    selection by its very brevity will be of minimal use to the experi-
    enced librarian or teacher of this age group.

Woy, Sara, ed. Richer by Asia: A Selected Bibliography of Books and
    Other Materials for Promoting West-East Understanding among
    Young Adults. Chicago: American Library Assn., 1959. 64p.
        Prepared by a committee of the Young Adults Services Division
    of the ALA, this bibliography was originally conceived as a pro-
    gram guide for a wider project on Asia sponsored by the division,
    and served as a handbook for adults interested in conducting
    programs on Asia besides providing an annotated listing for a
    wider audience. Free and inexpensive pamphlets, exhibit mate-
    rials, films, book talks and program outlines are included, as well
    as books about Asia, which are arranged under broad topical
    headings. Original and stimulating in its approach, it was a useful
    tool in its time but radical change in the area over twenty years
    has reduced it to a work of retrospective interest.

Wynar, Christine L. Guide to Reference Books for School Media
    Centers. Littleton, Colo.: Libraries Unlimited, 1973. 473p.
        Over 2,500 annotated entries for reference books and selection
    tools for children's materials and nonprint materials to be used in
    elementary, junior, and senior high schools are provided to cater
    to a wide range of reading level by students. The selected list is
    not intended as a buying list of best books, but rather "as a base for
    selecting reference books for purchase by listing, describing
    [and] evaluating." Arrangement is under fifty-four subject head-
    ings listed alphabetically, each with subdivisions. This classifica-
    tion is broad and easy to follow, but does not reflect any standard
    library science scheme. There is often a full paragraph of descrip-
    tive and critical annotation for each item. Professional reference
    tools are included. Indexing is thorough. Certainly the totality of
    the list and a number of the individual titles will be beyond the
    scope of any but the largest and best-supported school media
    centers, but there is corresponding compensation in that this is a
    very useful compilation for adult reference services. A supple-
    ment covering 1974-75 was published in 1976.

Yeager, Allan. Using Picture Books with Children. New York: Holt,
    1973. 203p.
        This paperback providing plot summaries of picture books,

designed to assist primary school teachers in instilling a love of reading in early childhood, is also directed to parents. Uniform treatment is applied to over seventy picture books arranged by title; the story is condensed to a brief paragraph, primary or intermediate interest level is assessed, illustrations are noted, and suggestions for use are given. A list of titles for further reading is provided. The selections are those which teachers, parents, and children should enjoy, and librarians can check.

Yonkers, N.Y. Public Library. Children's Services. A Guide to Subjects and Concepts in Picture Book Format. Dobbs Ferry, N.Y.: Oceana, 1974. 166p.

An unannotated listing of particular subjects, ideas, or themes found in the library's collection of picture books (strictly defined by the library) that are useful at the preschool or primary school levels. This longstanding project of the library was started in file form at the request of parents, teachers, and library-school students. Part 1 is arranged under fifty-two subject headings derived from the Sears list; part 2 is an author listing. Both refer to each other. Titles cited range from a few in the 1940s up to January 1974. More than the finding tool it is claimed to be, it forms a useful checklist for reading guidance that can serve the current trend towards developmental values. An updated second edition appeared in 1979.

Young, Beverly S., and Van de Garde, Linda. A Bibliography of High Interest-Low Vocabulary Books. Iowa City, Ia.: State Univ. of Iowa, 1967. 86p.

This unannotated list, published as a university extension bulletin, of titles with an interest level of two or more years above reading level, is arranged by grade reading level from pre-primary to sixth grade.

Zion, Mary Jo. A Bibliography of Reading Lists for Retarded Readers. Rev. ed. Iowa City, Ia.: State Univ. of Iowa, 1960. 19p.

First issued in 1949 and revised in 1953, this unannotated, non-evaluative list published as a university extension bulletin includes books, periodicals, bulletins, and information about series and textbooks. It is for teachers of retarded readers who need "printed materials which feature an interest level several grades higher than the level of reading difficulty."

Subject Index

●●●●●

Compiled by Margaret Cooter

Added Entry Index

•••••

Compiled by Margaret Cooter

Includes joint authors, titles, organizations, series. Authors and organizations appearing only as main entries are not repeated in this index; check body of text. Subtitles are used to distinguish identical titles, where possible.